SUBSTANCE ABUSE ASSESSMENT, INTERVENTIONS AND TREATMENT

SUBSTANCE ABUSE

PREVALENCE, GENETIC AND ENVIRONMENTAL RISK FACTORS AND PREVENTION

SUBSTANCE ABUSE ASSESSMENT, INTERVENTIONS AND TREATMENT

Additional books in this series can be found on Nova's website under the Series tab.

Additional e-books in this series can be found on Nova's website under the e-book tab.

SUBSTANCE ABUSE ASSESSMENT, INTERVENTIONS AND TREATMENT

SUBSTANCE ABUSE

PREVALENCE, GENETIC AND ENVIRONMENTAL RISK FACTORS AND PREVENTION

JEFFREY RAINES
EDITOR

nova publishers
New York

For permission to use material from this book please contact us:
Telephone 631-231-7269; Fax 631-231-8175
Web Site: http://www.novapublishers.com

Library of Congress Cataloging-in-Publication Data

ISBN: 978-1-63321-949-6

Library of Congress Control Number: 2014948898

Published by Nova Science Publishers, Inc. † New York

CONTENTS

PREFACE

In this book, the authors present current research in the study of alcohol and substance abuse. Topics discussed in this compilation include the correlation of alcohol misuse and team sport participation; the cutaneous effects of adultered cocaine; fetal alcohol syndrome; cocaine and the affects it has on the kidneys; coping and autonomic dysfunction act in tandem with alcohol-related subclinical atherosclerosis; alcohol consumption and alcoholism mortality in Russia; and oxycodone abuse prevention in cancer patients.

Chapter 1 – Team sports participation is positively associated with alcohol use. In this chapter the authors discuss reasons for this co-occurrence (i.e., coping with overtraining or injury, alcohol use to relax before or after competition, shared impulsivity/risk-taking tendencies, perceived performance enhancement, social group acceptability of engaging in both behaviors, quick dissipation of alcohol, media culture of drinking and sports, and common addiction elements). They also organize these reasons within a pragmatics, attraction, communications, and expectations (PACE) framework. The social climate when recruiting athletes, and events participation, often involves alcohol industry sponsorship and accessibility to alcohol products (pragmatics). Collegiality and festivities on athletic teams often involves alcohol use, and both may feel good to certain individuals (attraction). The authors posit that a shared language of sports and alcohol use develops, often promoted by the mass media (communication; e.g., "beer Olympics"). Finally, both activities may meet expectancies which could include subjective experience of adventure while controlling pain (expectations). Suggestions are made on how to dissociate the two activities.

Chapter 2 – *Introduction:* The cardiopulmonary, neurologic and psychiatric sequelae of cocaine are well documented. However, little is known of the devastating cutaneous manifestations of cocaine. When cocaine is cut with the common adulterant levamisole, significant impact on the integument ensues. Patients may suffer from a continuum of purpura and petichiae to full-thickness skin and soft tissue necrosis. These patients should be managed in a qualified burn center by an experienced Reconstructive Plastic Surgeon.

Rheumatologic Susceptability: Patients who present with these cutanous manifestations often have a history of rheumatologic disease or meet criteria for diagnosis of such. A variety of auto-antibodies have been serologically identified at presentation. These include Antinuclear Antibodies (ANA), Perinuclear Anti-Neutrophil Cytoplasmic Antibodies (P-ANCA), double-stranded DNA (dsDNA) , Lupus Anticoagulant (LA) titers, Rheumatoid Factor (RF), cyliccitrullinated peptide antibody (CCP), anti-proteus antibody (APA) and anti-streptolysin antibody (ASLO).

Adulterated Cocaine: The average cocaine bought on the streets today is only 45% cocaine hydrocholoride. Adulterants are added to potentiate the effects or increase the weight of the product. Since 2005, a new adulterant, levamisole, has been identified in cocaine. By 2011, 82% of cocaine imported into the United States already contained levamisole. This has been reported not just in the United States, but also in Canada, the United Kingdom and Italy. More recently, heroin samples laced with levamisole have also been identified.Levamisole is an anti-helminth, used solely in veterinary medicine to deworm livestock. In August of 2010, the New York State Department of Health issued a public advisory, warning of the dangerous health concerns of cocaine cut with levamisole.

Cutaneous Manifestations: Historically, levamisole was used in the treatment of cancer as well as nephrotic syndrome in children. Its use was abandoned due to the resulting vasculitis, purpura, agranulocytosis, hepatosplenomegaly and circulating autoimmune antibodies noted in patients. Health care professionals are now seeing a similar myriad of symptoms in cocaine users whose product is adulterated with the levamisole. Most patients present with vague constitutional symptoms and polyarthralgias. Upon further examination many have purpura or petechiae that mimic an autoimmune process. Even with abstinence from the drug, many of these patients go on to develop frank necrosis of their skin and soft tissue. This is commonly seen on the helix of the ear, the nasal tip, breasts, thighs, abdomen and upper extremities.

Surgical Mangement: Supportive local wound care is necessary to all cuteanous manifestations until the wounds have fully demarcated. Serial surgical debridement of non-viable tissue is necessary in a staged manner.

Once the wounds have stabilized, they may be closed via primary closure, skin grafting or local flaps.

Conclusions: The cutaneous manifestations of adultured cocaine have not been previously well described. It is necessary for health care professionals to have a heightened awareness of this emerging entity to aid in both prompt diagnosis and the appropriate medical and surgical management.

Chapter 3 – Fetal alcohol syndrome (FAS) is a serious global problem due to emergence of alcohol abuse among young pregnant women. Recently they have described biomarkers of FAS for early diagnosis, prevention, and treatment of FAS. Since the diagnosis and treatment of FAS can pose a significant challenge; it is prudent to prevent FAS at an early stage to avoid the deleterious consequences of alcohol abuse. Adults with FAS or fetal alcohol effects (FAE) suffer from mental illnesses and are more prone to drug addiction in stressful environment. Even in the absence of craniofacial abnormalities and intellectual handicap; children with FAS may experience psychiatric and developmental disorders. Adults with FAS have a high rate of brain anomalies as diagnosed by CT, MRI/spectroscopy, and PET neuroimaging. The FAS victims have also a higher rate of behavioral management problems. By performing high-resolution microPET neuroimaging with ^{18}F-DOPA and ^{18}FdG as biomarkers of dopaminergic and mitochondrial bioenergetics respectively, the authors established that chronic intoxication of cocaine and methamphetamine (METH) induces reduction in the striatal dopamine and glucose metabolism. A further reduction in ^{18}F-DOPA and ^{18}FdG uptake was noticed when cocaine and METH were co-administered along with ethanol, suggesting that alcohol may serve as a gateway to multiple drug abuse. In addition to fatty acid ethyl esters; the metabolite, cocaethylene is formed when cocaine and alcohol are abused concomitantly. Cocaethylene is more toxic as compared to ethanol and cocaine. Hence alcohol abuse along with other drugs during pregnancy may have significant impact on learning, intelligence, memory, and behavior. In addition to mtDNA, histone, and protein methylation; alcohol impairs microRNAs expression causing transcriptome and proteome abnormalities. Usually gastrulation period is highly vulnerable to the deleterious consequences of alcohol. Alcohol-induced cerebellar and hippocampal Charnoly body (CB) formation; involved in impaired motor learning and memory loss can be prevented by nutritional rehabilitation, physiological zinc, and metallothioneins (MTs). MTs as free radical scavengers, inhibit CB formation and α-synuclein index to provide ubiquinone-mediated mitochondrial protection and prevent neurodegenerative α-synucleinopathies.

MTs also regulate zinc-mediated transcriptional activation of genes involved in heavy metal ion detoxification, growth, development, differentiation, and maturation. Clinical manifestations of multidrug abuse were attenuated in MTs-over-expressing homozygous weaver mutant (wv/wv) mice. In addition, choline, folate, and vitamin–A are used for the treatment of FAS. As the deleterious effect of FAS can occur during any phase of fetal brain development, early prevention and differential diagnosis is essential for children born from mothers with history of alcohol abuse as it can pass through blood placental, brain, and milk barriers. Although some physicians allowed one drink during pregnancy; alcohol intake during any period of pregnancy should be avoided. Particularly pregnant women need to be educated regarding the deleterious consequences of FAS to avoid social, physical, mental, psychological, and economical burden on the society.

Chapter 4 – *Objective:* To report renal damage induced by cocaine itself, highlighting a special condition when cocaine is contaminated with levamisole.

Background: Levamisole is a veterinary antihelminthic agent, previously used to treat nephrotic syndrome, various autoimmune disorders and cancers in humans (colon and breast). It has been detected in seized cocaine samples and a levamisole-induced vasculopathy (LIV) has been described.

Discussion: There is evidence to support the existence of cocaine-induced renal changes, through multifactorial pathophysiology: vasoconstrictive effects and nonspecific glomerular, interstitial and tubular cell lesions. Levamisole has been detected in adulterated cocaine and a synergistic action resulting in increased nicotinic and dopaminergic effects, has been suggested. A typical serologic profile with ANCA-positivity differentiates cocaine-levamisole vasculopathy, mainly focused on skin, but can also appear involving kidney.

Conclusions: Kidney, as end organ involvement, is an uncommon presentation of ANCA-positive vasculitis induced by levamisole-adulterated cocaine. High index of suspicion should be considered in cocaine users with skin lesions and abnormal renal function.

Chapter 5 – *Introduction*: Alcohol abuse is among the Westernized world's most common lifestyle factors contributing to sensitization of vascular structure and pathology. Gamma glutamyl transferase (γ-GT), as a marker of alcohol abuse, may indicate increased sensitization and vascular disease risk when using chronic defense coping (DefS). DefS was contradicted as a promoter of health, as it was related with dissociation between self-reported behavioral ("in-control") albeit physiological ("loss-of–control") responses.

Therefore, the authors aimed to assess if DefS may *mask* autonomic dysfunction and induce alcohol-related subclinical atherosclerosis.

Methods: A black African male teacher cohort with similar socioeconomic standing and without atrial fibrillation (N=101) from the North-West Province of South Africa, was recruited and investigated. Fasting blood values, 24h ambulatory blood pressure (ABPM) and -ECG, Coping Strategy Indicator (CSI) scores and ultrasound left carotid intima media far wall scanning values, were obtained. The standard deviation between successful R-R intervals (SDNN) was utilized as a marker of time-domain 24h heart rate variability (HRV). Multivariate regression analyses were computed.

Results: A hypertensive state in the men was evident at a much lower ROC γ-GT cut point than the suggested MERCK cut-point of 78 U/L [55.7 U/L, sensitivity/specificity 60%/86% (AUC 0.78; 95% CI: 0.67; 0.88]. Hereafter, males were stratified into low (<55.7 U/l) and high (≥ 55.7 U/l) γ-GT groups. Overall, the high γ-GT group, revealed a poorer lifestyle profile, mean higher 24h ABPM, depressed 24h HRV and more 24h silent ischemic events (14 vs. 2) compared to their low γ-GT counterparts ($P \leq 0.01$). HRV responses were inversely associated with γ-GT when utilizing DefS ($r = -0.28$; $P = 0.015$). Additionally, ABPM predicted 24h silent ischemia (OR 1.11; $P \leq 0.01$) whereas 24h silent ischemia predicted a trend for structural vascular disease in the DefS African men (OR 1.06; $p \leq 0.06$).

Conclusion: DefS revealed behavioral "in-control" responses directly opposing or *masking* physiological "loss-of-control" responses, underpinning a dissociative response. Alcohol, which is a central nervous system depressant, enhanced vasoconstriction in the vasculature. Indeed, alcohol abuse was related to depressed heart rate variability, when utilizing DefS, sensitizing the vasculature, induced silent ischemia and ultimately structural vascular remodeling. The detrimental effects of DefS acting in tandem with autonomic dysfunction augment alcohol-related ischemia and may increase the risk for early sub-clinical atherosclerosis.

Chapter 6 – *Background:* Alcohol is increasingly implicated in the mortality crisis observed in Russia since the collapse of the communist system.

Objective: The aim of this study was to examine the aggregate-level relation between the alcohol consumption and alcoholism mortality rates in Russia.

Method: Age-standardized sex-specific male and female alcoholism mortality data for the period 1970-2005 and data on overall alcohol consumption were analyzed by means ARIMA (autoregressive integrated moving average) time series analysis.

Results: Alcohol consumption was significantly associated with both male and female alcoholism mortality rates: a 1 liter increase in overall alcohol consumption would result in a 23.1% increase in the male alcoholism mortality rate and in 27.1% increase in the female mortality rate.

Conclusions: The findings from the present study have important implications in regards alcohol-related mortality prevention indicating that a restrictive alcohol policy can be considered as an effective measure of prevention in countries with higher rate of alcohol consumption.

Chapter 7 – Reformulated OxyContin® (oxycodone-HCl controlled release) tablets became available in the United States in August 2010. The original formulation of the OxyContin® used a delivery system that did not prevent crushing and dissolving of the tablet.

Cancer patients experience three kinds of pain: (1) cancer related pain, (2) pain due to their treatments (such as chemotherapy induced peripheral neuropathy), and (3) chronic non-cancer pain (such as post herpetic neuralgia). However, physicians sometimes dispense similar opioid prescriptions for patients with (2) and (3) according to the three-step analgesic ladder framework of the World Health Organization, as well as for patients with (1). Thus, addiction or abuse of opioids in Japan has become a problem, especially in cancer survivors. Moreover, oxycodone consumption is increasing in Japan, as patients can be started on a low dose (5 mg tablet) that has few adverse effects.

This review discusses medical uses, potential adverse effects of oxycodone, and further reviews of recent pharmacotherapy for the prevention of its abuse, especially in cancer patients.

In: Substance Abuse
Editor: Jeffrey Raines

ISBN: 978-1-63321-949-6

Chapter 1

REASONS FOR CO-OCCURRENCE OF TEAM SPORTS PARTICIPATION AND ALCOHOL MISUSE*

Steve Sussman[1,†], Ph.D. and Nadra Lisha[2,††], Ph.D.
[1]Institute for Health Promotion and Disease Prevention Research,
University of Southern California Keck School of Medicine,
Los Angeles, CA, US
[2]Department of Psychiatry, UCSF School of Medicine,
San Francisco, CA, US

ABSTRACT

Team sports participation is positively associated with alcohol use. In this chapter we discuss reasons for this co-occurrence (i.e., coping with overtraining or injury, alcohol use to relax before or after competition, shared impulsivity/risk-taking tendencies, perceived performance enhancement, social group acceptability of engaging in both behaviors, quick dissipation of alcohol, media culture of drinking and sports, and

---

* This paper was supported by a grant from the National Institute on Drug Abuse (DA020138).
† Send correspondence to: Steve Sussman, Ph.D., FAAHB, FAPA., Institute for Health Promotion and Disease Prevention Research, University of Southern California, Soto Street Building, 2001 North Soto Street., Room 302A. Los Angeles, CA 90033. Telephone: 323-442-8220, Cell phone: 626-376-0389, FAX: 626-442-8201. E-mail: ssussma@usc.edu.
†† E-mail: nadra.lisha@ucsf.edu.

common addiction elements). We also organize these reasons within a pragmatics, attraction, communications, and expectations (PACE) framework. The social climate when recruiting athletes, and events participation, often involves alcohol industry sponsorship and accessibility to alcohol products (pragmatics). Collegiality and festivities on athletic teams often involves alcohol use, and both may feel good to certain individuals (attraction). We posit that a shared language of sports and alcohol use develops, often promoted by the mass media (communication; e.g., "beer Olympics"). Finally, both activities may meet expectancies which could include subjective experience of adventure while controlling pain (expectations). Suggestions are made on how to dissociate the two activities.

Keywords: Addictions, Team Sports, Alcohol Misuse, Co-occurrence

INTRODUCTION

The relationship of team sports participation and alcohol, tobacco, and other drug (ATOD) use has been a recent avenue of inquiry in health behavior research. There are several reasons to believe that the two activities would be inversely related. First, in risk factors research, exercise is related to a higher quality of life and increased lifespan, and is inversely related to participation various risky behaviors which would, in theory, include heavy levels of tobacco, alcohol, or other drug use (Lisha & Sussman, 2010). That is, exercise may reflect generalized embeddedness in a "wellness" lifestyle, whereas other behaviors such as heavy alcohol use may reflect a hedonistic (pleasure regardless of or in contradiction with health) orientation. Second, it has been thought by some researchers and practitioners that bringing youth and adults together in support of athletic teams would decrease the likelihood that team sports participation and drug use would be positively associated (Peretti-Watel, 2009). That is, the social venue for sports involvement would seem very different from the venues for substance use involvement (adult monitoring and supervision versus peer-only involvement). Third, sports can take a great deal of time if winning is important, and this might take away time from other activities such as alcohol or drug use (Wichstrom & Wichstrom, 2009).That is, simply "keeping busy" through a structured physical activity might preclude time spent engaging in risky behaviors. Fourth, enjoyment of exercise would potentially preclude the necessity to engage in drug use for enjoyment (Audrain-McGovern, Rodriguez, Cuevas, & Sass, 2013). In other words, youth may achieve a hedonic threshold that brings sufficient comfort such that another activity such as alcohol use is not needed. Finally, there is some evidence that alcohol or other drug use impairs athletic performance and recovery (Vella & Cameron-Smith, 2010), which would likely deter athletes interested in peak performance from drinking or using other drugs (e.g., dehydration, longer muscle recovery time, injuries). In fact, increasing levels of alcohol consumption has been found to be associated with an increasingly higher risk of sport injuries compared with other injuries (among women but not men) in Switzerland; also, men and women injured while exercising have been found to be much more often at-risk drinkers compared with those injured during other activities (Gmel, Kuendig, & Daeppen, 2009).

Indeed, cigarette or marijuana smoking, and other illicit drug use, generally are inversely related to sports participation and physical activity (e.g., Henchoz et al., 2014; Kwan et al., 2014; Lisha & Sussman, 2010), except through unique social networks, including groups of athletes who use illicit drugs and have relatively less formal education (Dunn & Thomas, 2012), or those athletes who appear to show a tendency to use any of a variety of drugs (including performance enhancing drugs, alcohol, and illicit drugs), which appears to reflect a general individual-level inclination towards enhancement of affect and substance addiction (Buckman, Farris, & Yusko, 2013; Buckman et al., 2011).

Surprisingly, however, alcohol use, including heavy drinking, getting drunk, and suffering alcohol-related consequences, is generally positively associated with physical activity and sports participation (e.g., Belanger et al., 2012; Cadigan, Littlefield, Martens, & Sher, 2013; Davies & Foxall, 2011; Diel et al., 2012; Henchoz et al., 2014; Hummer, LaBrie, & Lac, 2011; Kwan et al., 2014; Lisha, Crano, & Delucchi, 2014; Lisha & Sussman, 2010; Mays, DePadilla, et al., 2010; Mays, Thompson, et al., 2010; Sonderlund et al., 2014; Taliaferro, Rienzo, & Donovan, 2010).

Recently, several studies have attempted to better understand how it is that this positive relation exists. It is likely that this relationship is more central regarding team sports participation than engagement in regular physical activity *per se*, as the latter may involve any number of activities (e.g., yoga classes, jogging, health club workouts) which may be protective against later alcohol misuse and consequences (Korhonen, Kujala, Rose, & Kaprio, 2009; Wichstrom &Wichstrom, 2009). The reasons that team sports participation and alcohol use co-occur is discussed next.

Reasons Team Sports Participation and Alcohol Use Are Positively Associated

There are at least eight reasons that team sports participation and alcohol use may be positively associated. First, alcohol may be used by athletes who are tired or injured, to cope with stiff muscles, pain or inability to compete (Peretti-Watel, 2009). Alcohol historically has been used as an anesthetic and soporific (Makela, 1983). In the case of injury, alcohol may be used to "drown one's sorrows" due to the inability to compete. Second, alcohol may be used by athletes to manage stress associated with competition. That is, alcohol may be used to help an athlete calm down around the time of competition, either before competition (e.g., to get good night's sleep), or after competition (to unwind).

Third, both alcohol use and sports may involve sensation seeking or competitive tendencies (e.g., drinking games, with winners, losers, and spectators; Belanger et al., 2012; Hummer, LaBrie, & Lac, 2011; Lisha & Sussman, 2010; Leasure & Neighbors, 2013; Mays, Thompson, et al., 2010; Peretti-Watel, 2009). In fact, one recent study of Division 1 intercollegiate athletes found that 67% of the sample of 568 athletes engaged in pre-partying behavior (drinking prior to going to a club or other party-type event) and, of them, 54.5% also typically played competitive drinking games (Hummer, LaBrie, & Lac, 2011). A subjective sense of adventure may be achieved through either channel of activity. Fourth, athletes who misuse performance-enhancing drugs are also at relatively higher risk for heavy drinking (Buckman, Farris & Yusko, 2013). They may drink to obtain subjective performance benefits, perhaps self-medicating (getting numbed) to be able to engage in more strenuous workouts. Fifth, and related to the fourth reason, alcohol dissipates from the body rapidly (perhaps minimizing impairment of performance, or its detection; Lisha & Sussman, 2010), though some impairment exists (e.g., duration of muscle power recovery; Murphy et al., 2013). Sixth, alcohol is relatively accessible, and may be relatively tolerated among athletes, particularly in group-based sports (Bedendo, Opaleye, Andrade, & Noto, 2013; Kwan et al., 2014; Mays, Thompson, et al., 2010). This reason may be the most important one, and is discussed more below.

Seventh, and related to the sixth reason, the normative social climate may tend to reinforce a drinking culture (Davies & Foxall, 2011), as portrayed on television commercials, alcohol industry sponsorship of sporting events, and informal gatherings of athletes or casual competitors after competition (Lisha

& Sussman, 2010; O'Brien, Lynott, & Miller, 2013; Sawyer et al., 2012). Alcohol industry sponsorship may extend to payment for sports events naming rights, and 'direct to user' sponsorship (e.g., payment of club fees, uniform costs, and provision of free alcohol to athletes; O'Brien, Lynott, & Miller, 2013). Finally, as we will discuss more below, both types of activities (drinking and exercise) may become compatible addictions (e.g., one may increase sport involvement to burn excess calories from alcohol) for some persons and, as such, may tend to co-occur.

The Social Milieu of Drinking and Sports Participation. Certainly, the co-occurrence of drinking and sports participation is bounded by the social milieu. Terry-McElrath and O'Malley (2011) found that the positive relationship of alcohol use with athletic participation/physical activity was completely accounted for by participation in team sports, using Monitoring the Future Data. Mays, Thompson, et al. (2010) found that alcohol use was related to one's perceptions of relatively high peer use along with one's participation on competitive (varsity) teams. Further, Vest and Simpkins (2013) found that athletes' alcohol use was a function of the use prevalence among their peers/friends and teammates, using the AddHealth survey. The influence of prevalence overestimates on an athlete's drinking are greater when directed toward friends who are team members than non-athlete friends (Martens, Dams-O'Connor, Duffy-Paiement, & Gibson, 2006).

Team cohesion may be related to alcohol misuse. Zhou, O'Brien, and Heim (2013) found that hazardous drinking was partaken to enhance sports team cohesion, the latter which also mediated the relations of self-reported happiness with hazardous drinking. Interestingly, Grossbard et al. (2009) found that perceptions of drinking norms (prevalence estimates) were more strongly associated with individual alcohol use among athletes reporting higher levels of attraction to their intercollegiate sports teams, supporting the suggestion that team members drink to enhance group cohesion (to show support of perceived team norms). Through use of social network analysis on teen alcohol use and participation in high school activities, Fujimoto & Valente (2013) found that, after decomposing peer influence through activities by friendship status, peer influence through sport activities had a significant effect on drinking only when co-participant drinkers were also reciprocated friends (but not nominated friends), whereas influence through club activities had a significant effect on drinking, regardless of friendship reciprocation. This finding more directly illustrates the importance of attraction and cohesion to teammates and alcohol use.

Gender as a Moderator. Some studies also have found that alcohol use tends to be more strongly related to physical activity among males than females, and among young adults than younger teens (Lisha, Martens, & Leventhal, 2011; Taliaferro, Rienzo, & Donovan, 2010). Physical activity/team sports competition is positively related to alcohol use at the college level particularly among male fraternity members (Buscemi et al., 2011), perhaps indicating the extent to which the male group social fabric facilitates or deters drinking. Also, as found by Weaver et al. (2013), a construct of competitiveness was associated with greater alcohol consumption only among men in intercollegiate athletics (also see Hummer, LaBrie, & Lac, 2011). On the other hand, competitiveness was associated with less alcohol use among female athletes, suggesting that the trait may serve as a protective factor regarding alcohol-related outcomes among women. However, among elite athletes, females may be more likely to drink than males, at least in Norway (Martinsen & Sundgot-Borgen, 2014) and, in some populations (high school-level, majority African American) gender differences have failed to be found between sports participation and alcohol use (Mays et al., 2010). It is possible that a particularly heavy investment in exercise to the point of being an addiction may be positively associated with addiction to other activities including alcohol use, as is explored in the next section of this chapter.

Exercise and Alcohol Addictions

Sussman & Sussman (2011) provided a succinct definition of addiction, which involves (a) seeking an appetitive effect, (b) experience of brief periods of satiation, (c) eventual preoccupation with the behavior following repeated appetitive effect-satiation cycles, (d) loss of control over the behavior, and (e) occurrence of negative consequences. Recently, the scope of behaviors that has been considered potentially addictive has widened greatly (Demetrovics & Griffiths, 2012). For example, Sussman (2012) described 16 categories of addictive behaviors, placing them into potential sets of appetitive motives. These categories include: drug use, food-related, compulsive anti-social behavior, technology/communications related, gambling, working, social/group-related (e.g., sex, love) physical attractiveness seeking (e.g., tanorexia), fantasizing, exercise-related, spiritual obsession, pain seeking (e.g., trichotillomania), shopping, thrill/adventure seeking, hoarding, and voyeurism. Addiction to alcohol has been discussed for several hundred years. Exercise addiction is a less well-recognized phenomenon.

Exercise addiction, considered a "positive addiction" by some clinicians, may lead to repeated injuries and neglect of work and family life (Adams, 2009; Allegre, Souville, Therme, & Griffiths, 2006; Berczik et al., 2012; Freimuth, Moniz, & Kim, 2011). Amongst the scattering of research that has been completed, exercise addiction is said to include the presence of mood modification/regulation, tolerance, withdrawal symptoms, lack of control, detrimental social consequences, personal conflict, and several other negative effects such as disturbed psychological functioning, exercising despite medical contraindications, or interference with relationships or work (salience), and relapse (Freimuth, Moniz, & Kim, 2011; Hausenblas & Downs, 2002; Weinstein & Weinstein, 2014).

There is some scant evidence that 15-20% of exercise addicts are addicted to nicotine, alcohol or illicit drugs (see Freimuth, Moniz, & Kim, 2011; Sussman, Lisha, & Griffiths, 2011), though at least one study failed to find a difference in alcohol consumption between exercise dependent and nondependent participants of a fitness club (Lejoyeux et al., 2008), and two other studies found only correlations of Pearson $r=.06$ and $.09$ ($ps>.1$), respectively, between alcohol and exercise addiction among males and females in a chemical dependence recovery facility (Haylett, Stephenson, & Lefever, 2004) and college men and women (Greenberg, Lewis, & Dodd, 1999). Also, while physical activity has been found to be positively related to alcohol abuse in one large sample (NESARC data) it is not related to alcohol dependence (Lisha, Sussman, & Leventhal, 2013a & b), perhaps because at higher levels of alcohol use physical activity of necessity will diminish.

It has been asserted by some researchers that exercise addiction is not related to alcohol, cigarette smoking or other drug addictions, but might be related to eating (e.g., sometimes even being secondary to an eating disorder; Berczik et al., 2012; Lejoyeux et al., 2008), or internet or shopping addiction (Lejoyeux et al., 2008). We conjecture that there may be an overlap between both types of addiction under certain conditions.

Commonalities in the Addictive Process. For some persons, it is possible that both addictions co-exist. Both exercise and alcohol use increase release of mesolimbic dopamine, endorphins, and anandamide neurotransmitters (appetitive effects), and likely are met with counteradaptation processes (Weinstein & Weinstein, 2014). Thus, they could work off of each other, producing similar short-term impacts (satiation) and similar counteradaptations. Exercise/alcohol co-addicts may be preoccupied in engaging in both activities. For most such persons it is doubtful that they would engage in drinking and sports participation at the same time. Rather, they may over train (loss of control), leading to tiredness or injury, which may then lead to drinking alcohol. Conversely, they may drink too much alcohol (loss of control), leading to being hung over, and then they may exercise extensively to decrease the duration of feeling hung over, or feel a contrast effect while getting into shape. Certainly, engagement in both addictions may lead to a variety of negative consequences such as impaired performance and injury.

Potential Interplay of Exercise and Alcohol Addictions. Carnes, Murray & Charpentier (2005) discuss different ways in which co-occurring addictions may be related in their study which included over 1000 males who had sought treatment for a sexual disorder (46% reported a history of alcoholism and 11% reported a history of exercise addiction). Among the 10 types of co-occurrence patterns discussed by Carnes and colleagues, "withdrawal mediation", "alternating addiction cycles" and "intensification" appear reasonable explanations for how alcohol use and sports participation might be related. "Withdrawal mediation" refers to avoidance of withdrawal from one behavior by engaging in another. For example, outside of training an athlete may drink alcohol to obtain the same type of arousing effect (mediated mainly by social context, though some risk-taking athletes may engage in both activities regardless of social context). Likewise, an athlete may over train to attempt to obtain the same kind of arousing effect achieved by drinking.

"Alternating addiction cycles" refers to engaging in one addiction contingent on life event changes. For example, when injured an athlete may become a heavy drinker. When not drinking, possibly due to a drinking related consequence and need to at least temporarily stop drinking (e.g., suffering a DUI, or getting arrested for being drunk in public), a person may become engaged in excessive exercise.

Finally, "intensification" refers to establishing a means to intensify the effect of a behavior through a fixed pattern of involvement in a second behavior. An athlete may train hard to be able to (subjectively) drink more alcohol for the calories and sedating effects. Conversely, an athlete may drink alcohol, and then experience a more dramatic change in mood or sense of getting into shape by exercising. All three of these types of co-occurrence patterns may exist. Longitudinal research studies are needed to explore the potential interplay of these three types of co-occurrence patterns.

The PACE Model and Reasons for Overlap

One other means to approach conceptually, and suggest research directions regarding, the co-occurrence of these two activities is by utilizing the PACE theoretical model. The PACE model was created to explain the development of patterns of co-occurring or non-co-occurring addictive behaviors (Sussman et al., 2011). The four variables that compose this model are: pragmatics, attraction, communication, and expectations. *Pragmatics* variables operate to discern whether or not one can access a particular addictive behavior and then engage in this behavior regularly. One must have knowledge of and access to a bar, liquor store, sports lounge, gym area, or sports club, as examples. "Channels of introduction" to the addictive behavior likely contain cues specific to that behavior and begin a process of differential exposure to and learning of information related to the context of the addiction. For example, beer advertisements and packaging may indicate where to purchase the product and also suggest that when one drinks beer, one drinks multiple beers on a drinking occasion; thus, one also learns how much of the addiction object to purchase. Likewise, commercials or photos depicting sports competitions may suggest where one should go to exercise or compete (e.g., a track or baseball diamond) and how one should experience training (e.g., with how much exertion or how rough one should play). Interestingly, a sports bar or lounge is an establishment that caters to sports fans and participants and typically contains televisions that display sports events and sports memorabilia. This type of establishment, in particular, provides a clear introduction channel to the co-occurrence of, and creates cognitive associations regarding, alcohol drinking and sports teams participation.

Attraction plays an important role in addiction co-occurrence and specificity by impacting whether someone is likely to initiate and continue engaging in an addictive behavior or behaviors. Numerous variables can shape what determines if a behavior is attractive. These include individual difference variables that may influence selection of the addictive behavior. One may speculate that only persons who are relatively proficient at a sports activity (e.g., show some natural talent), or feel pleasure while working out, will tend to maintain a workout regimen and be a member of a sports team. Likewise, people who experience particular pleasure from an alcohol "buzz" are relatively likely to drink regularly. Attraction also involves the experiential pleasantness ascribed to addictive behavior-related stimuli and context. One may feel attracted to the sight, smells, sounds, tactile stimulation, or social stimuli inherent in the context of the addiction (e.g., the sight of a sports arena or a sports bar). Overtime, and through associative learning and memory processes, these contextual stimuli may come to represent the behavior and appetitive effects, affecting attraction to the behavior itself. Using alcohol as a reward for working out hard, and experiencing the sedation produced by the physical activity and then enhanced through drinking, all within a context of shared group collective experience, may reflect the sort of attraction that these behaviors may elicit in conjunction with each other.

Earlier life experiences, by perpetuating differential exposure and *communications* associated with addictive behavior, may prepare people for which types of addictions they pursue. That is, early experiences with differential vocabularies can direct behavior toward specific addictive behaviors. For example, as a child one may observe their older siblings or parents consuming beer and watching football on TV, view beer commercials during sports games, and hear conversation, laughter, and words such as "gusto" or "cheers", and phrases such as "you're out of the bar" (like you are out at the plate; http://www.beerhistory.com/library/holdings/beer_commercials.shtml; accessed 4-8-2014), or witness a toast to the winning score. As one engages in an addictive behavior, a relationship develops that involves craving, seeking, experiencing, and recovering from the effects of the addictive behavior. A system of communication about these aspects of the addiction may develop, encompass important features of one's daily life, and call upon quite distinct personal and intergroup communication styles and techniques. As one becomes differentially socialized, one may become an "expert" in the language of the addiction and feel like a "regular" or someone who belongs in that context. The person may self-identify with addiction-related groups or activities (e.g., regularly and ritualistically celebrating after team practice or after competitions). Communication about the addiction, therefore, can be a way of forming or solidifying social relationships with other addicts or addictive object providers.

Several words or phrases may be used to refer to alcohol use or sports participation, facilitating semantic associations. As examples, someone may be referred to as an "alcohol ace" (https://www.youtube.com/watch?v=zMNTKVM86fQ; accessed 4-8-2014), or able to imbibe a great deal, or as an ace athlete, a top player. One can go on a football "blitz" (a defensive attack) or a drinking "blitz". One can be in the "bush league" as a player or a drinker (amateur). Being "down for the count" can refer to being knocked out in boxing or football, or passing out from drinking. One can "fumble" a football, or say something embarrassing while drinking. ("Fumble" is also part of the name of a drinking game: http://www.fundrinkinggame.com/#!blind-mans-fumble/ctrb; accessed 4-8-2014).

Drinking games provide a context to express a common "competition" language as in team sports participation (Hummer, LaBrie, & Lac, 2011). "Quarters" and "Beer Pong" are drinking games involving bouncing a quarter or ping pong ball off a table into a glass of alcohol. These are competitions that have a sports competition-like tone (http://listverse.com/2007/10/20/top-10-drinking-games/; accessed 4-8-2014). A variation of "Quarters" is called "Baseball" in which one's score (single, double, triple, homerun) determines how many shots or glasses of beer one must drink (http://www.webtender.com/handbook/games/; accessed 4-8-2014). There are also sets of drinking games sometimes referred to as "beer Olympics" (http://www.urbandictionary.com/define.php?term=beer%20olympics; accessed 4-8-2014). Another game is referred to as the National Basketball Association Drinking Game (http://www.drinkinggamezone.com/drinking-games/national-basketball-association-nba/; accessed 4-8-2014) which involves drinking based on viewing scoring in a basketball game on TV. In summary, a language may exist among athletes to signal both alcohol consumption and sports team participation and group solidarity. More research is needed to better understand the language of alcohol intake-sports team participation co-occurrence.

Expectancy as a construct relevant to addiction involves the anticipated consequences of behavior or beliefs held about the likelihood of experiencing various appetitive effects. In terms of the PACE model, addiction expectancies or expectations are beliefs regarding the likelihood that or extent to which an addictive behavior is providing solutions to experiential requests. For example, heavier drinkers differ from light drinkers on activation of expectancies of positive arousing effects versus sedating effects of alcohol, similar, perhaps to the experience of participation in rigorous team sports (Sussman et al., 2011). That is, both activities may subjectively be expected to serve as arousing or adventurous events, which may be confirmed through experience.

Solutions and Conclusion

In this chapter we discussed reasons why alcohol use and sports participation co-occur. Perhaps the most important reason is that their co-participation may serve as a means to enhance peer group cohesion, as has been indicated in recent lab research (Kirkpatrick & de Wit, 2013). By drinking with other team members, who are also getting intoxicated, participants may derive more pleasure from the drinking, feel more intoxicated, and feel a relatively greater sense of comradery. This social cohesion aspect of drinking among sports team members does seem to be a key mediating variable of the relations among the two activities in studies that have been completed thus far.

Means to disassociate the two activities are needed in research and practice. Direct instruction of the negative aspects of engaging in alcohol misuse and team sports might be entertained by coaches who, in theory, should serve as role models for the team. Policy solutions also might be considered, such as enforcement of fines for going to clubs during the week, restricting serving of alcoholic beverages near sports venues, or restrictions on alcohol industry sponsorship of sports teams. As most alcohol misuse takes place on Friday or Saturday nights, having competitions take place on weekends might be a way to reduce athlete intoxication as any reduction in physical capacity will have immediate and recognizable consequences for peak athletic performance.

Relations between sports participation and alcohol use appear to be attenuated for those youth who are also actively involved in academic activities (Mays et al., 2010), or who are otherwise involved in executive processing operations. Interestingly, learning of cognitive-behavioral strategies which involve use of executive processing/planning appears to sever relations of alcohol use with negative affect among college athletes. For example, planning involved in stopping/limiting drinking (e.g., "stop drinking at a predetermined time"), changing manner of drinking (e.g., "avoid drinking games"), and use of serious harm reduction strategies (e.g., "use a designated driver") have been found to moderate the relations of negative urgency with alcohol use or use problems (Weaver, Martens & Smith, 2012).

After exercising, a person may become tired causing inhibitory executive cognitive processes to become temporarily less functional. Persons vulnerable toward drinking alcohol may be relatively likely to drink when tired out after training. Daily exercise may suppress the relationship between sports team participation and alcohol use (Terry-McElrath, O'Malley, & Johnston, 2011), perhaps suggesting that a serious investment in training may be protective, possibly reflecting more investment in health or a better muscular foundation (i.e., one doesn't get very tired out after training) so that executive processes continue to operate maximally. In summary, involvement in additional activities (e.g., academics) that involve deliberate cognitive processing appears to decrease the tendency to engage in drinking while serving as a participant on a sports team.

Possibly, providing athletes with a better lifestyle balance, or having them think through the implications of drinking while participating in sports (decision making exercises), may assist in decreasing self-defeating co-occurrence. Potentially, having athletes take five minutes of quiet, alone time after practices, along with provision of planning lists for that evening, may assist in not engaging in drinking events frequently. Other types of "hangouts" might be considered such as coffee sports clubs.

Future research is needed to better understand the co-occurrence of drinking and sports participation. However, the conceptual framework has been laid to test out a variety of ideas. Certainly, prevention and control strategies need better conceptualization and implementation to decrease the physical, financial, and social problems that may become created through their continued co-occurrence.

REFERENCES

Adams, J. (2009). Understanding exercise dependence. *Journal of Contemporary Psychotherapy, 39*, 231-240.

Allegre, B., Souville, M., Therme, P., & Griffiths, M. (2006). Definitions and measures of exercise dependence. *Addiction Research and Theory, 14*, 631-646.

American Psychiatric Association (APA). (2013). *Diagnostic and statistical manual of mental disorders (DSM-V)*. Washington, DC: Author.

Audrain-McGovern, J., Rodriguez, D., Cuevas, J., & Sass, J. (2013). Initial insight into why physical activity may help prevent adolescent smoking uptake. *Drug and Alcohol Dependence, 132*, 471-478.

Bedendo, A., Opaleye, E. S., Andrade, A. L. M., & Noto, A. R. (2013). Heavy episodic drinking and soccer practice among high school students in Brazil: the contextual aspects of this relationship. *BMC Public Health, 13*, 247, 8 pages.

Belanger, R. E., Ohl, F., Berchtold, A., Akre, C., & Suris, J.-C. (2012). Social contexts of sports-practicing youths' hazardous drinking. Swiss Medical Weekly: *The European Journal of Medical Sciences, 142*, 4 pages.

Berczik, K., Szabo, A., Griffiths, M. D., Kurimay, T., Kun, B., Urban, R., & Demetrovics, Z. (2012). Exercise addiction: Symptoms, diagnosis, epidemiology, and etiology. *Substance Use & Misuse, 47*, 403-417.

Buckman, J. F., Farris, S. G., & Yusko, D. A. (2013). A national study of substance use behaviors among NCAA male athletes who use banned performance enhancing substances. *Drug and Alcohol Dependence, 131*, 50-55.

Buckman, J. F., Yusko, D. A., Farris, S. G., White, H. R., & Pandina, R. J. (2011). Risk of marijuana use in male and female college student athletes and nonathletes. *Journal of Studies on Alcohol and Drugs, 72*, 586-591.

Buscemi, J., Martens, M. P., Murphy, J. G., Yurasek, A. M., & Smith, A. E. (2011). Moderators of the relationship between physical activity and alcohol consumption in college students. *Journal of American College Health, 59*, 503-509.

Cadigan, J. M., Littlefield, A. K., Martens, M. P., & Sher, K. J. (2013). Transitions into and out of intercollegiate athletic involvement and risky drinking. *Journal of Studies on Alcohol & Drugs, 74*, 21-29.

Carnes, P. J., Murray, R. E., & Charpentier, L. (2005). Bargains with chaos: Sex addicts and addiction interaction disorder. *Sexual Addiction & Compulsivity, 12*, 79-120.

Davies, F. M., & Foxall, G. R. (2011). Involvement in sport and intention to consume alcohol: An exploratory study of UK adolescents. *Journal of Applied Social Psychology, 41*, 2284-2311.

Demetrovics, Z., & Griffiths, M. D. (2012). Behavioral addictions: Past, present and future. *Journal of Behavioral Addictions, 1*, 1-2.

Diel, K., Thiel, A., Zipfel, S., Mayer, J., Litaker, D. G., & Schneider, S. (2012). How healthy is the behavior of young athletes? A systematic literature review and meta-analyses. *Journal of Sports Science and Medicine, 11*, 201-220.

Dunn, M., & Thomas, J. O. (2012). A risk profile of elite Australian athletes who use illicit drugs. *Addictive Behaviors, 37*, 144-147.

Freimuth, M., Moniz, S., & Kim, S. R. (2011). Clarifying exercise addiction: Differential diagnosis, co-occurring disorders, and phases of addiction. *International Journal of Environmental Research and Public Health, 8*, 4069-4081.

Fujimoto, K., & Valente, T. W. (2013). Alcohol peer influence of participating in organized school activities: A network approach. *Health Psychology, 32*, 1084-1092.

Gmel, G., Kuendig, H., & Daeppen, J.-B. (2009). Sport and alcohol: An emergency department study in Switzerland. *European Journal of Sports Science, 9*, 11-22.

Goodman, A. (2008). Neurobiology of addiction: An integrative review. *Biochemical Pharmacology, 75*, 266-322.

Greenberg, J. L., Lewis, S. E., & Dodd, D. K. (1999). Overlapping addictions and self-esteem among college men and women. *Addictive Behaviors, 24*, 565–571.

Grossbard, J., Hummer, J., LaBrie, J., Pederson, E., & Neighbors, C. (2009). Is substance use a team sport? Attraction to team, perceived norms, and alcohol and marijuana use among male and female intercollegiate athletes. *Journal of Applied Sport Psychology, 21*, 247-261.

Hausenblas, H. A., & Downs, D. S. (2002). How much is too much? The development and validation of the Exercise Addiction scale. *Psychology and Health, 17*, 387-404.

Haylett, S. A., Stephenson, G. M., & Lefever, R. M. H. (2004). Covariation in addictive behaviors: A study of addictive orientations using the shorter PROMIS Questionnaire. *Addictive Behaviors, 29*, 61-71.

Henchoz, Y., Dupuis, M., Deline, S., Studer, J., Baggio, S., N'Goran, A. A., Daeppen, J.-B., & Gmel, G. (2014). Associations of physical activity and sport and exercise with at-risk substance use in young men: A longitudinal study. *Preventive Medicine, 64*, 27-31.

Hummer, J. F., LaBrie, J. W., & Lac, A. (2011). Warming up and staying loose: The prevalence, style, and influence of prepartying behavior and drinking games among intercollegiate athletes. *Athletic Insight Journal, 3*, 135-152.

Kirkpatrick, M. G., & de Wit, H. (2013). In the company of others: social factors alter acute alcohol effects. *Psychopharmacology, 230*, 215-226.

Korhonen, T., Kujala, U. M., Rose, R. J., & Kaprio, J. (2009). Physical activity in adolescence as a predictor of alcohol and illicit drug use in early adulthood: A longitudinal population based twin study. *Twin Research and Human Genetics, 12*, 261-268.

Kwan, M., Bobko, S., Faulkner, G., Donnelly, P., & Cairney, J. (2014). Sports participation and alcohol and illicit drug use in adolescents and youth adults: A systematic review of longitudinal studies. *Addictive Behaviors, 39*, 497-506.

Leasure, J. L. & Neighbors, C. (in press). Impulsivity moderates the association between physical activity and alcohol consumption. *Alcohol.*

Lejoyeux, M., Avril, M., Richoux, C., Embouazza, H., & Nivoli, F. (2008). Prevalence of exercise dependence and other behavioral addictions among clients of a Parisian fitness room. *Comprehensive Psychiatry, 49*, 353-358.

Leshner, A. I. (1997). Addiction is a brain disease, and it matters. *Science, 278*, 45-47.

Lisha, N. E, Crano, W. D., & Delucchi, K. L. (2014). Participation in team sports and alcohol and marijuana use initiation trajectories. *Journal of Drug Issues, 44*, 83-93.

Lisha, N. E., Martins, M., & Leventhal, A. M. (2011). Age and gender as moderators of the relationship between physical activity and alcohol use. *Addictive Behaviors, 36*, 933-936.

Lisha, N. E., & Sussman, S. (2010). Relationship of high school and college sports participation with alcohol, tobacco, and illicit drug use: a review. *Addictive Behaviors, 35*, 399-407.

Lisha, N. E., Sussman, S., & Leventhal, A. M. (2013). Physical activity and alcohol use disorders. American *Journal of Drug and Alcohol Abuse, 39*, 115-120.

Lisha, N. E., Sussman, S., & Leventhal, A. M. (2013). Correction to "Physical activity and alcohol use disorders". *American Journal of Drug and Alcohol Abuse, 39*, 136-137.

Makela, K. (1983). The uses of alcohol and their cultural regulation. *Acta Sociologica, 26*, 21-31.

Martens, M. P., Dams-O'Connor, K., Duffy-Paiement, C., & Gibson, J. T. (2006). Perceived alcohol use among friends and alcohol consumption among college athletes. *Psychology of Addictive Behaviors, 20*, 178-184.

Martinsen, M. & Sundgot-Borgen, J. (2014). Adolescent elite athletes' cigarette smoking, use of snus, and alcohol. *Scandinavian Journal of Medicine & Science in Sports, 24*, 439-446.

Mays, D., DePadilla, L., Thompson, N. J., Kushner, H. I., & Windle, M. (2010). Sports participation and problem alcohol use. *American Journal of Preventive Medicine, 38*, 491-498.

Mays, D., Thompson, N., Kushner, H. I., Mays, D. F., Farmer, D., & Windle, M. (2010). Sports-specific factors, perceived peer drinking, and alcohol-related behaviors among adolescents participating in school-based sports in Southwest Georgia. *Addictive Behaviors, 35*, 235-241.

Murphy, A. P., Snape, A. E., Minett, G. M., Skein, M., & Duffield, R. (2013) The effect of post-match alcohol ingestion on recovery from competitive rugby league matches. *Journal of Strength and Conditioning Research,* 27, 1304–1312.

O'Brien, K. S., Lynott, D., & Miller, P. G. (2013). Alcohol industry sponsorship and alcohol-related harms in Australian university sportspeople/athletes. *Drug and Alcohol Review, 32*, 241-247.

Peretti-Watel, P. (2009). Sports and drugs: Further interpretive hypotheses are necessary. *Addiction, 104*, 150-151.

Potenza, M. N. (2010). What integrated interdisciplinary and translational research may tell us about addiction. *Addiction, 105*, 790-796.

Sawyer, A. L., Wolfenden, L., Kennedy, V. J., Kingsland, M., Young, K. G., Tindall, J., Rowland, B. C., Colbran, R. W., & Wiggers, J. H. (2012). Alcohol sponsorship of community football clubs: the current situation. *Health Promotion Journal of Australia, 23*, 70-72.

Sonderlund, A. L., O'Brien, K., Kremer, P., Rowland, B., De Groot, F. Staiger, P., Zinkiewicz, & Miller, P. G. (2014). The association between sports participation, alcohol use and aggression and violence: A systematic review. *Journal of Science and Medicine in Sport, 17*, 2-7.

Sussman, S. (2012). Steve Sussman on Matilda Hellman's "Mind the Gap!" Failure in understanding key dimensions of an addicted drug user's life: Addictive Effects. *Substance Use & Misuse, 47*, 1661-1665.

Sussman, S., Lisha, N., & Griffiths, M. (2011). Prevalence of the addictions: A problem of the majority or the minority? *Evaluation & the Health Professions, 34*, 3-56.

Sussman, S. & Sussman, A. N. (2011). Considering the definition of addiction. *International Journal of Environmental Research and Public Health, 8*, 4025-4038.

Taliaferro, L. A., Rienzo, B. A., & Donovan, K. A. (2010). Relationships between youth sport participation and selected health risk behaviors from 1999 to 2007. *Journal of School Health, 80*, 399-410.

Terry-McElrath, Y. M., & O'Malley, P. M. (2011) Substance use and exercise participation among young adults: Parallel trajectories in a National cohort-sequential study. *Addiction, 106*, 1855-1867.

Terry-McElrath, Y. M., O'Malley, P. M., & Johnston, L. D. (2011). Exercise and substance use among American youth, 1991-2009. *American Journal of Preventive Medicine, 40*, 530-540.

Vella, L. D., & Cameron-Smith, D. (2010). Alcohol, athletic performance and recovery. *Nutrients, 2*, 781-789.

Vest, A. E., & Simpkins, S. D. (2013). When is sport participation risky or protective for alcohol use? The role of teammates, friendships, and popularity. In J. A. Fredricks & S. D. Simpkins (Eds.), *Organized Out-of-School Activities: Settings for Peer Relationships. New Directions for Child and Adolescent Development, 140,* 37–55.

Weaver, C. C., Martens, M. P., & Smith, A. E. (2012). Do protective behavioral strategies moderate the relationship between negative urgency and alcohol-related outcomes among intercollegiate athlctics? *Journal of Studies on Alcohol & Drugs, 73*, 498-503.

Weaver, C. C., Martens, M. P., Cadigan, J. M., Takamatsu, S. K., Treloar, H. R., & Pedersen, E. R. (2013). Sport-related achievement motivation and alcohol outcomes: An athlete-specific risk factor among intercollegiate athletes. *Addictive Behaviors, 38*, 2930-2936.

Weinstein, A., & Weinstein, Y. (2014). Exercise addiction-diagnosis, bio-psychological mechanisms and treatment issues. *Current Pharmaceutical Design, 20*, in press.

Wichstrom, T., &Wichstrom, L. (2009). Does sports participation during adolescence prevent later alcohol, tobacco and cannabis use? *Addiction, 104*, 138-149.

Zhou, J., O'Brien, K. S., & Heim, D. (2013). Alcohol consumption in sportspeople: The role of social cohesion, identity and happiness. *International Review for the Sociology of Sport*, 1-16, in press.

In: Substance Abuse
Editor: Jeffrey Raines

ISBN: 978-1-63321-949-6

Chapter 2

THE CUTANEOUS EFFECTS OF ADULTERED COCAINE

Ashley N. Amalfi[1], M.D. and
Michael W. Neumeister,[2,*] M.D., FRCSC, FACS

[1]PGY 6 Plastic Surgery Resident,
Southern Illinois University School of Medicine
Institute for Plastic and Reconstructive Surgery
[2] Professor & Chair – Department of Surgery, the
Elvin G. Zook Endowed Chair in Plastic Surgery,
Southern Illinois University School of Medicine
Institute for Plastic and Reconstructive Surgery

ABSTRACT

Introduction: The cardiopulmonary, neurologic and psychiatric sequelae of cocaine are well documented. However, little is known of the devastating cutaneous manifestations of cocaine. When cocaine is cut with the common adulterant levamisole, significant impact on the integument ensues. Patients may suffer from a continuum of purpura and petichiae to full-thickness skin and soft tissue necrosis. These patients should be managed in a qualified burn center by an experienced Reconstructive Plastic Surgeon.

---

* Corresponding Author: 747 N Rutledge – 3rd Floor, PO Box 19653. Springfield, IL 62794, (217) 545-7018 Phone, (217) 545-2588 Fax, mneumeister@siumed.edu E-mail.

Rheumatologic Susceptability: Patients who present with these cutanous manifestations often have a history of rheumatologic disease or meet criteria for diagnosis of such. A variety of auto-antibodies have been serologically identified at presentation. These include Antinuclear Antibodies (ANA), Perinuclear Anti-Neutrophil Cytoplasmic Antibodies (P-ANCA), double-stranded DNA (dsDNA), Lupus Anticoagulant (LA) titers, Rheumatoid Factor (RF), cyliccitrullinated peptide antibody (CCP), anti-proteus antibody (APA) and anti-streptolysin antibody (ASLO).

Adulterated Cocaine: The average cocaine bought on the streets today is only 45% cocaine hydrocholoride. Adulterants are added to potentiate the effects or increase the weight of the product. Since 2005, a new adulterant, levamisole, has been identified in cocaine. By 2011, 82% of cocaine imported into the United States already contained levamisole. This has been reported not just in the United States, but also in Canada, the United Kingdom and Italy. More recently, heroin samples laced with levamisole have also been identified. Levamisole is an anti-helminth, used solely in veterinary medicine to deworm livestock. In August of 2010, the New York State Department of Health issued a public advisory, warning of the dangerous health concerns of cocaine cut with levamisole.

Cutaneous Manifestations: Historically, levamisole was used in the treatment of cancer as well as nephrotic syndrome in children. Its use was abandoned due to the resulting vasculitis, purpura, agranulocytosis, hepatosplenomegaly and circulating autoimmune antibodies noted in patients. Health care professionals are now seeing a similar myriad of symptoms in cocaine users whose product is adulterated with the levamisole. Most patients present with vague constitutional symptoms and polyarthralgias. Upon further examination many have purpura or petechiae that mimic an autoimmune process. Even with abstinence from the drug, many of these patients go on to develop frank necrosis of their skin and soft tissue. This is commonly seen on the helix of the ear, the nasal tip, breasts, thighs, abdomen and upper extremities.

Surgical Mangement: Supportive local wound care is necessary to all cuteanous manifestations until the wounds have fully demarcated. Serial surgical debridement of non-viable tissue is necessary in a staged manner. Once the wounds have stabilized, they may be closed via primary closure, skin grafting or local flaps.

Conclusions: The cutaneous manifestations of adultured cocaine have not been previously well described. It is necessary for health care professionals to have a heightened awareness of this emerging entity to aid in both prompt diagnosis and the appropriate medical and surgical management.

INTRODUCTION

The cardiopulmonary, neurologic and psychiatric sequelae of cocaine have been well documented since its earliest recorded use in the fifteenth century. Peruvians in the Andes mountains relied heavily on the cocoa plant, *Erythroxylum Coca* for its stimulant properties on the central nervous system that curbed the cold, hunger and monotony of early civilization in this region. Medical practitioners are accustomed to treating patients in the emergency setting for similar stimulating neurologic sequelae of cocaine.

Each year in the United States, cocaine consumption is linked to over 500,000 visits to emergency rooms and acute care settings (National Survey on Drug Use and Health). As its use continues to rise, it is now estimated that nearly 2 million Americans abuse cocaine on a regular basis, and each day 1,700 new individuals try cocaine for the first time (National Survey on Drug Use and Health). Fortunately, few patients require hospitalization and mortality remains low, occurring in less than 1% of users presenting for medical attention [Brody].

In the past few years, a new reaction to cocaine has been encountered by health care practitioners. Cocaine is now causing medical sequelae on the skin and soft tissue of the body. When cocaine is cut with the common adulterant levamisole, significant impact on the integument ensues. Patients who are affected suffer from a continuum of purpura and petichiae that progresses to full-thickness skin and soft tissue necrosis. The drug levamisole has been linked as the culprit adulterant, due to its historic side effect profile that closely mimics the cutaneous and immune response seen in these patients.

The Rise of Levamisole Adultered Cocaine

The cocaine bought on the streets today contains only 45% cocaine hydrocholoride, but can vary between 20 and 90% purity in the United States (World Drug Report). A variety of substances are added or "cut" into the powder, causing such a range in purity. Some cocaine seized in the United States in found to contain almost no cocaine at all upon analysis. An adulterant is something that is added to cocaine purposefully to potentiate its effects based on its own drug profile. Medications and other drugs including lidocaine, caffeine and methamphetamine may also be added for their stimulant properties. A bulking agent is also intentionally cut into the product to increase the amount and weigh of the product. Low cost items such as talc and baking soda are cut into cocaine by dealers to increase the quantity of the drug for sale, and thus their profit.

In 2005, a new adulterant, levamisole, was detected in cocaine seized in the United States. Not only was this a new substance never before detected in cocaine, it was peculiar that the product was already cut into the cocaine before it reached the United States. Typically, cocaine is transported into the United States in its pure powder form, and ranges from 90 to 100% purity. The drug is usually adultered within the country of distribution by metropolitan hubs and drug organizations before it is distributed to local dealers who often add bulking agents, and the product finally reaches the consumer.

After its entry into the market, just three years later in 2008, the U.S. Drug Enforcement Administration (DEA) estimated that 10% of cocaine imported into the United States was laced with levamisole. In 2011, this increased eight-fold, with 82% of cocaine imported into the United States already contained the dangerous chemical. These exponentially growing numbers have been reported not just in the United States, but also in Canada, the United Kingdom and Italy [Arkanjel]. More recently, heroin samples laced with levamisole have also been identified in the United States [Casale].

Historically, levamisole was an investigational drug used for the treatment of metastatic colon cancer. Its use quickly fell out of favor as it showed no benefit in the treatment of the disease. It was then used for its immune-modulating effects in nephrotic syndrome in children. After prolonged clinical trials in Europe, numerous case reports linked the drug to autoimmune vasculitis in many of the children being treated for renal disease. The resultant vasculitis consisted of diffuse purpura, agranulocytosis, hepatosplenomegaly and circulating autoimmune antibodies. In one clinical trial, 5 of the 150 enrolled children developed a severe vasculitis, leading to the premature termination of the study [Barbano]. Levamisole was then promptly removed from the United States market in 2000, and in Canada in 2003.

Since the moratorium within the oncologic community, Levamisole is now used solely in veterinary medicine for its anti-helminthproperties. It is one of the most common medications used to deworm cattle, pigs, sheep and other livestock here in the United States and also globally. It has been suggested that this inexpensive drugs presence in large quantities in rural farming communities of Central and South America may be the driving force behind its escalating presence in imported drugs.

In August of 2010, the New York State Department of Health issued a public advisory, warning of the dangers of cocaine cut with levamisole. Early symptoms reported included a profound agranulocytosis. Those affected were also noted to have purpura of the helices and lobules of the ears and diffusely across the face. In this initial report, all cutaneous manifestations eventually subsided with cessation and continued abstinence of the contaminated cocaine (NYS-DOH). Unfortunately for health care workers, levamisole has a very short half-life of just four hours, making its detection difficult unless consumption is suspected promptly.

Canada experienced a similar surge in health related complications of cocaine use, also incriminating levamisole as the most likely culprint. In Alberta and British Columbia, mandatory reporting of neutropenia associated with levamisole tainted cocaine was instituted, and forty-two cases of confirmed or probable agranulocytosis were identified and linked to levamisole. Once awareness was raised, patients were tested for the metabolites of both cocaine and levamisole in the urine. Other patients also had drug paraphernalia that was confiscated and analyzed in the laboratory, revealing levamisole in the cocaine. Most patients readily admitted to daily smoking of crack cocaine. Unforuntately, only the hematologic sequelae were included in this database, and no records indicate either the autoimmune profile or cuteanous manifestations experienced among this Canadian cohort [Lewinda].

Initial public health concern related to agranulocytosis, but as more cases were reported, medical practicioners began to notice similar skin manifestations and rheumatologic concerns among those affected. Patients at the University of Rochester Medical Center in Rochester, NY were noted to have agranulocytosis as well as purpuritic plaques on the malar eminence of their cheeks, helical rim and lobule of the ear. This further emphasized the link to levamisole, as an almost identical purpuritic pattern was seen in the cohort of children treated with levamisole for nephrotic syndromealmost a decade prior [Dumyati].

Many similar reports followed, noting now both the serologic concerns as well as the skin manifestations commonly encountered. It was also apparent that the earliest cases noted complete resolution of cutaneaous manifestations with cessation of the drug. But as the medical concern continued to mount, so did the severerity of the encountered illness. There were now reported deaths linked to agranulocytosis [Waller], as well as frank necrosis of the skin that required operative intervention, skin grafting and prolongedsurgical treatment in a burn unit [VanWiren]. Emergency Medicine literature now urged practicioners to screen drug abusers presenting for treatment for both cocaine and levamisole metabolites to aid in early diagnosis [Kinzie].

Rheumatologic Profile

Patients who develop cutaneous manifestations from adultered cocaine have a unique rheumatologic profile. Their autoimmune history makes them susceptible to the effects of levamisole, while those who lack such a profile appear to have some element of immunity. Patients medical histories are often quite similar with the most common rheumatologic diagnoses including Systemic Lupus Erythematosis (SLE), Antiphosopholipid Antibody Syndrome, Wegener's Granulomatosis, Churg-Strauss Granulomatosis, p-ANCA Necrotizing Vasculitis, Rheumatoid Arthritis (RA) and Scleroderma. If a patient's medical history does not reveal an autoimmune diagnosis, a more thorough history, physical and serology workup should ensue. Often, the evaluating physician will arrive at a rheumatologic diagnosis that has since been previously undiagnosed. The patients who carry a diagnosis are not always on medical therapy for such, and no correlation between medications used to manage these rheumatologic diseases and the development of cutaneous manifestations after cocaine use have been identified.

The workup of patients should include a thorough history and physical as well as a complete serology panel to test for autoantibodies and inflammatory markers. A varied cocktail of autoantibodies is found in each patient. As their skin manifestations develop and evolve, so too will their serologic profile. We recommend screening for autoantibodies at the time of presentation and weekly throughout the progression of their illness. Titers will often rise over time and dissipate in a pattern that closely parallels their cutaneous manifestations. After complete healing and re-epithelialization of their wounds, some serologic studies may normalize, while others remain constant. The serologic antibodies most commonly identified in this population include Antinuclear Antibodies (ANA), Perinuclear Anti-Neutrophil Cytoplasmic Antibodies (p-ANCA), double-stranded DNA (dsDNA) , Lupus Anticoagulant (LA) titers, Rheumatoid Factor (RF), Anticardiolypin Antibody, Anti-Human Neutrophil Elastase (HNE), Cylic Citrullinated Peptide Antibody (CCP), Anti-Proteus Antibody (APA) and Anti-Streptolysin Antibody (ASLO). Testing should also include Erythrocyte Sedimentation Rate (ESR) and C-Reactive Protein (CRP) throughout the course of the illness. Some practicioners believe that HNE antibodies are the most specific for cocaine-related skin necrosis, however our patient experience has not demonstrated such a profile in patients who subsequently tested positive for cocaine and levamisole [Walsh].

The immune-modulating effects of levamisole have been studied extensively, yet its method of action remains elusive. Levamisole has been found to alter the delicate balance of cytokines and shift the immune response from a type 2 response (predominantly interleukin-4) to a type 1 response (interferon-gamma) in a rat model [Szeto]. Patients with certain autoimmune diseases also display a similar imbalance, with an overactive type 1 immune response, and high circulating levels of interferon-gamma. In patients with SLE and other mixed connective tissue diseases, this higher expression of serum interferon-gamma directly correlates with active clinical disease in patients [Funauch]. Similarly, in patients with a known autoimmune disease, the administration of interferon-gamma results in a fulminant and aggressive form of SLE [Mariani].

Extrapolating from these known autoimmune phenomena, we can propose a similar method of action in this subset of patients. The at-risk population consists of patients with a concomitant autoimmune history, and therefore these patients have a known innate over-expression of a type 1 immune response. Subsequent exposure to levamisole further augments this imbalance and causes a surge of interferon-gamma culminating in clinical disease. This would explain why certain individuals display such a severe response when exposed to levamisole while other who lack a predisposition for autoimmunity consume the contaminated cocaine without consequence. It is common for patients to report that they shared the same adultered cocaine with other users who seemed to experience no cutaneous effects of the cocaine, while they themselves suffered devastating medical consequences.

Cutaneous Manifestations

The initial public health concern was centered on the neutropenia caused by cocaine laced with levamisole. It became apparent with time however, that perhaps the most critical and life-threatening of the effects encountered is the effects on the integument.

The natural history of the disease varies in its severity, but follows a very similar pattern among patients. Most patients present to a primary care physician or Emergency Department with vague, constitutional symptoms. Upon further questioning, many recall a new onset rash that was progressing along with their other symptoms. Initially this resembles a vasculitis, with multiple scattered petechiae or more confluent purpura of the skin. (Figure 1) As the patient continues to use the contaminated drug, the skin reactions progress as well. These patchy areas often coalesce, forming larger, more distinct areas of concern. (Figure 2)

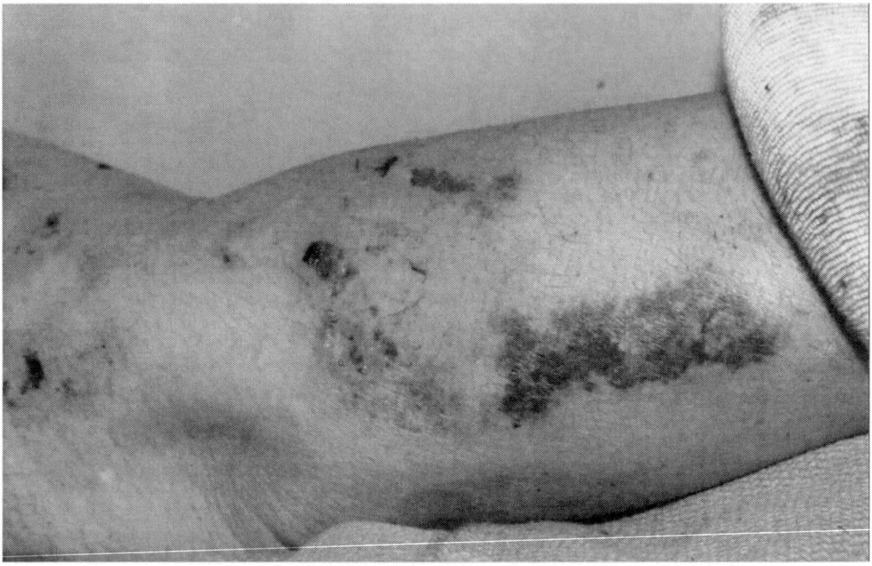

Figure 1. Early skin manifestations include scattered petechiae and purpura.

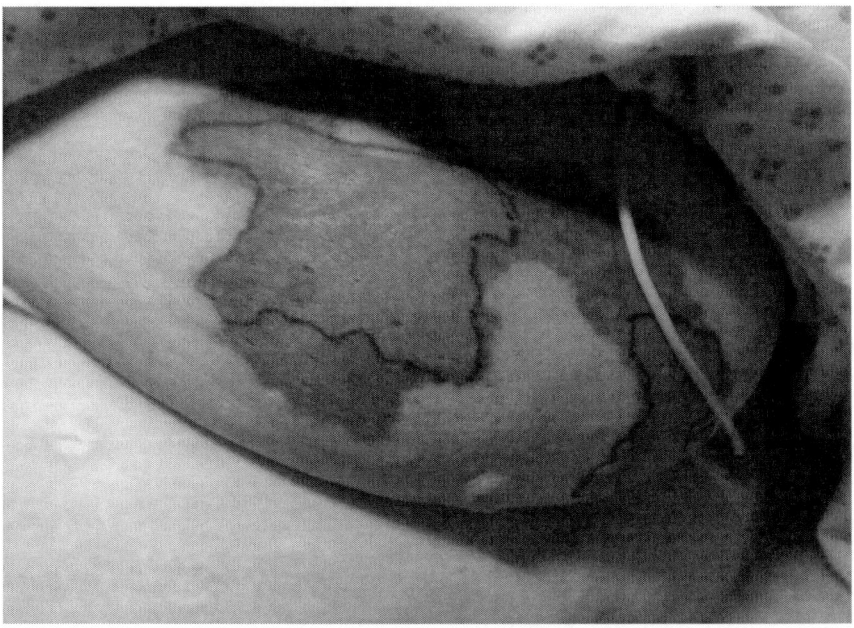

Figure 2. Scattered petechiae continue to progress into coalescing areas of purpura and soft tissue damage.

The location of the lesions is very specific to levamisole. As seen in the historical literature, almost all patients have purpura of the ears, often found along the helical rim and on the lobule as well. Other areas of the face affected include the malar eminence and cheeks. The lesions have a predilection for soft tissue areas with increased adiposity, and the distribution over the entire body reflects this. Purpura were often seen on the female breast as well as the infraumbilical abdomen. (Figure 3) The fleshy inner and outer thighs were similarly affected (Figure 4), mirroring a predilection to the inner arm of the upper extremity as well. (Figure 5 and 6).A thorough physical exam should be conducted, with care to look at the ears, breasts upper arms and and thighs for hallmarks of the disease process.

The differential diagnosis for these skin manifestations includes autoimmune processes, vasculitis and purpurafulminans. It is often prudent to obtain a dermatology consult to rule out these more common disease processes. This will lead to the diagnosis of levamisole induced skin necrosis via exclusion of other, more common entities.

It is also recommended that full thickness biopsies of the skin be obtained. These biopsies should be performed via a punch biopsy or an incisional biopsy. The core central area of necrosis should not be biopsied, as it will simply show advanced necrosis without contributing to the diagnosis. The ideal site should include early purpura and include the border with unaffected skin at the periphery of a lesion.

All tissue specimens should be examined by a dermatopathologist, accustomed to diagnosing rare skin conditions. Evaluation of the tissue by Hematoxylin and Eosin (H & E) staining will show microthrombi within both the superficial and deeper dermal blood vessels. (Figure 7). However, unlike a true vasculitis, a paucity of inflammatory cells in seen histologically. This absence of inflammatory cells can be used to distinguish levamisole induced necrosis from a true autoimmune vasculitis, where leukocytes would commonly populate the tissue around each of the coagulated vessels. (Figure 8)

The other distinguishing characteristic of these skin lesions are the propensity to progress in a vertical fashion, rather than a radially spreading process. As such, the tissue loss often is much more severe than a superficially spreading epidermolysis. The tendency for the thrombi to extend deeper has been observed in many patients. This results in a much more devastating loss of not just the dermal and epidermal elements, but the subcutaneous tissue as well.

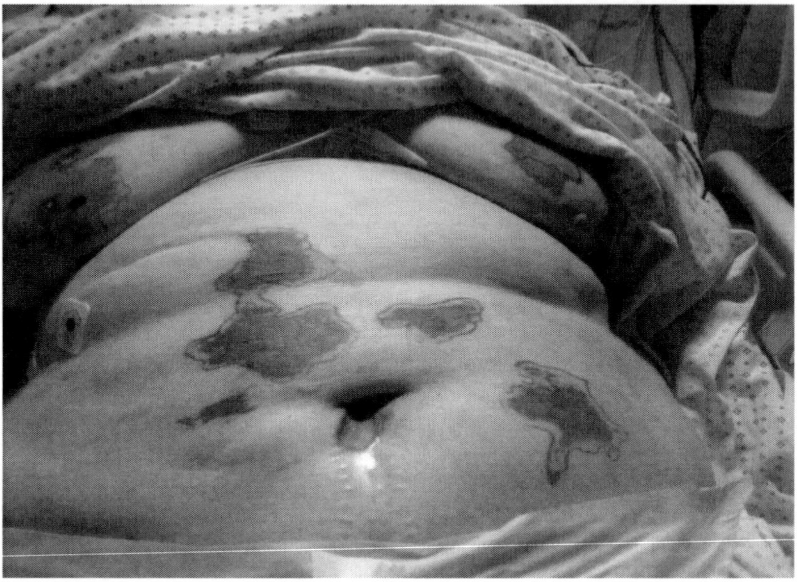

Figure 3. Areas of increased adiposity, including the breasts and abdomen are commonly affected.

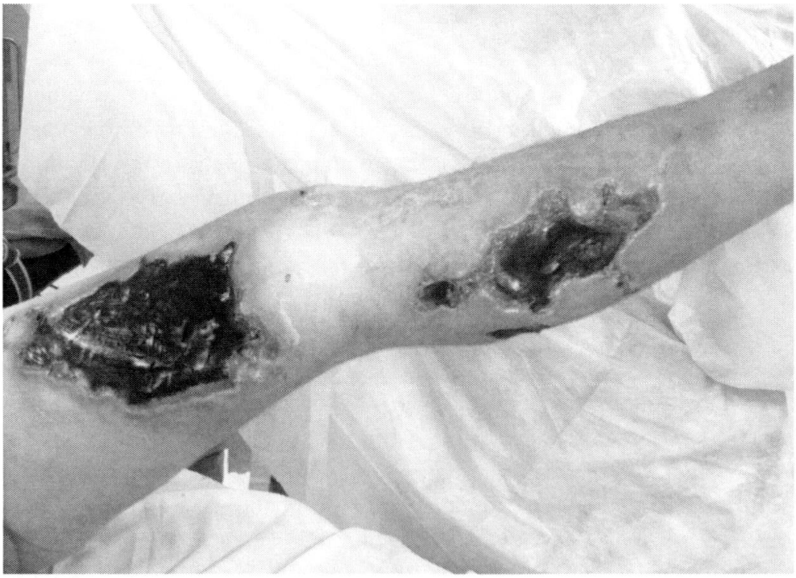

Figure 4. Full thickness necrosis depicted in inner thighs, a sight commonly affected by adultered cocaine.

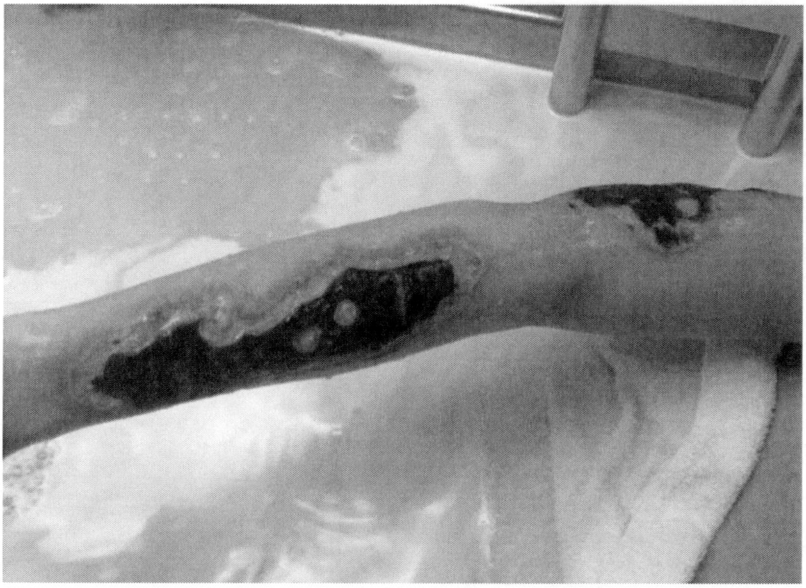

Figure 5. The upper extremities are similarly affected by the disease process.

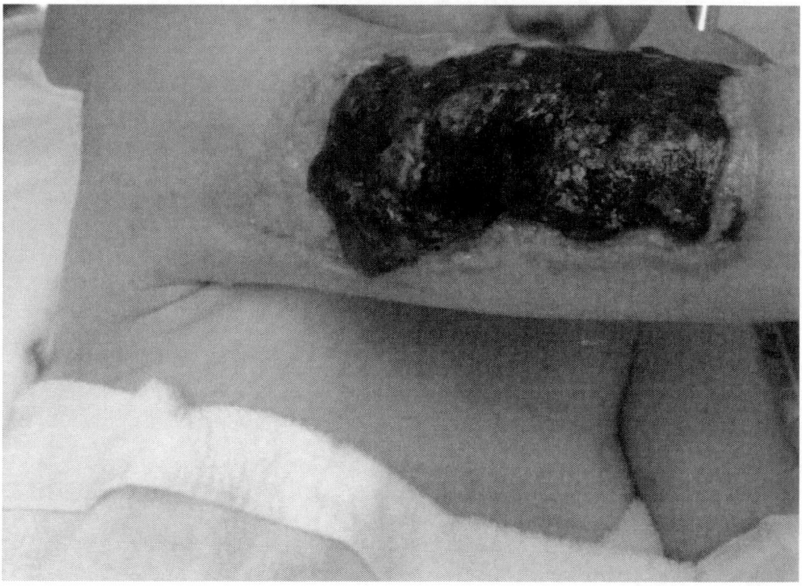

Figure 6. Large eschar representing full thickness necrosis of the upper extremity.

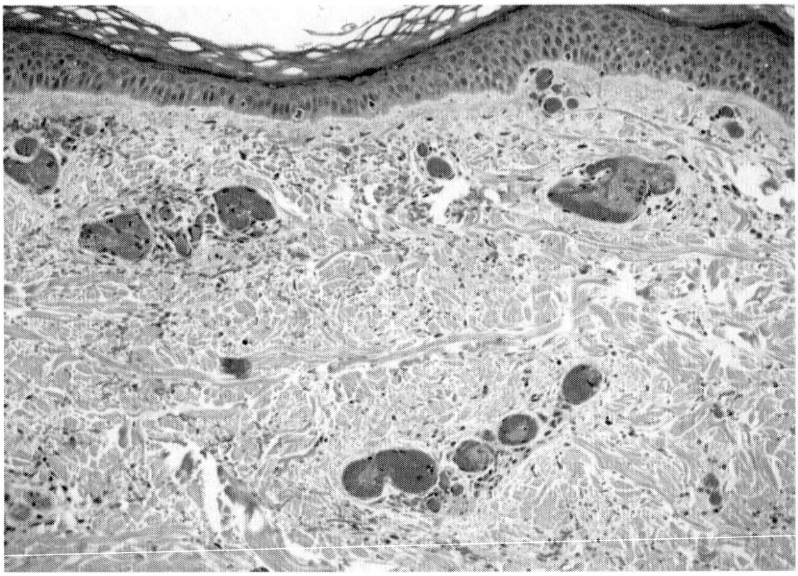

Figure 7. H &E of biopsy of lesions showing microthrombi with a paucity of inflammatory cells.

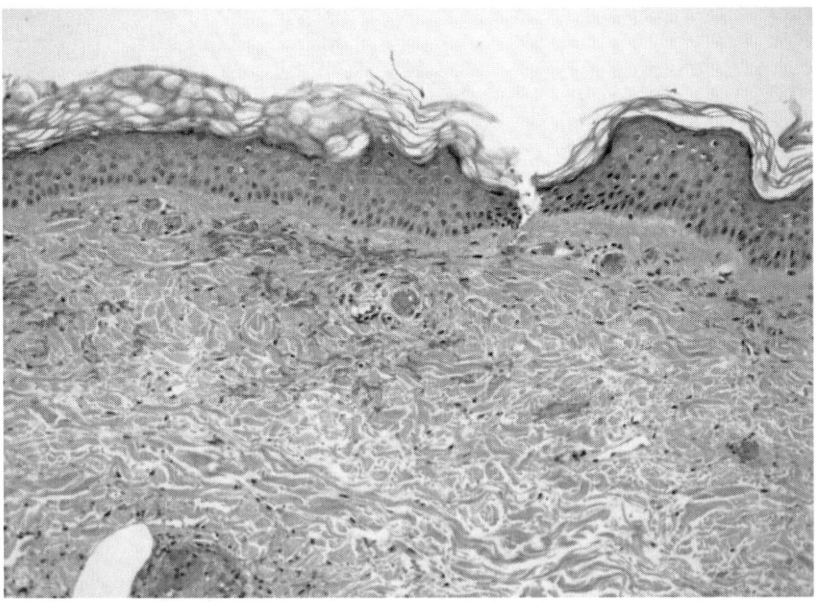

Figure 8. H&E demonstrating thromboses but no true inflammation, as would be seen in a true vasculitis.

Due to the poor vascularity of adipose tissue and the predilection for levamisole induced necrosis to target fatty areas of the body, this often results in devastating loss of soft tissue for the patient and significant deformity results. (Figure 9)

In the literature, one patient experienced life-threatening evisceration due to these phenomena. She presented with what appeared to be superficial purpura on her abdominal pannus. The patient had multiple medical comorbidities including a known ventral hernia at a previous pfannenstial incision. The purpura involved her breasts as well as the soft tissue of her abdomen which had abundant adipose tissue, especially at the level of her pannus. Because the process progressed in a vertical fashion, she developed full thickness necrosis and spontaneously eviscerated at the level of her hernia. Urgent surgical intervention was pursued in this case [Amalfi].

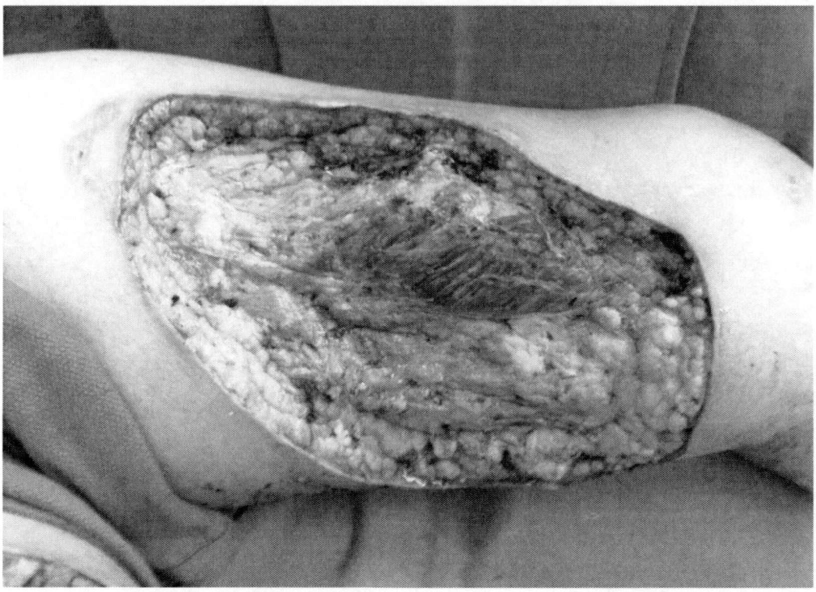

Figure 9. Significant soft tissue deficit that results from vertical progression of full thickness necrosis.

Medical and Surgical Management

The care of the cutaneous manifestations of adultered cocaine should include a multidisciplinary approach. As mentioned previously, a

Rheumatology as well as Dermatology consult are helpful in establishing the diagnosis. However, an expert in complex wound care and closure is necessary for the treatment of these complicated wounds. It is recommended that patients whose lesions comprise full thickness tissue loss greater than 1 percent Total Body Surface Area (TBSA) be transferred to a regional burn center for surgical intervention.

At presentation, many of these patients have petechiae or purpura without any loss of the epidermal layer of skin. At this most early stage, treatment is topical and supportive only. The area should be treated with a moist dressing, preferably a gauze impregnated with antimicrobial ointment such as xeroform™ petrolatum gauze (Covidien, Mansfield, MA) and bacitracin ointment. Patients should also be taken to the whirpool tub daily for washing of the affected areas with antimicrobial soap before daily dressings. Adequate hygiene is paramount to preventing concomitant bacterial or viral super-infection in the wounds.

As the disease progresses, the epidermal layer often sloughs, revealing deeper necrosis and tissue loss. Open wounds should be treated with similar moist gauze dressings to allow for re-epithelialization when possible. If dry eschar develops, dressing management should include an ointment with deeper penetration such as silver sulfadiazine cream. This is similar to the treatment of full thickness burns, and these wounds almost always require debridement for adequate healing.

Before scheduling a patient for surgical intervention, the treating physician must be sure that the disease process has plateaued, and no further necrosis will continue. It is imperative to monitor the patient for continued use of cocaine and levamisole to ensure abstinence, even during their hospital stay.

Operative debridement should be performed by a Reconstructive Plastic Surgeon who is accustomed to soft tissue debridement and current concepts in burn care. Sharp surgical debridement of the wounds is performed, excising necrotic tissue tangentially until healthy, bleeding and viable tissue is identified. For more superficial areas of nerosis, this would involve the use of a Weck Blade of Watson Blade for serial tangential excision. For areas of full thickness loss, a fascial excision may be more appropriate, using electrocautery and controlling blood loss for such significant necrosis. The surgical endpoint is marked by the viability of the tissue. It is common that upon separation of the eschar from deeper tissue, purulence is encountered. Intraoperative cultures should always be taken to treat for any infectious process that would complicate wound healing. Thorough intraoperative irrigation should be used to clean the wound bed of any bacterial contamination or biofilm development. Once healthy, bleeding tissue is encountered, a temporary dressing should be applied, such as E-Z Derm® Porcine Xenograft (Brennen Medical LLC, Saint Paul, Minnesota) (Figure 10).

Xenograft should be left in place under an occlusive dressing for three to five days. The removal of outer dressings will reveal if the graft is adherent to the wound bed, signifying viability of the tissue present, and a vascularized bed that is ready for skin grafting. Should the xenograft slough off, then further debridement to healthier tissue with a better blood supply is needed to support the imbibition, insoculation and revascularization of a skin graft. (Figure 11) Fat often is a poorly vascularized bed to support a skin graft, and excision down to muscle fascia may be necessary for definitive closure.

Once a healthy bed is achieved and the cutaneous disease is stable, the patient is ready for definitive wound coverage. We recommend the use of split thickness skin grafts on a healthy wound bed when feasible. Due to the contour irregularities that often develop from this vertically progressing process, it is often necessary to use negative pressure dressing therapy (V.A.C. Therapy®, KCI Incorporated, San Antonio, TX) to help contour the graft into the concavity of the soft tissue defect. Grafts should be protected via a semi-permeable membrane to protect it from the negative pressure dressing. Similarly, a bolster type dressing could be fashioned to help contour the grafts into the defect as well to promote vascularization of the skin graft.

Other options for wound coverage include delayed closure of the wounds directly when skin laxity allows. When primary closure is not an option, local tissue rearrangement via local flaps may be needed to cover the defects. This is most critical if vital structures are found at the wound base such as tendons, arteries or nerves. Working up the reconstructive ladder, in some cases free tissue transfer may be the only option for stable wound coverage when vital structures are exposed and no local options are available. A reconstructive plastic surgeon should manage such complicated wound closure to achieve ultimate healing of these cutaneous wounds.

Patients are suitable for discharge upon healing of their wounds. It may be necessary to arrange for social services to help with home dressings until grafts are stable. Hygiene remains of prime importance, and patients should bathe daily, washing all grafted areas before new dressings are applied. (Figure 12) Services should also be provided to the patient for substance abuse counseling. Education remains a key component to long term success, as any further consumption of adultered cocaine will lead to a similar cutaneous eruption in this at-risk population.

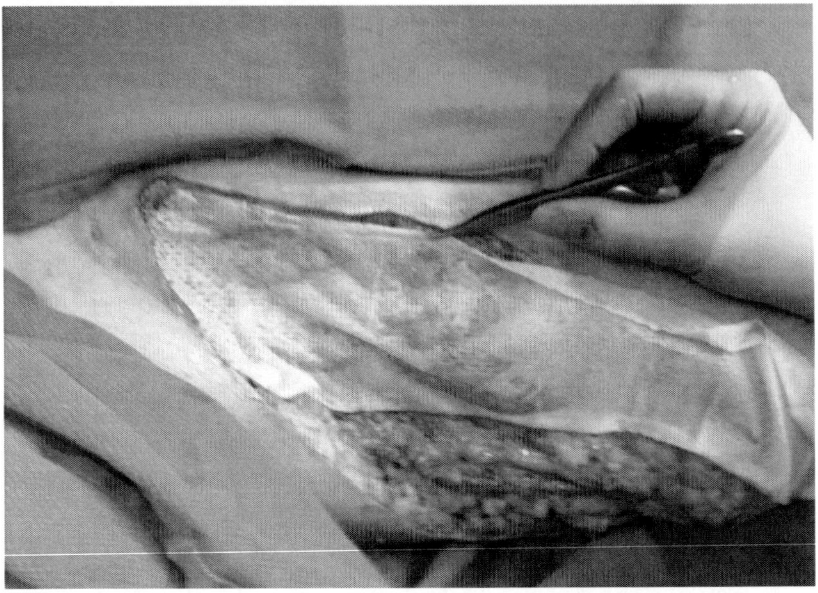

Figure 10. The application of porcine xenograft to temporize deeper wounds.

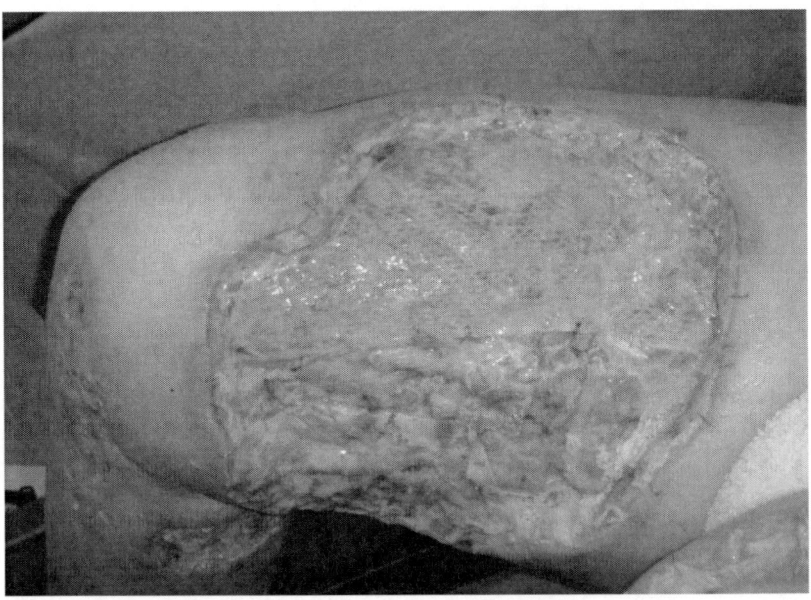

Figure 11. The appearance of xenograft in the wound bed.

Figure 12. Healed split thickness skin grafts indicate that the patient is suitable for discharge.

CONCLUSION

Although the reason for the sudden appearance of levamsiole in cocaine and its mechanism of action have yet to be elucidated, its medical sequelae have hastily demanded the attention of medical professionals. It is critical for emergency room physicians and primary care doctors to promptly recognize and diagnose the cutaneous effects of adultered cocaine. Timely diagnosis will help confirm the presence of cocaine and levamisole via urine testing. The care for these patients should involve inpatient monitoring in an accredited burn unit. A multidisciplinary approach utilizing rheumatologists, dermatologists, dermatopathologists and plastic and reconstructive surgeons is necessary to both arrive at an accurate diagnosis and treat the devastating cutaneous effects of adultered cocaine.

REFERENCES

Amalfi AN, Neumeister MW, Bueno RA, Sommer NZ, Henkelman EK. Cocaine-Induced Full-Thickness Tissue Necrosis: A Case Series. *Plastic and Reconstructive Surgery*. 132(5): 887e-892e, Nov 2013.

Arkangel, C. Cocaine Abuse Medicine Health. http://www.emedicinehealth.com/cocaine abuse/page11 em.htm. Accessed Dec,2011

Barbano G, Ginevri F, Ghiggeri J, Gusmano R. Disseminated autoimmune disease during levamisole treatment of nephrotic syndrome. *Pediatr. Nephrol.* 1999; 13:602-3.

Brody SL, Slovis CM, Wrenn KD. Cocaine-related medical problems: Consecutive series of 233 patients. AmJnl Med. 1990: 88(4); 325-331.

Casale EM, Casale JF. Identification of levamisole and Lidocaine Acetylation Reaction Impurities Found in Heroin Exhibits.US Dept of Justice Drug Enforcement Administration. *Microgram. Jnl.* 8(1):16-23.

Dumyati G, Bradford M, Rosenberg B, Moreno J. Bilateral Necrosis of Earlobes and Cheeks: Another Complication of Cocaine Contaminated with Levamisole. *Annals of Int. Med.* 2010;152(11):758-9.

Funauchi M, Sugishima H, Minoda M, Horiuchi A. Serum level of interferon-gamma in autoimmune diseases. *Tohoku J. Exp. Med.* 1991; 164(4):259-67.

Kinzie E. Levamisole found in patients using cocaine. *Ann. Emerg. Med.* 2009;53(4):546.

Lewinda K, Buxton JA, Skuridina N et al. Levamisole tainted cocaine causing severe neutropenia in Alberta and British Columbia. *Harm. reduction Jnl.* 2009;6(30).

Mariani SM. Silencing Autoimmunity: Manipulating interferon in systemic lupus erythmatosus. *Medscape Modular Medicine*. 2003;5(1).

National Survey on Drug Use and Health. US Dept. of Health and Human Services.*http://oas.samhsa.gov/nsduh/2k9nsduh/2k9resultsp.pdf.*Accessed March, 2011

NYSDOH-OASAS Health Advisory: Levamisole-Contaminated Cocaine. Department of Health: New York State. *http://www.health. ny.gov/diseases/aids/harm_reduction/opioidprevention/healthadvisorylevamisole-contaminated cocaine.htm.* Accessed August, 2011.

Szeto CC, Gillespie KM, Mathieson PW. Levamisole induces interleukin-18 and shifts type 1/type 2 cytokin balance. *Immunology*.2000; 2:217-24.

Van Wieren A. A new low for an old high: Neutropenia Induced by Levamisole-adultered cocaine. *Medicine and Health Rhode Island*.2010: 93(10)320-1.

Waller JM, Feramisco JD, Alberta-Wszelok L, et al. Cocaine-associated retiformpurpua and neutropenia: is levamisole the culprit? *J. Am. Acad. Dermatol.* 2010;63(3):530-5.

Walsh, NMG, Green PJ, et al. Cocaine-related retiformpurpura: evidence to incriminate the adulterant levamisole. *J. Cutan. Pathol.* 2010: 37;1212-1219.

World Drug Report. Volument 2: Statistics. *http://www.unodc.org/pdf/WDR 2006/wdr2006 chap5 cocaine.pdf.* Accessed December, 2011.

In: Substance Abuse
Editor: Jeffrey Raines

ISBN: 978-1-63321-949-6

Chapter 3

FETAL ALCOHOL SYNDROME: PREVENTION, DIAGNOSIS AND TREATMENT

Sushil Sharma*, Sonal Gawande, Abhijeet Jagtap, Reem Aboulela and Zara Salman

Saint James School of Medicine, Bonaire, Dutch Caribbean, The Netherlands

ABSTRACT

Fetal alcohol syndrome (FAS) is a serious global problem due to emergence of alcohol abuse among young pregnant women. Recently we have described biomarkers of FAS for early diagnosis, prevention, and treatment of FAS. Since the diagnosis and treatment of FAS can pose a significant challenge; it is prudent to prevent FAS at an early stage to avoid the deleterious consequences of alcohol abuse. Adults with FAS or fetal alcohol effects (FAE) suffer from mental illnesses and are more prone to drug addiction in stressful environment. Even in the absence of craniofacial abnormalities and intellectual handicap; children with FAS may experience psychiatric and developmental disorders. Adults with FAS have a high rate of brain anomalies as diagnosed by CT, MRI/spectroscopy, and PET neuroimaging. The FAS victims have also a higher rate of behavioral management problems. By performing high-

* Sushil Sharma, Ph. D; D.M.R.I.T, Professor of Pharmacology & Course Director, Saint James School of Medicine, Plaza Juliana 4, Kralendijk, Bonaire, Dutch Caribbean, The Netherlands, Tel (599) 717-7550; Fax (599) 717-7570, Email Sharma@mail.sjsm.org.

resolution microPET neuroimaging with 18F-DOPA and 18FdG as biomarkers of dopaminergic and mitochondrial bioenergetics respectively, we established that chronic intoxication of cocaine and methamphetamine (METH) induces reduction in the striatal dopamine and glucose metabolism. A further reduction in 18F-DOPA and 18FdG uptake was noticed when cocaine and METH were co-administered along with ethanol, suggesting that alcohol may serve as a gateway to multiple drug abuse. In addition to fatty acid ethyl esters; the metabolite, cocaethylene is formed when cocaine and alcohol are abused concomitantly. Cocaethylene is more toxic as compared to ethanol and cocaine. Hence alcohol abuse along with other drugs during pregnancy may have significant impact on learning, intelligence, memory, and behavior. In addition to mtDNA, histone, and protein methylation; alcohol impairs microRNAs expression causing transcriptome and proteome abnormalities. Usually gastrulation period is highly vulnerable to the deleterious consequences of alcohol. Alcohol-induced cerebellar and hippocampal Charnoly body (CB) formation; involved in impaired motor learning and memory loss can be prevented by nutritional rehabilitation, physiological zinc, and metallothioneins (MTs). MTs as free radical scavengers, inhibit CB formation and α-synuclein index to provide ubiquinone-mediated mitochondrial protection and prevent neurodegenerative α-synucleinopathies. MTs also regulate zinc-mediated transcriptional activation of genes involved in heavy metal ion detoxification, growth, development, differentiation, and maturation. Clinical manifestations of multidrug abuse were attenuated in MTs-over-expressing homozygous weaver mutant (wv/wv) mice. In addition, choline, folate, and vitamin–A are used for the treatment of FAS. As the deleterious effect of FAS can occur during any phase of fetal brain development, early prevention and differential diagnosis is essential for children born from mothers with history of alcohol abuse as it can pass through blood placental, brain, and milk barriers. Although some physicians allowed one drink during pregnancy; alcohol intake during any period of pregnancy should be avoided. Particularly pregnant women need to be educated regarding the deleterious consequences of FAS to avoid social, physical, mental, psychological, and economical burden on the society.

Keywords: Fetal Alcohol Syndrome, ^{18}F-DOPA; ^{18}FdG; Cocaine, Methamphetamine, Cocaethylene, N-Acetyl Aspartate, Charnoly Body, Charnolophagy, Metallothioneins

ABBREVIATIONS

ARND: Alcohol-related neurodevelopmental disorders; ATP = adenosine triphosphate BAC: Blood alcohol concentration; CB: Charnoly body; CDT: Carbohydrate-deficient transferrin; BHMT = betaine homocysteine methyltransferases; DIV: Days in vitro, EWD: Ethanol withdrawal; EtS: Ethyl sulfate. ETOH ethanol; EtG: Ethyl glucronide; eIF4A: Eukaryotic initiation factor 4A; FAE: Fetal alcohol effects; FAEE: Fatty acid ethyl ester; FAS fetal alcohol syndrome, Fetal alcohol spectrum disorder; FASD: Fetal alcohol spectrum disorders; GSH = glutathione GGT: Gamma glutamyl transferase; 8-OH-dG: 8-Hydroxy, 2-deoxy-guanosine HCC = hepatocellular carcinoma; IGF-1: Insulin-like growth factor; mtDNA: Mitochondrial DNA; RhO_{mgko}: Mitochondrial genome knock out; MCV: Mean corpuscular volume; MAT: Methionine adenosyltransferase; MTs: Metallothioineins; MTHFR: Methylene tetrahydrofolate reductase; $\Delta\Psi$: Mitochondrial membrane potential; PAE: Prenatal Alcohol Exposure; PCNs: Primary cortical neurons; PEth: Phosphatidylethanol; PDCD4: Programmed cell death protein 4; SES: Socioeconomic status; TLFB: Total enteral nutrition; TEN: Time-line follow back procedure to assess alcohol exposure; UTR: Untranslated region.

HIGHLIGHTS

- Social, physical, mental, psychological, economical, and demographic factors play a significant role in the etiology of FAS
- Differential diagnosis of FAS in a clinical setting may be challenging
- Carniofacial dysmorphogenesis may or may not be evident in all FAS victims
- Neurobehavioral deficits exist in at least 70% cases of FAS
- Fatty acid ethyl esters provide sensitive analysis of FAS even after three months of delivery
- Hippocampal and cerebellar N-acetyl aspartate, 8-hydroxy, 2 deoxy-guanosine, Charnoly Body (CB), Metallothioneins (MTs), and α-synuclein index may be used as early sensitive biomarkers of FAS
- Animal models of FAS can provide more objective measures of FAS prevention, diagnosis, and treatment

- Mitochondrial and nuclear epigenetics, microRNA, one carbon metabolism (OCM), and omics analyses promise to discover novel biomarkers for better clinical management of FAS
- Nutritional rehabilitation, physiological zinc, and MTs prevent alcohol-induced neurodegenerative α-synucleinopathies by inhibiting free radicals-induced CB formation in the developing brain
- Ethanol induces nuclear and mitochondrial genetic and epigenetic changes in FAS
- Specific CB antagonists and Charnolophagy agonists may be developed for the prevention and treatment of FAS during pre-zygotic phase

INTRODUCTION

About forty years ago, alcohol was unknown as a teratogen; an agent that can disrupt the development of the fetus (Thomas et al 2010). Despite centuries of alcohol abuse, the first two reports on fetal alcohol syndrome (FAS) appeared in 1973, which described dysmorphic and developmental problems in eight children from alcoholic women (Jones et al. 1973). The second publication described three children and introduced the term FAS to highlight the deficits of intrauterine alcohol abuse (Jones and Smith 1973). Now we know that FAS is the most common and leading preventable cause of mental retardation. Prenatal alcohol exposure (PAE), induces deleterious effect on physical, neurological, and behavioral development of the child. Since the incidence of FAS is increasing and its diagnosis and treatment can pose a serious challenge, it is important to prevent FAS at an early stage to avoid its deleterious consequences in adult life. Intrauterine exposure to alcohol is the leading cause of developmental abnormalities (O'Connor, 2011). Adults with FAS or fetal alcohol effects (FAE) suffer from mental illnesses and are prone to drug addiction particularly in a stressful environment. Hepper et al (2014) reported that maternal alcohol abuse damages the brain, causing decreased information processing, poor habituation, and increased variability in performance. Hence maternal alcohol abuse should be avoided at any stage of pregnancy to prevent damage to brain regional synaptic neurotransmission for normal learning, intelligence, memory, and behavior. Not only does FAS affect the phenotype and brain, but also the metabolic pathways to increase adiposity and abnormal pancreatic morphology (Dobson et al., 2014; Qi et al.,

2014). Ethanol-induced brain damage and abnormal neuron development are associated with impaired protein synthesis in primary cortical neurons in the developing brain (Narasimham et al., 2012). It is also involved in inhibiting transport of proteins, folate, zinc, glucose, amino acids, and many other essential nutrients through the placental barrier, all of which can affect the normal fetal development (Hutson et al., 2012).

FAS is a serious global problem due to increased prevalence of alcohol abuse among young women during pregnancy. Fetal alcohol spectrum disorder (FASD), caused by PAE, can result in craniofacial dysmorphism, cognitive impairment, sensory and motor disabilities. FASD incidences are as high as 2% to 5% in the U.S, and its prevalence is higher in low socioeconomic populations. Even in the absence of intellectual handicap, children and adolescents with FAS or FAE may experience psychiatric and developmental abnormalities. Adults with FAS have a higher rate of brain abnormalities as diagnosed by multimodality CT, magnetic resonance imaging (MRI)/ spectroscopy, and PET neuroimaging. The FAS victims also have a high rate of behavioral management problems. FASD is the term used to describe the wide range of deleterious outcomes following PAE, associated with serious pregnancy and birth defects (Bailey and Sokol, 2011). Alcohol abuse during pregnancy may increase the risk of miscarriage, stillbirth, preterm delivery, and sudden infant death syndrome (SIDS). FAS research has inherent limitations including; the collection of accurate information about alcohol abuse during pregnancy and controlling for comorbid exposures and conditions. Creeley and Olney (2013) reported that alcohol abuse during pregnancy can cause craniofacial malformations, structural pathology in the brain, and neuropsychiatric disturbances in the developing child. The exposure to alcohol during 4th week of gestation can cause apoptosis of cells that are highly crucial for the normal development of the face and brain. Craniofacial malformations and brain anomalies, in many cases may be absent, and the FASD syndrome manifests primarily as neurobehavioral disorder. It remains unknown how alcohol causes these neurobehavioral changes. As a consequence, attributing poor birth outcomes to PAE is a challenging task, requiring improved methodology and accurate knowledge of specific biological mechanisms.

Alcohol triggers massive apoptosis of neurons and oligodendroglia (OLs) in the developing brain when administered to animals, including primates, during a period equivalent to the human third trimester of gestation. This is associated with reductions in brain mass and neurobehavioral disturbances. Drugs, such as general anesthetics (GAs) and anti-epileptics (AEDs), mimic alcohol in triggering apoptosis of neurons and OLs, and children exposed to GAs during early infancy, or to AEDs during the third trimester, have increased incidence of FASD-like neurobehavioral problems, suggesting that all these agents during late gestation, can cause FASD-like abnormal developmental syndromes. Therefore, there is a need to further explore the basic molecular mechanisms by which these agents induce apoptosis to prevent neurodevelopmental disorders. Mattson and Riley (2011) reported that FAS is associated with a broad range of neurobehavioral deficits. The term FASD is used to encompass a spectrum of effects that includes FAS towards the extreme end as well as alcohol-related birth defects (ARBD) and alcohol-related neurodevelopmental disorder (ARND). The term ARND refers to individuals who, after heavy PAE, exhibit neurobehavioral effects without qualifying the physical criteria of FAS (Hoyme et al. 2005; Vaurio et al. 2010).

By performing high-resolution microPET neuroimaging with ^{18}F-DOPA and ^{18}FdG as biomarkers of dopaminergic neurotransmission and mitochondrial bioenergetics respectively, we established that chronic intoxication of cocaine and methamphetamine induces significant reduction in the dopamine and glucose metabolism in the striatum (Sharma and Ebadi, 2008). A further reduction in the striatal ^{18}F-DOPA and ^{18}FdG uptake was observed when cocaine and methamphetamine were co-administered along with ethanol, suggesting that alcohol may serve as a gateway to multiple drug abuse and may induce more deleterious changes in the developing fetal brain when consumed in combination with other drugs such as cocaine. In addition to fatty acid ethyl esters, the metabolite, cocaethylene is formed when cocaine and alcohol are consumed in combination. Cocaethylene is more toxic as compared to ethanol and cocaine. Hence multiple drug abuse along with alcohol during pregnancy may have more deleterious life-long consequences in learning, intelligence, memory, and behavior. Although some physicians allowed one drink during pregnancy, it is now recommended that alcohol consumption during any period of pregnancy must be avoided. Usually gastrulation period is considered most sensitive to the deleterious consequences of alcohol. We discovered that clinical manifestations of multidrug abuse are attenuated in metallothioneins (MTs)-over-expressing homozygous weaver mutant (wv/wv) mouse model of drug addiction (Sharma and Ebadi, 2014).

As the deleterious effect of FAS can occur at any phase of fetal brain development, early prevention and differential diagnosis is essential for developing children born from mothers with history of alcohol abuse as it can easily pass through blood placental, brain, and milk barriers. Nuñez et al (2011) reported that PAE children experience deficits in cognitive and psychosocial functioning as well as alterations in brain structure and function. These impairments may or may not present in children with FAS and in children with intrauterine alcohol exposure who do not exhibit facial dysmorphology, important for the FAS diagnosis. Neuropsychological and behavioral studies demonstrated deficits in cognitive parameters, including intellectual performance, attention/working memory, executive skills, speed of processing, and academic skills in children and adolescents with FASD. Neuroimaging can detect differences in brain structure related to PAE and abnormalities in the white matter. Several studies have found relationships between these morphological differences and cognitive functions, suggesting the clinical significance of morphological abnormalities in FAS. Furthermore, the concentrations of neurotransmitter metabolites of PAE children is altered, and functional neuroimaging has revealed significant differences in learning, intelligence, memory, and behavior in children and adolescents with FASD.

Worldwide prevalence and high costs of FASD warrants the need for further research on FASD as there are no known safety levels of alcohol abuse during pregnancy. FAS babies are born to non-alcoholic women as well as to women who have problem with alcohol abuse. All types of alcohols (beer, wine, liquors) can be harmful during pregnancy. There does not seem to be safe period in pregnancy for drinking. FAS victims become burden to society, and may experience early morbidity and mortality. Hence it is prudent to initiate early preventable measures, discover novel biomarkers for the differential diagnosis, and effective treatment because FAS predisposition is random and unpredictable. Astley and Larren (1995) described FAS screening tool and we reported that maturation of adolescent brain is significantly impacted by drug abuse, including PAE (Arain et al., 2013). We have also described various biomarkers used for the prevention, diagnosis, and/or treatment of FAS (Chabenne et al., 2014). In this chapter, we have described recent trends in the prevention, diagnosis, and treatment of FAS with a primary objective to provide basic knowledge to young doctors, researchers, and scientists on the deleterious consequences and possible ways to prevent/treat FAS employing sensitive and specific universal biomarkers such as Charnoly Body (CB), and therapeutic agents such as choline, vitamin A, folic acid, and neuroprotective peptides. (*To be specific, we have used the word "ethanol" instead of "alcohol" at certain places in the text)*

FAS Risk Factors & Prevalence Risk factors include race, low socioeconomic status, women with partners who abuse alcohol, binge drinking during pregnancy, emotional stress, and use of tobacco and other drugs along with alcohol. The estimated prevalence in the U.S. is 8 for every 1000 live births, and there is no single diagnostic parameter for FAS, hence further research is needed for the accurate assessment of FAS for providing better treatment strategies to affected children (Landgraff et al., 2014). FAS is preventable by counseling, interventions to improve knowledge on FAS, and abstinence of alcohol during pregnancy. Popova et al., (2011) estimated the prevalence of PAE and the number of children (0–18 years) with FASD to determine the cost by age group, gender, and province/territory in Canada. The number of children with FASD ranged from 2,225 to 7,620, with an annual cost ranging from $57.9 to $198.3 million dollars. The highest cost ($29.5 to $101.1 million CND) was for 11–15 year-olds, indicating that FASD places huge economic burden on the child welfare system. Similarly, Russia has one of the highest incidence of alcohol abuse, yet limited information is available about the impact of PAE and FASDs. Recently Popova et al., (2014) reviewed epidemiological studies on various aspects of PAE and FASD. This study indicated a high prevalence of PAE and FASD, with significant impact of alcohol on morbidity, disability, and mortality. Hence prevention efforts to reduce FASD incidence are urgently needed.

In addition to socioeconomic and educational status, nutritional, physical, and genetic factors could play a significant role in FASD. Besides amount, dose, and stage of alcohol exposure, only 5% of alcohol drinking women have a newborn with FAS. Although the incidence of alcohol abuse is increasing in the western world, the nutritional and physical status of these woman may have significant impact on the FAS occurrence. In general, balanced diet consumed by young pregnant western women is rich in iron, folic acid, choline, and vitamin A essential for the normal growth and development of the fetus. Therefore even if the alcohol consumption rate is high, the deleterious effects of intrauterine alcohol seem to be nullified. Detailed studies are needed to define the quantity of maternal alcohol consumption from specific populations that produce children with FASD. For example, frequency of drinks per episode, episodes per week, and time during pregnancy does it take to produce a child with FAS, pFAS, or ARND (Hannigan et al., 2010). Although animal models can provide clues; more specific studies on alcohol abuse in humans are needed to determine maternal risk factors. Once this specificity is accomplished from maternal interviewing, the differential effects of gravidity, maternal age, body mass, nutrition, and other influences may be analyzed to determine the risk and/or cause. Accurate data on maternal risk from mothers of FASD children with all levels of severity; from those who drank, but did not have children with FASD; and also from those who did not drink are needed. These data can determine maternal risk for FASD especially since most women are reluctant to share such information. Collecting information about drinking during pregnancy is one of the most challenging tasks of studying FASD. This information is crucial to linking specific risk factors to diagnosis within the FASD. May et al., (2011) emphasized that maternal risk is multidimensional including; factors associated with quantity, frequency, and timing of alcohol consumed; age; number of pregnancies; frequency of child birth; the body size; nutritional status; body mass index; socioeconomic status; metabolism; religion; spirituality; depression; other drug abuse; and social relationships. Further studies are needed to delineate specific type of individual behavioral, physical, and genetic factors that may lead to having children with FASD. Although there is lot of information about individual maternal factors that may increase or decrease risk of FASD, the warning for public health remains the same: "*don't drink alcohol when pregnant*". In 2005, the Surgeon General's office provided the advisory on alcohol abuse and pregnancy which states that: "*We do not know what, if any, amount of alcohol is safe. But we do know that the risk of a baby being born with any of the FASDs, increases with the amount of alcohol a pregnant woman drinks, as does the likely severity of the condition. And when a pregnant woman drinks alcohol, so does her baby. Therefore, it is in the child's best interest for a pregnant woman to simply not drink alcohol during any phase of pregnancy*"

Recent evidence suggests that FAS incidence may be correlated with the socio-economic and educational status of the pregnant mother. Any type of alcohol, including beer and wine, can cause birth defects due to blood traveling through mother's placenta to baby and affects the baby's development, particularly the heart and brain. Ethanol can easily pass through blood, placental, and milk barriers; hence its exposure during pregnancy can cause apoptotic cell death, leading to craniofacial malformations, microcephaly, musculoskeletal abnormalities, short palpebral fissures, smooth philtrum, thin upper lip, and stunted growth (Creely et al, 2013). However, in many cases, these clinical symptoms may be absent and the syndrome is represented as neurobehavioral disorders due to the deleterious effects of alcohol on neurons and oligodendrocytes. Oligodendrocytes are involved in myelinogenesis for proper nerve conduction. Impairment in myelinogenesis results in abnormal electrical conduction due to improper insulation. Particularly, alcohol's deleterious effect on the developing cerebellar Purkinje neurons may cause delayed eye blink conditioning and impaired hand-writing in the FAS victims.

The National Institute on Alcohol Abuse and Alcoholism (NIAAA) has been the lead Federal agency responsible for scientific research on alcohol and its effects for 40 years (Warren and Hewitt, 2010). NIAAA has funded research, disseminated research findings to a broad audience to improve public health. Significant contributions are the National Epidemiologic Survey on Alcohol and Related Conditions; investment in research to identify the genes underlying vulnerability to alcoholism; collaborative studies on genetics of alcoholism; exploring the effects of alcohol on fetal development and on a variety of diseases; alcoholism treatment including supporting medications development program; international collaborations; research on preventing alcohol problems through community programs as well as policy changes; and the translation of research findings to routine clinical practice, including the production of training materials.

FAS causes deleterious consequences on the developing fetus and is characterized by growth retardation, facial abnormalities, functional CNS abnormalities, structural CNS abnormalities, and impaired growth and development as illustrated in Figure 1. Since animal as well as human studies have variability in the manifestations of intrauterine alcohol exposure, the term FASD is used to reflect the effects of alcohol exposure. Shannon et al (2013) reported that women who drink alcohol during pregnancy are at increased risk of giving birth to children with neurodevelopmental disorders. These investigators demonstrated that third trimester equivalent binge alcohol exposure at a dose of 1.75 g/kg/day results in significant Purkinje neuron loss in fetal sheep and that both maternal and fetal adrenocorticotropin (ACTH) and cortisol levels are elevated in response to alcohol treatment. It was hypothesized that repeated elevation in cortisol from chronic binge alcohol is responsible for neuronal deficits. These investigators used four treatment groups: normal control, pair-fed saline control, alcohol and cortisol. The elevation in cortisol in response to alcohol was mimicked in the cortisol group by infusing pregnant ewes with hydrocortisone for 6 hours/day, and saline during the first hour for three consecutive days followed by four days without treatment beginning on gestational day (GD) 109 until GD 132. The number, volume, and density of Purkinje neurons remained unchanged in response to glucocorticoid infusion in the absence of alcohol, suggesting that elevations in maternal glucocorticoids during the third trimester does not produce Purkinje neuron loss during the brain growth spurt. However, the elevations in cortisol along with alcohol could lead to serious brain injury in the FASD.

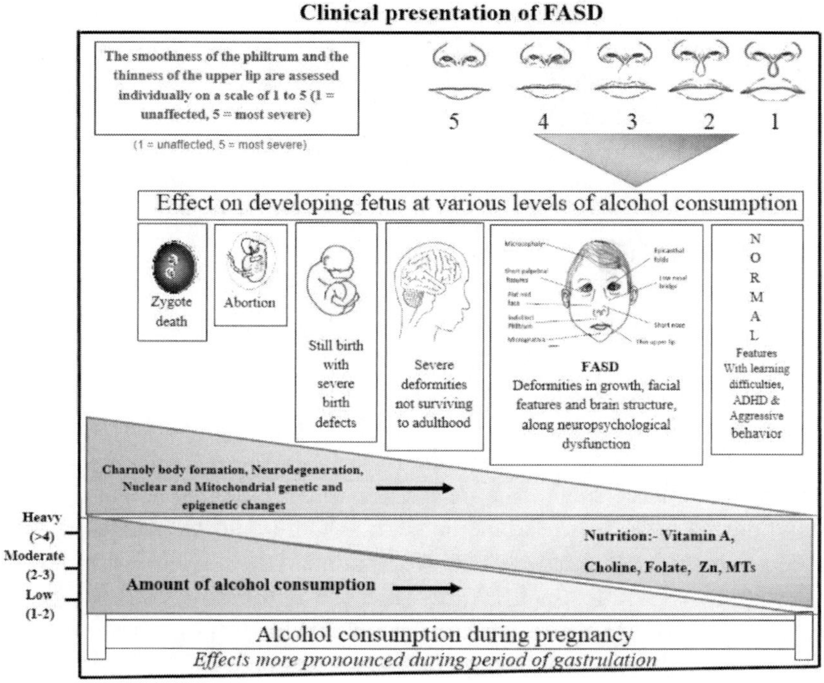

Figure 1. A pictorial diagram illustrating clinical presentation of FASD.

Ethnic Differences in FAS Predisposition Ethnicities have a crucial role to play with higher rates of risky behavior and drinking harms. There is limited information on how drinking differentially affects in breast and colorectal cancers, in diabetes, and HIV/AIDS onset, and how its effects vary across ethnic subgroups. Chartier et al., (2014) reported that alcohol abuse is differentially associated with social and health harms across U.S. ethnic groups. Native Americans, Hispanics, and African Americans are disadvantaged by alcohol-associated harms compared with Whites and Asians due to social disadvantage, acculturation, drinking preferences, and genetic differences in alcohol metabolism. The relationship of ethnicity and drinking to injuries, FAS, gastrointestinal diseases, cardiovascular diseases, cancers, diabetes, and infectious diseases warrant further studies to elucidate the relationship of alcohol abuse and these diseases across ethnic groups, and to delineate the molecular mechanisms that give rise to these disparities to recommend prevention strategies for local and federal government. Native Americans have higher incidence of alcohol-related motor vehicle fatalities, suicide, violence, FAS, and hepatic disease mortality. Unlike other ethnic groups, in which men are primarily at risk for alcohol-related harms, both Native American men and women are high-risk groups. Hispanics have higher rates of alcohol-related motor vehicle fatalities, suicide, and mortality due to liver cirrhosis. African Americans have higher rates of FAS, spouse violence, head and neck cancers, with limited support for a protective health effect from moderate drinking, indicating health disparities in alcohol-induced harms across ethnicities. The contributing factors include the higher rates of alcohol consumption in Native Americans and Hispanics.

Pfinder (2014) highlighted social inequalities in low birth weight (LBW) children/adolescents with PAE and the contribution of anthropometric and health-related behavioral factors to social inequalities. A total of 2,159 participants with parental self-reported moderate to regular PAE were examined. At similar levels of PAE, the risk of LBW was increased in women with a low and middle socioeconomic status (SES). Maternal height, BMI, and smoking during pregnancy also mediated the association. The mediating effect of maternal height was 12.5% to 33.7%. Maternal BMI explained 7.9% of the socioeconomic difference in LBW between the high and low SES groups in children with PAE. The mediating effect of smoking during pregnancy was 17.3% to 31.5%. Maternal height, BMI and smoking during pregnancy explained 24.4% to 60.1% of the socioeconomic differences in LBW in children with PAE. A significant proportion of the socioeconomic differences in LBW in children with PAE could be attributed to anthropometric and health-related behavioral factors. The development of FASD in alcohol-exposed children is related to LBW and that smoking during pregnancy, lower maternal height, and underweight trigger the risk of LBW. Both anthropometric and health-related behavioral factors mediate the association between SES and alcohol-related disorders. To reduce social inequalities in the health of children with PAE at an early stage, it is important to advice women with a lower SES about the adverse effects of smoking and being underweight on the embryo/fetus. Furthermore, prevention strategies related to the deleterious effects of alcohol and tobacco during pregnancy could be designed to reach women from all social classes.

Chartier and Caetano (2010) performed surveys to show variations across ethnicities in drinking, alcohol use disorders, alcohol problems, and treatment use. Higher rates of high-risk drinking among ethnic minorities were reported for Native Americans and Hispanics, although within-ethnic group differences (e.g., gender, age-group, and other subpopulations) were also evident. Whites and Native Americans have increased risk for alcohol use disorders relative to other ethnic groups. However, once alcohol dependence occurs, Blacks and Hispanics experience higher rates than Whites of recurrence or dependence. The consequences of drinking appear to be more profound for Native Americans, Hispanics, and Blacks. Disparities in alcohol treatment utilization are most apparent for Hispanics due to risky drinking behavior, immigration experiences, racial/ethnic discrimination, economic and neighborhood disadvantage, and variations in alcohol-metabolizing genes.

It has been nearly 10 years since NIAAA addressed alcohol-related health disparities (Russo et al., 2004). Native Americans, Hispanics, and Blacks remain impacted by drinking compared with other ethnic groups. Despite the progress, the current picture for ethnic groups, related to alcohol consumption, disorders, and related consequences is fragmented. There is no one place to look for a complete account of alcohol research on all ethnic groups in spite of large surveys conducted, and comparisons between existing studies are made difficult by the use of different surveys. There should be caution in interpreting between-ethnic-group differences in alcohol abuse and related behaviors until within-group differences are investigated. Generalizations about Asians drinking less than other ethnic groups may not apply to Pacific Islanders, and risky drinking for Hispanic men and Native Americans may be less applicable to Cuban-American men and Southwest Indians. Immigrant groups must go through a process of acculturation to U.S. society that can lead to increased stress and tension within families. Together with Blacks and Native Americans, these groups also can face socioeconomic disadvantage and potential racial/ethnic discrimination. These factors are associated with, poor job opportunities, residential segregation, life in unsafe neighborhoods, constant exposure to alcohol advertising, police profiling and brutality, and lack of access to adequate health care.

Scott and Taylor (2007) reported that alcohol metabolism involves two key enzymes—alcohol dehydrogenase (ADH) and aldehyde dehydrogenase (ALDH). There are various types of ADH and ALDH, each of which may exist in several isoforms that differ in their ability to metabolize alcohol and its toxic metabolite, acetaldehyde. These isoforms are encoded by different alleles whose distribution among ethnic groups differs. One variant of ADH is ADH1B, is encoded by several alleles. An allele, *ADH1B*3* is pertinent to people of African descent and some Native American tribes. This allele is associated with more rapid breakdown of alcohol, leading to a transient accumulation of acetaldehyde. African Americans with this allele are less likely to have a family history of alcoholism. Moreover, children of mothers with this allele are less vulnerable to ARBD. The enzyme ALDH1 also is encoded by several alleles. Two of these alleles that are found in African Americans—*ALDH1A1*2* and *ALDH1A1*3*—may be associated with a reduced risk of alcoholism. Several *ADH* and *ALDH* alleles primarily in African Americans, appear to offer protection from the risk of alcoholism. The *ADH1B*3* allele, found in up to one-fourth of people of African descent results in a higher rate of alcohol metabolism, was associated with a reduced likelihood of a family history of alcoholism, less positive response to alcohol, and protection against ARBD. Similarly, the *ALDH1A1*3* allele, in African Americans, also may be associated with a reduced risk of alcoholism. Further studies in this direction will improve our understanding of the relative risks of alcohol dependence and health consequences for people of all ethnicities.

Prevention of FAS Increased alcohol abuse by women of childbearing age, reduced contraceptive use, and limited knowledge of health care professionals regarding PAE can put more risk of alcohol-affected pregnancies. France et al (2013) reported that the public awareness-raising campaigns targeting alcohol abuse during pregnancy are essential for preventing PAE and FASD. These investigators evaluated three different concepts of alcohol and pregnancy: (i) a threat appeal, (ii) a positive appeal promoting a self-efficacy message, and (iii) a concept that combined the two appeals to determine the effectiveness in increasing women's intentions to abstain from alcohol during pregnancy. Childbearing and pregnant women from Perth (Australia) participated in a computer-based questionnaire where they viewed either a control or one of the three concepts. Participants' intentions to abstain from and reduce alcohol intake during pregnancy were assessed. Other measures included perceived main message, diagnostics, and potential to promote defensive responses or unintended consequences.

The analysis indicated that threat appeal was more effective than the self-efficacy message and the control. The combined threat and self-efficacy was recommended as it has persuasive potential, provides balanced positive and negative emotional responses, and is unlikely to result in defensive or unintended consequences. This study enhanced the effectiveness of preventing PAE, and has potential for promoting women's intentions to abstain from alcohol during pregnancy. Based on this study, it was recommended that servers should offer FAS information to the customer in a non-threatening manner, promote non-alcohol beverages, listen to customer's concerns, respond respectfully and with accurate information, explore what customers know about drinking and pregnancy, support pregnant customers who choose not to drink alcohol, encourage a pregnant women's network (partner, friend, and family) to remain alcohol-free during pregnancy.

Table 1. Longitudinal Analysis of FAS Biomarkers

Level of alcohol consumption		Detectable biomarkers	Gestational time Window
Low (< 1drink/day)	A	Breath/Blood/Urine alcohol	Hours to days
	B	Urine EtS / EtG	
Moderate	A	%CDT	Within a month
	B	PEth	1st trimester
	C	Hair analyses (FAEE, EtG)	
High (>14 drinks/week or Binge)	A	GGT MCV	Within a month
	B	Meconium FAEE	1st trimester
	C		2nd & 3rd trimester

Temporal detection window of FAS biomarkers (Landgraf et al, 2013).

Biomarkers in FAS. Presently established biomarkers of alcohol abuse are insensitive for many pregnant women and screening questionnaires are unreliable. These limitations warrant the need to develop novel biomarkers with enhanced sensitivity for detecting moderate levels of drinking during pregnancy for a prolonged period after the last drinking episode. Recently we have described various biomarkers for the early prevention, diagnosis, and treatment of FAS (Cahbenne et al., 2014). In addition, Bakhireva and Savage (2011) studied the biomarkers of fetal alcohol exposure and fetal alcohol effects and suggested that developing reliable biomarkers of fetal alcohol effects that can identify children at risk for adverse neurobehavioral outcomes could lead to behavioral interventions earlier in life. Moreover the use of animal models of FASD in biomarker development could accelerate progress in FASD recovery. The longitudinal analysis of biomarkers which can help in the differential diagnosis of FAS are presented in Table 1.

Epigenetic Biomarkers of FAS The genetic and epigenetics of FASD are becoming intertwined and inseparable, however epigenetic medicine is still in its infancy. The epigenetic processes are linked to the chromatin and involve chemical modifications (e.g., methylation, which may result in altered gene expression). Even alcohol exposure prior to conception may induce epigenetic changes that can affect off-springs. Epigenetic processes may occur as a result of maternal alcohol abuse during the period between fertilization of the egg and implantation in the uterus. As a regulator of gene expression, DNA methylation is gaining importance as an epigenetic biomarker, allowing for a role in CNS development, which is spatiotemporally organized, protracted, and influenced by alcohol. Kobor and Weinberg (2011) reported that epigenetic changes result in changes in gene expression but do not involve changes in the DNA sequence. Epigenetic changes can induce deleterious effects of PAE and contribute to FAS abnormalities. Studies are ongoing to answer this question by characterizing genome-wide expression, allele-specific expression (ASE), gene polymorphisms (SNPs) and maternal genetic factors that influence alcohol vulnerability. Chromatin (i.e., DNA, histones, and other proteins) remodeling resulting from histone modifications in the amygdala may be important in the effects of both acute and chronic ethanol exposure. Starkman et al., (2012) reported that genetic and environmental factors play a significant role in the development of alcoholism. Whole-genome expression profiling has highlighted the importance of genes that may contribute to alcohol abuse disorders. Both acute and chronic ethanol exposure can alter gene expression in specific neuronal circuits involved in physical tolerance and dependence. The vicious cycle of alcohol abuse includes satiation and self-medication with alcohol, followed by withdrawal symptoms and relapse, which reflects both the positive and negative symptoms of alcohol addiction. Behavioral changes induced by acute and chronic ethanol exposure may involve chromatin remodeling resulting from histone modifications and DNA methylation in the neuronal circuits involving the amygdala. These findings have facilitated identifying enzymes such as the histone deacetylase, histone acetyl transferase, and DNA methyl transferase, as novel targets for the development of pharmacotherapies for the treatment of alcoholism. Acute ethanol exposure can inhibit both histone deacetylase (HDAC) and histone acetyltransferase. A possible epigenetic mechanisms acting in neuronal circuits of the amygdala may contribute to the development of anxiety-like behaviors during ethanol withdrawal after chronic exposure in rats.

Resendiz et al., (2013) discussed DNA methylation during development, taking alcohol as a mediator of the epigenetic impact in disease etiology, particularly the growth retardation and neurodevelopmental deficits of FASD. The backbone of epigenetics is cytosine methylation (methylcytosine: 5mC) and the coding of the histone protein. Recent discovery of 5-hydroxymethylcytosine (5hmC), and high-throughput DNA methylation analyses have provided insight into development, maintenance, and neuroplasticity. Adverse maternal condition impacts on the developing fetus and predisposes the offspring to develop metabolic and cardiovascular diseases later in life. Furthermore, nutritional stress can alter fetal development through epigenetic modifications, even though growth restriction is modest.

Epigenetic reprogramming in early life could cause altered DNA transcription and gene expression into adulthood and contribute to disease susceptibility.

Laker et al., (2013) reported the impact of maternal high fat diet to the offspring in early life and the adult health consequences and role of epigenetic modification, such as DNA methylation and histone modifications, as a mechanism underlying developmental programming. Studies on genetic variation in the gene encoding methylenetetrahydrofolate reductase (MTHFR), is a key enzyme in the methionine–homocysteine cycle (Lutz 2008). A genetic variation in the MTHFR gene, called *MTHFR C677T*, results in higher plasma homocysteine levels, an effect similar to that seen during chronic alcohol abuse. Because homocysteine is involved in the metabolism of methyl groups for DNA and histone methylation, such variants influence the epigenetic regulation of gene expression. The homocysteine pathway is sensitive to environmentally altered gene activity indicating that the *MTHFR* gene is under epigenetic control through smoking-induced methylation of its promoter regions (Vaissière et al., 2009). Altered DNA methylation of the regulatory region of a gene encoding monoamine oxidase A (MAOA) in the lymphoblasts is associated with alcohol dependence in females but not in males The degree of DNA methylation in the MAOA regulatory region is correlated with genetic variation in the DNA sequence located in that region in females (Philibert et al., 2008).

Ungerer et al., (2013) recently reported epigenetic etiology in the development of FASD Following conception, epigenetic mechanisms ensure normal differentiation and embryonic development. Evidence from studies on DNA methylation and histone modification that affect chromatin structure, and on the role of microRNAs in regulating mRNA supports the contribution of epigenetic mechanisms to the development of FASD. These effects are difficult to study because they are cell-type specific and transient in nature. Therefore rodent models could play a significant role in FASD research. *All three types of epigenetic modulators; DNA methylation, histone modifications, and regulation of microRNAs, are impaired by PAE and can* affect developmental genes and pathways, involved in cell proliferation, differentiation, and organogenesis. In mouse models, ethanol exposure can be controlled and other environmental parameters, such as diet and stress, can be kept constant allowing for investigation of the effects of PAE on epigenetic regulatory mechanism and their association with FAS-like symptoms. Furthermore, one-carbon-metabolism (OCM) provides protein precursors for DNA replication and repair, and in DNA methylation for transcriptional regulation, histone modification, and genomic stability. Ethanol or its metabolites, are known antagonist to OCM that transports one-carbon groups for methylation reactions in the cell. Abnormal OCM impairs the intracellular homeostasis. Alcohol-induced interference in methylation disturbs cell differentiation and eventually organogenesis during embryonic development. Both folate deficiency combined with ethanol are teratogenic. In addition to neurodegeneration, impaired OCM can affect other organs of the body. Since these epigenetic alterations may be reversible, these can be used as potential therapeutic targets for FAS recovery (Kruman and Fowler, 2014).

To identify ethanol-sensitive genes, McCarthy et al., (2013) investigated five known craniofacial mutants: *cyp26b1, gata3, pdgfra, smad5,* and *smoothened in zebra fish.* Only *platelet-derived growth factor receptor α* (*pdgfra*) interacted with ethanol during craniofacial development. Analysis of the PDGF family in a human FASD genome-wide dataset linked *pdgfra* to craniofacial phenotypes in FASD, providing a molecular mechanism of this interaction. Untreated *pdgfra* mutants had cleft palate due to defective neural crest cell migration, whereas *pdgfra* heterozygotes developed normally. Ethanol-exposed *pdgfra* mutants had craniofacial defects including the loss of the palatal skeleton and hypoplasia of the pharyngeal skeleton. Furthermore, ethanol treatment caused haplo-insufficiency, associated with palatal defects in ~62% of *pdgfra* heterozygotes. Neural crest apoptosis caused defects in *pdgfra* mutants, suggesting the protective role of pdgfra, mediated by the PI3K/mTOR pathway. This model suggested combined genetic and environmental inhibition of PI3K/mTOR signaling for variability within FASD. Furthermore, Veazey et al., (2013) reported that exposure to alcohol alters the developmental trajectory of progenitor cells and compromises histogenesis. Thus ethanol can impair development by interfering with the molecular events regulating differentiation, whereas MTs regulate zinc-mediated transcriptional activation of genes involved in growth, proliferation, and differentiation (Sharma et al., 2013; Sharma and Ebadi 2014). Normally, lineage-specific transcription factors establish the networks of new cell type; the cell's identity is maintained through epigenetic alterations in which the DNA encoding each gene becomes packaged within the chromatin. Ethanol exposure disrupts cell migration, changes cell–cell interactions, and alters growth factor signaling pathways. Two enzyme complexes—the *Polycomb and Trithorax proteins*—are significant to the epigenetic programs which control the balance between self-renewal and cell differentiation. PAE may disrupt the functions of these two enzymes, altering differentiation. Hence characterizing the involvement of Polycomb and Trithorax groups may enhance understanding the crucial role epigenetic programming plays in FASD.

Mitochondrial Epigenetics in FAS Epidemiological studies are now being conducted on mitochondrial epigenetics which is sensitive to oxidative stress, with particular consideration to study design and analytical challenges (Byun and Baccarelli, 2014). Metabolites, including those generated during ethanol metabolism, can impact disease by binding to transcription factors and/or modifying chromatin structure, thereby altering gene expression. For example, the activities of enzymes involved in epigenetic modifications such as DNA and histone methylation and histone acetylation, are influenced by the levels of metabolites such as nicotinamide adenine dinucleotide (NAD), adenosine triphosphate (ATP), and S-adenosylmethionine (SAM). Chronic alcohol consumption leads to reductions in SAM, thereby contributing to DNA hypomethylation. Similarly, ethanol metabolism alters the ratio of NAD+ to reduced NAD (NADH) and promotes the formation of ROS and acetate, all of which impact epigenetic regulatory mechanisms. In addition to altered carbohydrate metabolism, induction of cell death, and changes in mitochondrial permeability transition, these changes can lead to modulation of epigenetic regulation of gene expression (Zakhari 2013). Methionine, which is formed by methylation of homocysteine (using either 5-methyl tetrahydrofolate [5-methyl THF] or betaine as methyl donors), is essential for the production of S-adenosylmethionine (SAM), which is used to methylate DNA. In addition, chronic heavy drinking reduces folate levels and inhibits methionine synthase (MS), resulting in the reduction of methionine and SAM and eventually increase in homocysteine and S-adenosylhomocysteine (SAH). SAH further inhibits DNA methyltransferases (DNMTs), resulting in global hypomethylation of DNA, which can induce craniofacial and neurobehavioral abnormalities in FAS.

Recently Jia et al., (2013) reported that mitochondrial oxidative phosphorylation (OXPHOS) plays an important role in energy homeostasis by controlling electron transport chain and ATP synthesis. Maternal malnutrition during pregnancy affects mitochondrial (mt) DNA-encoding OXPHOS in offspring, yet it remains unknown whether epigenetic mechanism is involved in the transcriptional regulation of mtDNA-encoded OXPHOS genes. These researchers fed 14 primiparous purebred Meishan sows either standard-(SP) or low-protein (LP) diets during gestation, and analyzed hepatic expression and transcriptional regulation of mtDNA-encoding OXPHOS genes in newborn piglets. Maternal low protein diet decreased hepatic mtDNA copy number in males, but not in females. LP male piglets had higher hepatic AMP concentration and low energy charge, with increased mRNA expression of NADH dehydrogenase subunits 6, cytochrome *c* oxidase subunit 1, 2, 3 and cytochrome *b*, and increased cytochrome *c* oxidase activity. In contrast, LP female piglets showed lower hepatic AMP concentrations and higher energy charge with no alterations in OXPHOS gene expression. LP males exhibited higher glucocorticoid receptor (GR) binding to the mtDNA promoter compared with SP males, with reduced cytosine methylation and hydroxymethylation on mtDNA promoter. Females showed diminished GR binding, increased cytosine methylation, and hydroxymethylation on mtDNA promoter suggesting that maternal low protein diet during pregnancy causes sex-dependent alterations in mtDNA-encoding OXPHOS gene expression and possibly GR is involved in the transcriptional regulation of mtDNA. In addition, Sookoian et al., (2013) used a combination of gene–protein enrichment analysis along with functional annotations and protein interaction networks for understanding the mechanisms underlying fetal metabolic programming. Fetal adaptation to an impaired nutritional environment presumes profound changes in gene expression that involve regulation of tissue-specific patterns of methylated cytosine residues, modulation of the histone acetylation–deacetylation switch, cell differentiation, and stem cell pluripotency.

To test the hypothesis that mitochondrial changes may serve as a link between poor nutrition in early life and insulin resistance, the effect of protein malnutrition during gestation and lactation on mitochondria of the liver and skeletal muscle was investigated by Park et al (2003). The mtDNA of the liver and skeletal muscle were reduced in fetal and early postnatal malnourished rats even when adequate nutrition was provided after weaning. These changes were accompanied by a decrease in mtDNA-encoding gene expression; however, they were not dependent on mitochondrial transcriptional factor A, indicating that undernutrition causes long-lasting changes in mitochondria that may contribute to the development of insulin resistance. In addition, maternal obesity and high fat diet during pregnancy can elevate circulating lipid to increase their levels in the placenta and fetal circulation causing placental inflammation and oxidative stress. Lipids accumulate in the fetal tissue and cause nuclear receptor activation, altered gene expression, oxidative stress, and epigenetic changes can induce impairments in the insulin signaling, reduced muscle mass, and liver and CNS disorders. Thus obesity/high fat diet during pregnancy can have significant impact on the developing fetus that may contribute to maladaptation and adverse health outcomes in adult offspring. In addition, PEPCK gene plays a significant role in glucose homeostasis. A fetal compensatory response to nutrient restriction could prove to be maladaptive in a postnatal environment where nutrients are adequate, contributing to the development of metabolic diseases later in life (Laker et al 2013). Jousse et al (2011) studied the influence of prenatal maternal nutritional stress during gestation and lactation on DNA methylation, histone modification, and leptin gene expression. Animals born to mothers fed low protein diet had lower body weight/adiposity and exhibited a high food intake than animals born to mothers fed a control diet. These changes persist throughout life and were associated with lower levels of leptin mRNA in starved progeny, suggesting that maternal protein undernutrition affects the intricate balance between food intake and energy expenditure in adults. Nutritional stress resulted in removal of methyl residue at CpGs in the promoter region of the leptin gene causing modifications in the leptin gene expression which enhanced induction in low protein fed progeny in response to meal, suggesting environmental influences to phenotypic consequences (Jousse et al., 2011).

It is known that genetic analyses reveals gene sets vulnerable to alcohol exposure during early neurulation. PAE alters expression of genes involved in neural specification, hematopoiesis, methylation, chromatin remodeling, histone variants, eye, and heart development. Recently, quantitative map locusing (QTLs) that mediate alcohol-induced phenotype have been identified between two mouse strains. During development DNA methylation is dynamic, yet orchestrated as methylation progresses in a spatiotemporal manner during neurulation and coincides with neural differentiation. Alcohol can influence epigenetics through alterations of the methionine pathway and subsequent DNA or histone methylation/acetylation. Alcohol also alters noncoding RNA including miRNA and transposable elements (TEs). miRNA expression may mediate ethanol teratology, and TEs may be affected by alcohol through altering DNA methylation at LTR to intertwine epigenetic and genetics of FASD. Early epidemiological studies revealed infants with FASD-like features in the absence of maternal alcohol, where the fathers were alcoholics. Novel mechanisms for alcohol-induced phenotypes include altered sperm DNA methylation, hypomethylated paternal allele and heritable epimutation. These studies predict heritability of alcohol-induced epigenetic abnormalities and gene function across generations (Zhou and Mason 2014). Proposed mechanisms include cell death, cell signaling defects and changes in gene expression. More recently non-coding RNA, epigenetic changes and specific vitamin deficiencies which may interact, producing a wide spectrum of consequences has been explored. Recently Muralidharan et al., (2013) discussed manifestations of alcohol exposure on the developing CNS, including the neural crest cells and sensory neural placodes, and neurodevelopmental pathways as therapeutic targets for prevention or protection from FASD.

Two major apoptotic pathways, the death receptor and the mitochondrial pathway, have been documented in mammalian cells. Apoptosis of human gastric SNU-620 carcinoma cells induced by TGF-β 1 is caused by the Fas death pathway in a Fas ligand-independent manner, and that the Fas death pathway activated by TGF-β 1 is linked to the mitochondrial apoptotic pathway via Bid mediation. TGF-β 1 induced the expression and activation of Fas and the subsequent caspase-8-mediated Bid cleavage. Expression of dominant negative FADD and treatment with caspase-8 inhibitor prevented TGF-β 1-induced apoptosis, whereas treatment with an activating CH11 or a neutralizing ZB4 anti-Fas antibody, recombinant Fas ligand, or Fas-Fc chimera did not influence activation of Fas and the induction of apoptosis by TGF-β 1 which also activated the mitochondrial pathway demonstrating Bid-mediated loss of mitochondrial membrane potential ($\Delta\Psi$) and subsequent cytochrome c release associated with the activations of caspase-9. TGF-β 1-induced apoptotic events were inhibited by Smad3 knockdown and also abrogated by Smad7 expression, suggesting the involvement of the Smad3 pathway in the Fas death pathway by TGF-β 1 (Kim et al., 2004). In addition, mitochondrial dysfunction and activation of onco-metabolites production might pave the way for the epigenetics of carcinogenesis (Menendez et al., 2014). Evolutionary theories of aging predict the existence of genes that provide selective advantage early in life with deleterious consequences on lifespan later in life (*antagonistic pleiotropy theory*) or longevity insurance genes (*disposable soma theory*). Furthermore, recent genetic analyses have identified "gerontogenes" as new genes that increase lifespan when overexpressed or mutated. In addition, genetic and epigenetic mechanisms have a positive effect on longevity. The gerontogenes are considered as lifespan regulators, mediators, effectors, housekeeping genes, genes involved in mitochondrial function, regulating cellular senescence, and apoptosis. The majority of the genes as well as genetic and epigenetic mechanisms that are involved in regulation of longevity are related to stress response (Moskalev et al., 2014). Recent discoveries of novel iron-sulfur proteins are also involved in epigenetics and DNA metabolism. Hence further understanding of intracellular iron trafficking is opening up new strategies to discover iron distribution between iron cofactor assembly pathways and its regulation in the cell (Balk and Schaedler 2014).

Recently Pandhare et al., (2014) reported that substance abuse is a major barrier in eradication of the HIV epidemic because it acts as a powerful cofactor for viral transmission, disease progression, and AIDS-related mortality. Cocaine, one of the commonly abused drugs among HIV-1 patients accelerates HIV disease progression. Therefore, these researchers tested whether cocaine augments HIV-1-associated $CD4^+$ T-cell decline, a predictor of HIV disease progression by examining apoptosis of resting $CD4^+$ T cells from HIV-1-negative and HIV-1-positive donors, because decline of uninfected cells plays a significant role in HIV-1 disease progression. Treatment of resting $CD4^+$ T cells with cocaine (up to 100 μmol/L) was ineffective, but 200-1000 μmol/L induced apoptosis. Treatment of $CD4^+$ T cells with both HIV-1 virions and cocaine increased apoptosis compared with the apoptosis induced by cocaine or virions alone suggesting that cocaine induces $CD4^+$ T-cell apoptosis by increasing ROS and by mitochondrial depolarization, suggesting synergy between cocaine and HIV-1 on $CD4^+$ T-cell apoptosis that may explain the accelerated disease in HIV-1-infected drug abusers.

It is known that DNA damage is associated with aging and tumorigenesis. A high-sensitivity long-run real-time PCR has been developed for quantifying DNA-damage (LORD-Q) in both the mitochondrial and nuclear genome. While most conventional methods are of low-sensitivity or restricted to abundant mtDNA samples, a protocol that enables the accurate sequence-specific quantification of DNA damage in >3-kb probes for any mitochondrial or nuclear DNA sequence. LORD-Q was compared with a previously published qPCR-based method and single-cell gel electrophoresis, demonstrating a better performance of LORD-Q. Induction of DNA damage and repair processes in induced pluripotent stem cells and isogenic fibroblasts suggested that LORD-Q provides a better method to quantify DNA damage, thereby allowing assessment of DNA repair, genotoxicity screening and other processes for biological applications including FAS (Lehle et al., 2013).

Clinical Diagnosis of FAS Coles (2011) reported that FAS and FASD remain underdiagnosed in general treatment settings and it is challenging to accurately diagnose the FAS victims without accurate information from the mother. Unfortunately mothers remain reluctant to disclose that they consumed alcohol during pregnancy even when their infants are diagnosed with FAS. Moreover, confirmation of intrauterine alcohol exposure is not considered a pre-requisite for the diagnosis of FAS even when CNS abnormalities are lacking. PAE causes a continuum of effects. The neurodevelopmental effects of PAE, include: learning and memory, motor and sensory/motor effects, visual/spatial skills, and executive functional anomalies. The most severe phenotype, FAS, involves facial dysmorphism, growth deficits, and neurocognitive problems. Therefore, we need to discriminate the effects of PAE from other clinical conditions which may require more education and training but will improve outcomes for affected children.

Usually, FAS and other conditions associated with PAE are underdiagnosed in clinical settings that focus on behavior and developmental problems. Attributing the effects of the neurodevelopmental impact of alcohol exposure to other factors (like ADHD or behavioral disorders) may not help the individuals with FASD and to their families. Earlier studies have identified typical behavioral and cognitive patterns associated with FASD. Among the factors involved in identifying the effects of PAE are: the effects of the caregiving environment; comorbidities and differential diagnosis, which includes identifying the developmental defects of alcohol and discriminating these effects from other clinical conditions.

Preliminary diagnosis of FAS can be made by detecting facial features such as: skin folds of the corners of the eyes, low nose bridge, short nose, indistinct philtrum, small head circumference, small eye opening, small mid face, and thin upper lip, low nasal bridge, epicanthal fold of eye (Thomas et al 2010; Mattson et al 2011). Although facial characteristics, growth deficits, CNS abnormalities are considered diagnostic for the clinical evaluation; only facial phenotype is universally-acceptable as a screening tool for the diagnosis of FAS (Landgrof et al., 2013).

The diagnostic features of FAS can be broadly divided as growth deficits and facial characteristics. At least one of the growth deficits should be present such as: birth weight or body weight; birth length or body length; and body mass index (BMI) should be less than 10th percentile as illustrated in Table 2.

The facial characteristics: should be present simultaneously at any age; short palperbral length should be less than or equal to 3rd percentile along with thin upper lip. Clinical judgment based on functional CNS abnormality with global intellectual deficit $<2SD$ or developmental delay associated with loss of more than two functions with or without epilepsy. The structural abnormalities include microcephaly in less than 10th percentile.

The loss of CNS functionality is measured by assessing language/speech; fine motor functions such as spatial-visual perception, spatial-constructive skills; learning and memory skills; executive functions; arithmetic skills; attention; social skills, and behavior.

Table 2. Clinical Criteria of FAS Diagnosis

Diagnostic features	Parameter	Recommendation
Growth deficits (At least one should be present)	1. Birth weight or body weight 2. Birth length or body length 3. Body mass index	< 10th percentile
Facial characteristics (All should be present simultaneously at any age)	1.Short palpebral fissure length 2. Smooth philtrum 3. Thin upper lip	≤ 3rd percentile 4 or 5 on Astley scale
Structural /functional evidence of neuro-behavioral /cognitive deficiency with or without epilepsy	1. Head circumference 2. global intellectual deficit 3. social, fine motor & learning/memory skills	< 10th percentile < 2SD < 2SD

Alcohol consumption should be confirmed throughout gestation to ascertain: > 1 Oz absolute alcohol/day or >4 drinks/day (Landgraf et al, 2013).

In the mother, the age, gravidity, parity, stillbirths and miscarriages, inadequate practices of religion/spirituality, low maternal education, cigarette smoking, depression/psychological stress, short stature, low weight, low BMI, nutritional deficiency, specific alcohol dehydrogenase polymorphism; and agents exposure: High blood alcohol levels from large quantities of ethanol consumption, binge drinking (3 + per occasion), length of drinking career, frequent smoking, low birth weight, (*Beer is the most common beverage of a majority of FASD mothers*), drinking outside the meals, poly-substance abuse in urban population, changes in gastric ADH activity, change in nutritional status during pregnancy, environment: Low SES, unmarried but living with sex partners, cultures accepting heavy drinking, family of origin of heavy drinkers, sex partner with heavy binge drinking, popular alcohol-centered recreation, social isolation from main stream economy and society, and little or no knowledge or awareness of FASD can be evaluated.

It is important to elucidate the dangers of PAE at precise gestational time points, such as first, second, and third trimester, to clarify the stages of human fetal development during which alcohol exposure may cause auditory and vestibular deficits. Development of the human's ear begins as early as the fourth week of gestation and by about the twenty-second week the inner ear is fully developed. Zamora and Lu (2013) examined the morphological effects of alcohol on the developing octavolateral system (the inner ear and lateral line) using the zebrafish. The embryos of 2 hours post fertilization (hpf) were treated in 2% alcohol for 48 hours and screened at 72 hpf for morphological defects of the inner ear and lateral line. Octavolateral organs were examined. Several otolith phenotypes for alcohol-treated zebrafish were noticed including zero, one, two abnormal, two normal, and multiple otoliths, suggesting that alcohol exposure during early development impairs the inner ear (smaller ear, abnormal otoliths, and fewer sensory hair cells) and the lateral line (smaller neuromasts, fewer neuromasts and hair cells per neuromast, and kinocilia of hair cells), which result in defective hearing, balance, and hydrodynamic function of zebrafish. Thus embryonic alcohol exposure from 2 to 50 hpf causes early developmental deformities in octavolateral organs. Alcohol-induced defects in the mechanosensory system could also be present in the human auditory-vestibular system affected by FAE.

The developing fetus is differentially and temporally–susceptible to FAS. Typical symptoms of FAS are represented as smoothness of philtrum as shown in the upper panel (Figure 1). The middle panel illustrates the effect of ethanol on developing fetus depending on the levels of alcohol consumed during pregnancy, which is associated with deleterious consequences including: zygote death, abortion, still birth and severe birth defects, craniofacial deformities, stunted body growth, and neurobehavioral anomalies. Lower panel illustrates CB formation as a consequence of alcohol-induced mitochondrial degeneration which may occur during pre-zygotic phase in the young male and female reproductive system even before marriage. In addition, nuclear and mitochondrial epigenetic changes can influence cell proliferation, differentiation, migration, and organogenesis. We can arbitrarily categorize alcohol abuse as low (1-2 drinks/day), moderate (2-3 drinks/day), and heavy (>4 drinks/day or >14 drinks/week). FASD spectrum can be attenuated by nutritional supplementation of Vitamin-A, Choline, Folate, physiological zinc (Zn^{2+}), and MTs induction which serve as free radical scavengers to prevent mitochondrial degeneration and CB formation implicated in apoptosis and progressive neurodegeneration (Sharma 2014).

3D Face Shape Analysis of FAS Face photography is becoming frequently available with the 3D shape analysis. To overcome size difference, average FAS, PFAS, and HE faces can be scaled using ratio of nasion to gnathion length before normalization to render signatures reflecting FASD. When the upper lip is reduced in size compared with matched controls, convexity can be highlighted. Face signature graph of 18 clusters arising from normalization against controls of 107 children with clinical categorization of FAS, PFAS, or HE were acquired. Magnified insets showed links between individuals. This study identified novel strategies for detecting facial effects of PAE. Heat maps and dynamic morphs to matched controls enhanced the appreciation of facial form. More testing has been planned for USA, South Africa, and Ukraine. This collaborative initiative on FASD plans is to make face visualization tools available in future. After evaluation and modification, these 3D facial maps can be distributed globally. The mobile devices and websites are now offering conversion from 2D to 3D. Moreover stereo webcams in laptops for face recognition are available which can facilitate FAS diagnosis. Recently a study was performed to develop novel strategies to detect facial dysmorphism across the FASD, in children with heavy alcohol exposure but without classic facial characteristics. Of 192 children recruited, 69 were born to women who reported abstaining from alcohol during pregnancy. The remainder were categorized as the FAS, partial FAS, or nonsyndromal HE. These investigators used dense surface modeling and signature analyses of 3-D facial photographs to visualize facial differences, and to determine links between face shape and behavior. The most severe phenotype, FAS, involved facial dysmorphism, growth deficits, and cognitive problems. Face signatures delineated dysmorphism across the FASD and in half of the nonsyndromal HE category detected facial characteristics consistent with PAE. This group performed less well on IQ and learning tests than did nonsyndromal subjects without typical facial characteristics, suggesting that heat Map and morphine visualization of face signatures may help physicians detect facial dysmorphogenesis across the FASD. Thus face signature graphs have potential for identifying nonsyndromal heavily exposed children who lack the classic facial phenotype but have cognitive impairment (*NIAAA Director's Report, June 2013*).

Neuroimaging in FAS Diagnosis Recognition of FAS consequences is essential for accurate diagnosis and prevention. The application of Magnetic resonance imaging (MRI) to the study of FASD in animal models promises to facilitate the definition of the FASD spectrum of birth defects along with their developmental stage and dose-dependency. MRI, diffusion tensor imaging (DTI), and magnetic resonance spectroscopy (MRS) provide valuable information for examining brain structure and neurochemistry of FASD. As compared to clinical studies of the effects of alcohol on development, animal models allows better control over dose, duration, and pattern of alcohol exposure. Although the application of MRI–based methodologies to the study of FASD in animal models is in its infancy, it has provided clinically-relevant information and holds promise to further extend our understanding of alcohol's effects on the developing fetus. O'Leary-Moore et al (2011) reviewed the utility of these neuroimaging methods to study FASD in animal models. Rodent studies confirmed the vulnerability of the brain to alcohol-mediated damage at developmental stages that occur in humans prior to pregnancy detection, emphasizing the importance of pre-pregnancy counseling. In addition, the ex vivo analyses are expected to allow longitudinal analyses of both the brain and behavior in individual animals. In the mouse brain, cortical heterotopias have been noticed following acute gestational day 7 alcohol exposure using 3D reconstructions of MRI and confirmed by routine histology. Furthermore, MRI in combination with MRS can provide data that will be beneficial for clinical practice as well as ongoing research. Generally N-acetyl aspartic acid (NAA), creatine, and choline, are estimated for the clinical assessment and severity of FASD. By performing magic angle spinning, high-resolution MRS analyses, we discovered significantly reduced N-acetyl aspartic acid (NAA) in chronic morphine-treated rats as seen in FASD children (Sharma et al., 2003). In addition, reduced hippocampal NAA has been used as a biomarker in obesity (Coplan et al., 2014) and in traumatic brain injury (Moffett et al., 2013).

Omics Analysis of FAS Indeed omics analysis provides excellent opportunities to discover novel biomarkers for the early detection, prevention, and treatment of diseases including FASD. Two studies used rodent models of FASD in combination with high-throughput screening to discover novel biomarker candidates. By using a proteomic screening procedure, Datta et al (2008) reported a significant increase in α-fetoprotein expression in amniotic fluid taken from gestational day (GD) 17 mouse fetuses after a single high-dose alcohol binge–like exposure on GD 8. By using a rat model of moderate drinking throughout pregnancy that produces offspring with learning deficits, Rosenberg et al (2010) identified 22 placental genes whose expression was significantly altered in alcohol-consuming dams. The alcohol-altered genes encode growth factors important for placental as well as fetal brain, vascular, endocrine, and immune system development, suggesting that these and other high-throughput screening procedures could facilitate developing sensitive and specific biomarkers for the diagnosis of FAE and for earlier prognostication of fetal alcohol damage in exposed offspring. Kietzman et al (2014) recently reported implications of the abnormal Hedgehog signaling pathway as a molecular mechanism in the pathogenesis of FAS. In severe cases, the abnormalities of the face and brain that result from PAE fall within the spectrum of holoprosencephaly. Single allele mutations in the Hh pathway genes *Sonic Hedgehog* (*SHH*) and *GLI2,* cause holoprosencephaly with variable phenotypic penetrance in humans. These investigators tested whether mutations in these genes alter the frequency or severity of ethanol-induced dysmorphology in a mouse model of FAS. Pregnancies were established by mating *Shh*$^{+/-}$ or *Gli2*$^{+/-}$ male mice backcrossed to C57BL/6J strain, with wild-type females. On gestational day 7, dams were treated with two i.p doses of 2.9 g/kg ethanol, administered 4 hrs apart. Fetuses were then genotyped and imaged to assess the severity of facial dysmorphology. Following ethanol exposure, dysmorphology scores were increased by 3.2- and 6.6-fold in *Shh*$^{+/-}$ and *Gli2*$^{+/-}$ groups, respectively. A cohort of heterozygous fetuses exhibited phenotypes not produced in this model but associated with severe holoprosencephaly, including exencephaly, median cleft lip, otocephaly, and proboscis. A correlation between the severity of facial dysmorphology and medial forebrain deficiency was observed in affected animals. While *Shh*$^{+/-}$ and *Gli2*$^{+/-}$ mice have been described as normal, these results demonstrated haploinsufficiency of both genes in combination with ethanol exposure. By demonstrating an interaction between specific genetic and environmental risk factors, this study provided information into the multifactorial etiology and complex pathogenesis of FAS and holoprosencephaly. Thus the severity of FAS can be evaluated by estimating facial dysmorphology rating scale to predict medial forebrain deficiency. These findings support that even a low ethanol exposure is sufficient to cause clinically significant abnormalities in fetuses with genetic mutations in the Hh signaling pathway. Thus mutations in *SHH* are the cause of non-chromosomal HPE, while 7.6% of women in the U.S consume ethanol during pregnancy. By demonstrating an interaction between PAE and genes in the Hh pathway, this study has provided insights into the multifactorial etiology and pathogenesis of both FAS and HPE. Translation of these findings would benefit by future studies examining the dose-response relationship of ethanol exposure in models of relevant genetic predisposition. In addition to the commonly seen FAS and FASD outcomes, many other adverse pregnancy and birth outcomes have been linked to PAE. These studies suggest that drinking during pregnancy may increase the risk of miscarriage, stillbirth, preterm delivery, and SIDS as discussed earlier. Whether these effects are attributed to true biological effects, sociodemographic and lifestyle factors that co-occur with pregnancy drinking, or a combination and possibly synergistic effect remains unknown.

By employing large-scale microarray technology, Shankar et al (2006) examined the changes in the expression of 8,800 genes in the livers of pregnant rats fed alcohol in either adequate or undernourished states and determined the number of genes that were altered in response to alcohol treatment in the maternal liver. The genes differed by approximately 10-fold (369 vs. 37 genes, respectively) following ethanol exposure. In general, genes involved in cellular metabolism; response to stress and stimulus; protein, carbohydrate, and lipid metabolism; cell-cycle regulation and DNA transcription; cell communication and development; and cell and tissue differentiation were altered in the undernourished alcohol group. Particularly, IGF-1 was decreased in alcohol-fed rats during undernutrition. Several genes known to be regulated by IGF-1 also were altered, making it a candidate for further investigation. The activity of the enzyme casein kinase, which is increased with IGF-1, was also decreased in correlation with IGF-1. Gene expression of the binding protein GH and IGF binding protein 3 (IGFBP-3) was also significantly altered to decrease IGF-1 signaling, suggesting that undernutrition is a significant risk factor in alcohol-associated fetal growth retardation, and optimal nutritional management during pregnancy may be effective strategy to reduce fetal alcohol toxicity in high-risk pregnancies.

MicroRNAs and FAS Recently microRNAs (miRNAs) have been identified as master regulators of the cellular transcriptome and proteome which play a crucial role in shaping the differentiation and function of tissues and organs in both health and disease. New evidence showing that ethanol-sensitive miRNAs are indeed regulatory master-switches has been put forth. Balaraman et al (2013) reported that microRNAs (miRNAs) are members of non–protein-coding RNA (ncRNA) molecules that represent cell regulation. Assessment of the generation and function of miRNAs suggests that these ncRNAs are vulnerable to fluctuations in genetic, epigenetic, and environmental factors including ethanol. Currently the role of epigenetic mechanisms in neurogenesis and how it is affected by PAE, causing FASD is being explored. Animal-and cell culture–based models have demonstrated that miRNAs are targets of alcohol during fetal development and that their dysregulation plays a significant role in the etiology of FASD. Hence, an analysis of the regulation and function of the miRNAs may yield clues in the clinical management of FASD. Miranda et al (2010) reported that ethanol exerts complex effects on human physiology and health. Ethanol is not only addictive, but it is also a fetal teratogen, an adult neurotoxin, and an etiologic agent in hepatic and cardiovascular disease, inflammation, osteoporosis, and fracture susceptibility. miRNAs control the development of tolerance, a crucial component of ethanol addiction. Other drugs of abuse also target some ethanol-sensitive miRNAs suggesting common biochemical mechanisms of drug addiction. There is evidence that miRNAs mediate several ethanol pathologies, including disruption of neural stem cell proliferation and differentiation in the exposed fetus, gut leakiness that contributes to endotoxemia and liver disease, hepatocellular carcinomas, and gastrointestinal cancers. Finally, investigations into potential roles of miRNAs as mediators of ethanol's effects on inflammation and fracture healing, and as diagnostic biomarkers and targets for therapeutic interventions for alcohol-related disorders are now emerging.

Animal Models of FASD The development of sensitive biomarkers of FASD based exclusively on clinical research is difficult due to variability in patient populations, variable drinking pattern among pregnant women, and the time intervals between an optimal time for collecting biological samples during pregnancy or at birth, and the time at which measures of functional brain damage and/or adverse behavioral outcomes are evaluated. One alternative solution is to first identify and validate biomarkers in animal models of FASD and then, based on this information, pursue human studies to assess their clinical potential. Despite translational research challenges, the preclinical approach to novel biomarker development has merits. Preclinical studies increase the prospects of identifying novel biomarkers without the confounding variables associated with patient populations. Biomarker validation can be performed in a systematic and controlled fashion over a shorter period of time and in a cost-effective manner. An animal model provides an opportunity to assess directly how a biomarker signature may change as a function of alcohol dosing, patterns of exposure, and the influence of other risk factors during pregnancy, such as nicotine, ethanol, other drugs of abuse, stress, malnutrition, or environmental toxins, and heavy-metals exposure. How a biomarker pattern is altered by concurrent exposure to other risk factors would be highly significant for the interpretation of data from clinical studies. Moreover, an animal model allows for direct correlation of biomarker patterns with markers of functional damage to the fetus and with longer-term behavioral outcomes. Above all, animal model could provide insights about the molecular mechanism of ethanol-induced teratogenic damage; assessments that may be extremely difficult to examine in a clinical setting.

Susceptibility of Purkinje Neurons The cerebellum and hippocampus are the most sensitive regions that are specifically affected by ethanol, resulting in delayed motor learning, cognitive disabilities, poor memory, attention deficits, impulsive behavior, and poor cause-effect reasoning. Alcohol causes selective loss and/or degeneration of Purkinje neurons, which results in sensory-motor impairments. The numbers and density of Purkinje neurons decreased with increasing daily alcohol intake but not with age. Long-term moderate daily consumption was associated with significant loss of Purkinje neurons (Karhunen et al., 1994). A study demonstrated delayed cerebellar maturation in the progeny of intrauterine ethanol associated with impaired maturation of Purkinje neurons. The Purkinje neuron nuclei were smaller than normal and had a delayed cytoplasmic maturation (Volk et al., 1981). Cerebellum is particularly vulnerable to ethanol-induced Purkinje neuron loss during the third trimester-equivalent, with striking regional differences in vulnerability in which early-maturing regions in the vermis show more loss than the late-maturing regions (Sawant et al., 2013).

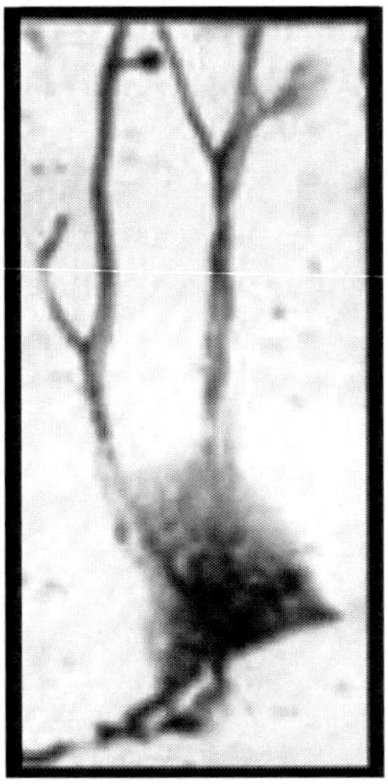

Figure 2. Alcohol-induced deficits on motor coordination tasks due to synaptic degeneration of 30 days undernourished Purkinje neurons. (X1000).

A study was performed to test the hypothesis that the sheep model will show similar regional differences in Purkinje neuron loss when binge ethanol exposure is restricted to the prenatal period of brain development equivalent to the third trimester and also compared the pattern of loss to that produced by ethanol exposure during the first trimester-equivalent. Pregnant sheep were assigned to four groups: first trimester-equivalent saline control group, first trimester-equivalent ethanol group (1.75 g/kg/day), third trimester-equivalent saline control group, and third trimester-equivalent ethanol group. Ethanol was administered as an i.v infusion on 3 consecutive days followed by a 4-day ethanol-free interval, to mimic a weekend binge drinking pattern. Animals were sacrificed and fetal brains were harvested on gestation day 133. Purkinje neuron counts were performed in an early-maturing region (lobules I-X) and a late-maturing region (lobules VIc-VII) from mid-sagittal sections of the cerebellar vermis. The third trimester-equivalent ethanol exposure caused a significant reduction in the Purkinje neuron volume density and number in the early-maturing region, but not in the late-maturing region. However, the first trimester-equivalent ethanol exposure resulted in significant reductions in both the early and late-maturing regions, supporting that PAE in the first trimester interferes with the genesis of Purkinje neurons in a nonselective manner, whereas during the third trimester selectively kills post-mitotic Purkinje neurons in specific vermal regions during differentiation and synaptogenesis. Thus ethanol exposure during first trimester caused Purkinje neuron loss, independent of cerebellar region, whereas the third trimester exposure caused Purkinje neuron loss in the early maturing region only.

Purkinje neurons are highly susceptible to nutritional stress, environmental neurotoxins, and ethanol. This picture of an isolated Purkinje neuron was taken from 30 days developing undernourished rat cerebellar cortex (Figure 2). The apical dendrites exhibit structurally intact synaptic terminal exhibiting dense rounded grape-like appearance, whereas degenerating synaptic terminal appears club-shaped, swollen, and with cloudy appearance due to CB formation implicated in synaptic degeneration, apoptosis, and neurodegeneration (Sharma et al., 2013, Sharma, 2014; Sharma and Ebadi, 2014). The incidence of CB formation was maximum in the apical dendrites as compared to basal dendrites and oblique branch of apical dendrites. Delayed motor learning in FAS victims occurs due to CB-mediated degeneration of synaptic terminal in the developing Purkinje neurons (Sharma and Ebadi 2014). Impairments in cerebellar-dependent eye-blink conditioning and impaired handwriting in FAS victims may be induced by CB formation in the developing Purkinje neurons, implicated in synaptic terminal degeneration. Nutritional rehabilitation attenuated alcohol-induced deficits in acquisition of eye-blink conditioning in females but not in males.

Wagner et al., (2013) generated binge-like alcohol exposure model in neonatal rats during the period of brain development comparable with that of the human third trimester, which causes structural and functional damage to the cerebellum and disrupts cerebellar-dependent eye-blink conditioning. The eye-blink conditioning deficits demonstrated in this rat model predicted the similar deficits as noticed in children with FASD. This study extended this translational approach by testing the hypothesis that rehabilitation involving 20 days of training on traversal of an obstacle course (complex motor learning) would ameliorate the deficits on classical conditioning of eye-blink responses produced by the neonatal alcohol exposure. This training stimulated cerebellar synaptic plasticity and improved alcohol-induced deficits on motor coordination tasks and attenuated alcohol-induced deficits in acquisition of eye-blink conditioning in females but not in males.

Nutrition in FAS: Animal studies have demonstrated important roles for maternal nutrition in FASD, but the impact of prenatal maternal body composition has not been studied in humans. Carter et al (2013) reported that fetal alcohol-related growth restriction persists through infancy but its impact later in life is less understood. These investigators examined the effects of PAE on longitudinal growth from birth through young adulthood and the degree to which maternal weight and BMI moderate these effects. 480 mothers were admitted at their first prenatal clinic visit to over-represent moderate-to-heavy use of alcohol during pregnancy, including a 5% random sample of low-level drinkers and abstainers. They were interviewed at every prenatal visit about their alcohol abuse. Their children were examined for weight, length/height, BMI, and head circumference at birth, 6.5 and 13 months, and 7.5, 14, and 19 years. PAE was associated with reductions in the above parameters. At low-to-moderate levels of exposure, these effects were more severe in infancy than in later childhood. By contrast, effects persisted among children whose mothers drank at least monthly and among those born to women with alcohol abuse and/or dependence who had consumed ≥4 drinks/occasion. Alcohol-related growth restriction was less severe in later childhood and adolescence among low-to-moderately exposed children. In addition, effects on aforementioned parameters were stronger among children born to mothers with lower pre-pregnancy weight which may have been due to attainment of higher BAC in smaller mothers for a given amount of alcohol intake or to increased vulnerability in infants born to women with poor nutrition, suggesting that smaller maternal pre-pregnancy weight and BMI exacerbate alcohol-related growth restriction. Creeley et al. (2013) reported that intrauterine exposure of the fetal non-human primate (NHP) brain to alcohol on a single occasion during early or late third-trimester triggers widespread apoptosis of cells in both gray and white matter (WM) regions of the fetal brain. The degenerating gray matter cells are primarily neurons. The degenerating WM cells belong to the oligodendrocyte (OL) lineage which become vulnerable when they just begin to generate myelin basic protein and remain vulnerable throughout later stages of myelination. The mean density of dying WM cells in alcohol-exposed brains was 12.7 times higher than the density of WM cells degenerating by natural apoptosis in control brains. A similar apoptosis of both neurons and OLs occurs following exposure of the developing brain to anesthetic and anticonvulsant drugs, which raise concerns regarding the role neuro and oligo-apoptosis play in the FASD, and pose a question whether other apoptogenic drugs such as general anesthetics, and antiepileptic drugs may also cause FASD-like syndromes. Shankar et al (2007) reported that metabolism of ethanol is regulated by genetic and environmental factors as well as physiologic state. The rate of alcohol clearance, which ultimately determines tissue ethanol concentrations, may be the most significant risk factor for many of the deleterious effects of alcohol. Faster ethanol clearance would help minimize target tissue concentrations, and in pregnant women, mitigate FAE. Among pregnant rats allowed unrestricted access to alcohol and those fed alcohol containing liquid diets under experimental conditions via a feeding tube (total enteral nutrition [TEN]), urine ethanol concentrations were lower in pregnant rats compared with non-pregnant females given the same dose of ethanol. Maternal nutritional status also is an important determinant of fetal alcohol toxicity. Thus TEN system demonstrated that alcohol-induced fetal growth retardation is potentiated by undernutrition via impaired alcohol metabolism and clearance.

FAS and ADHD: Children with PAE with and without ADHD need to be further differentiated, as they may have different behavioral outcomes and clinical presentations. ADHD is explained by multiple neurodevelopmental pathways (Sonuga-Barke, 2005). Hence, exploring the direct effects of PAE, with and without the presence of ADHD, will allow to create effective interventions for children with PAE. Mattson et al (2013) reported that PAE results in neurobehavioral deficits. Their studies were aimed to build neurobehavioral profile in order to improve classification accuracy and test the specificity of the resulting profile. A neuropsychological test battery was used to three groups of children: subjects with PAE, controls (CON), and subjects with ADHD. A representative sample from six sites in the U.S and South Africa was subjected to latent profile analyses (LPA) including: (1) subjects with FAS and controls, (2) subjects with PAE without FAS and controls, (3) subjects with PAE (with or without FAS) and subjects with ADHD. This study indicated that the neuropsychological effects of PAE can be used to distinguish alcohol-affected children from both normally developing children and children with ADHD. 70% of children with heavy PAE were neuro-behaviorally affected while the remaining 30% were spared. These studies suggested that; alcohol-affected children are likely to also have ADHD and thus may be confused with non-exposed children with ADHD. While there are similarities, these two clinical conditions are not synonymous. Differences in treatment effectiveness between FASD and ADHD, warrants the need for accurate identification of alcohol-affected children (Frankel et al., 2006, Doig et al., 2008; Collins et al., 2009). Recently Graham et al (2013) reported that children with PAE meet criteria for ADHD. ADHD research has examined subtype differences in symptomology, such as sluggish cognitive tempo (SCT), represented by behavioral symptoms including, hypo activity and day-dreaming, and has been linked to increased internalizing behaviors. Alcohol-exposed children exhibited elevated SCT scores related to increased parent ratings of internalizing and externalizing behaviors and attention. These findings were observed in alcohol-exposed children regardless of ADHD symptoms and specific SCT items proved useful in distinguishing exposed children. Distinguishing teratogenic effects of PAE from those associated with ADHD may help to clarify whether PAE causes ADHD directly, or that PAE causes deficits in cognition and behavior that then cause a child to meet criteria for ADHD. Ware et al (2013) examined the prevalence of psychiatric disorders and behavioral problems in children with and without PAE and ADHD employing computerized diagnostic interview for children-IV (C-DISC-4.0) and reported that presence of both PAE and ADHD lead to psychiatric and behavioral symptoms, which are greater in severity and distinguishable from those seen in PAE without ADHD. Future research should examine whether children with PAE with and without ADHD differ in attention, executive function, learning, and memory.

FAS and Neurotransmitter System: Valenzuela and Puglia (2011) reported that neurotransmitter systems have been recognized as important targets for the developmental actions of alcohol. Short-and long-term effects of ethanol on amino acid (e.g., γ-aminobutyric acid and glutamate) and biogenic amine (e.g., serotonin and dopamine), and peptide neurotransmitters have been demonstrated in animal models of FASD. Researchers have detected ethanol effects during developmental period equivalent to the first, second, and third trimesters of human pregnancy. Recent studies have elucidated new mechanisms and/or consequences of the actions of ethanol on amino acid and biogenic amine neurotransmitter systems. Alterations in these neurotransmitter systems could be responsible for (a) learning, memory, and attention deficits; (b) impairments in motor coordination; (c) abnormal responsiveness to stress; and (d) increased susceptibility to neuropsychiatric disorders, drug addiction, depression, and neurological disorders, such as epilepsy and SIDS. Neurotransmission in the developing brain does not always respond to ethanol as in the adult brain and that components of developing neurotransmitter systems have unique properties that make them sensitive to the adverse effects of ethanol, even at low levels of exposure. Ethanol-induced abnormalities in the formation of developing neuronal circuits are responsible for the persistent structural and functional brain deficits that characterize FASD. These deficits are responsible for the behavioral and cognitive alterations and increased propensity to neuropsychiatric and neurological disorders. It is important to investigate the effects of developmental ethanol exposure on modulators of neurotransmission, as these may be targets for the development of effective therapeutic interventions against FASD. Ethanol exposure during development can act in conjunction with genetic susceptibility factors. Murawski and Stanton (2010) reported that neonatal ethanol exposure in the rat partially damages the hippocampus, but such exposure causes only modest or inconsistent deficits on hippocampus-dependent behavioral tasks. This may reflect variable sensitivity of these tasks following partial hippocampal injury. The pre-exposure facilitation effect (CPFE) is a variant of context conditioning in which context exposure and immediate shock occur on successive occasions. During testing, pre-exposed rats freeze more than non-pre-exposed controls. The CPFE is more sensitive to hippocampal injury than standard contextual fear conditioning (Rudy & O'Reilly, 2001). Rats exposed to a high binge dose of ethanol (5.25 g/kg/day) over postnatal days [PD] 4–9 failed to demonstrate the CPFE when pre-exposed to the conditioning context on PD31. Neonatal alcohol disrupted conditioned freezing to a lesser extent when context pre-exposure was followed by a standard context conditioning trial rather than immediate shock. Fear conditioning to a discrete auditory cue (tone) was unaffected by neonatal alcohol exposure ruling out possible performance effects suggesting that the CPFE is sensitive task for detecting hippocampal injury produced by alcohol. Mixed results with other tasks may reflect residual hippocampal function and/or the use of alternate neurobehavioral systems or "strategies" following alcohol-induced brain damage. An additional brain region contributing to contextual fear conditioning deficits may be the cerebellum. Neonatal ethanol exposure reduces the number of Purkinje neurons in rodents and there is evidence that sCFC is retrieved representation that becomes associated with shock, producing the CPFE. Rats that are not pre-exposed to the context show the ISD to immediate shock because the individual features of the context sampled prior to immediate shock are insufficient to support conditioning.

Hippocampal CA-3 region has been proposed to support the process of pattern completion due to its abundance of recurrent circuits. Rats with CA3 and DG lesions, but not with CA1 or sham lesions, were impaired during the test phase of a spatial pattern completion task. NMDA receptors of the CA-3 region are required for the rapid formation of context representation during contextual conditioning at short placement-to-shock intervals. Livy et al (2003) reported reductions in CA3 density and cell number at PD10 using an artificial rearing method for developmental ethanol exposure over PD4-9, though other studies could not confirm CA3 reductions. If dosing method produced CA3 reductions at PD31-33, the disruptions in the CPFE demonstrated by ethanol-exposed rats may represent a disruption in the pattern completion process during the training phase of the CPFE paradigm. An additional brain region contributing to contextual fear conditioning deficits is the cerebellum. sCFC is attenuated by inactivation of the cerebellar vermis, which was noted in studies using the Morris water maze assay in neonatally exposed rodents, for mutant mice with Purkinje neuron dysfunction show acquisition deficits in a spatial Morris water maze. Reductions in contextual conditioning on two variants of contextual fear conditioning in juvenile rats neonatally exposed to a high binge dose of ethanol during early development were observed. Masten et al., (2009) reported that underage alcohol use can be viewed as a developmental phenomenon because developmental changes and expectations influence this behavior and also because it has consequences for development. Data on alcohol use, abuse, and dependence show age-related patterns. Moreover, many of the short and long term effects that alcohol abuse has on the drinker, depend on the developmental timing of alcohol abuse or exposure. Finally, many developmental connections have been observed in the risk and protective factors that predict the likelihood of problem alcohol abuse in young people.

Brain Regional Neurocircuitry in FAS: Raineki et al., (2014) recently reported that individuals exposed to alcohol during gestation show higher rates of psychopathologies. The hyper-responsiveness to stress induced by PAE has been related to this increased rate of psychopathologies, especially because this population is likely to be exposed to stressful environments throughout life. Analysis of the neural activity within central areas known to play key roles in both emotional and stress regulation was performed. Adult male and female offspring from PAE, pair-fed, and *ad libitum*-fed control conditions were exposed to chronic mild stress (CMS). Following CMS, the neural activity (*c-fos* mRNA) of the amygdala, ventral hippocampus, medial prefrontal cortex (mPFC), and paraventricular nucleus of the hypothalamus (PVN) was assessed in response to an acute stress (elevated plus maze). In general, PAE decreased neural activity within the amygdala and hippocampus in males and increased neural activity within the amygdala and mPFC in females. CMS reduced neural activity within the mPFC and PVN in PAE males, but reduced activity in all areas in control males. By contrast, CMS reduced neural activity in the mPFC in PAE females and had no effects in control females. Principal component analysis revealed that these patterns of neural activity results in differential activation of the functional neural networks in males compared to females, indicating sexually dimorphic effects of PAE and CMS. Thus the altered networks of brain activation in PAE animals may underlie the hyper-responsiveness to stress and increased psychopathologies among PAE individuals, suggesting differential regulation of stress and emotion in individuals exposed to alcohol during gestation. Despite a relatively low number of animals in one of the experimental groups, the use of CPCA provided approach for assessing global changes in functional neural networks in PAE compared to control animals, allowing to go beyond simple assessments of changes in individual brain areas. These results highlighted how PAE and control males and females recruit different brain networks in the regulation of stress responses and emotion. Specifically, CPCA indicated that while control males rely more on the amygdala and hippocampal formation, PAE males rely more on the mPFC and mpdPVN when facing a stressful situation. In contrast, the functional neural networks underlying stress and emotional regulation in females are more restricted, as PAE females rely primarily on the mPFC and amygdala indicating that CMS differentially affected the neural networks regulating stress and emotion in PAE and control animals. Exposure to CMS reduced the activity of the *amygdala + hippocampal network* in control males, but reduced the activity of the *prefrontal cortex + paraventricular nucleus network* in PAE males. CMS reduced the activity of the p*refrontal cortex network* in PAE animals suggesting that PAE, regardless of its association with CMS, results in a sexually dimorphic dysregulation of the neurocircuitry that underlies stress and emotional regulation, implicated in the stress hyper-responsiveness and increased vulnerability to anxiety and depressive disorders among individuals exposed to alcohol during gestation.

Narasimhan et al., (2013) reported that PAE elicits a range of neuro-developmental abnormalities, microcephaly to behavioral deficits. Impaired protein synthesis has been connected to pathogenesis of ethanol-induced brain damage and abnormal neuron development. These investigators elucidated the effects of ethanol on programmed cell death protein 4 (PDCD4), a tumor and translation repressor. Primary cortical neurons (PCNs) were treated with ethanol for 2.5mg/ml and 4mg/ml for different time points (4h to 24h) and PDCD4 expression was detected. A 2-day acute 5-dose binge model with ethanol (4 g/kg body wt, 25% v/v) was performed in Sprague Dawley rats at

12h intervals and analyzed for PDCD4, eukaryotic initiation factor 4A (eIF4A) and eIF4A-methyl cap association. Ethanol increased PDCD4 expression in PCNs which inhibited the association of eIF4A with methyl-cap. Ethanol and ectopic PDCD4 expression suppressed *in vivo* translation in PCNs and RNAi targeting of PDCD4 blocked the inhibitory effect of ethanol on protein synthesis. *In utero* exposure of pregnant rats to ethanol resulted in a significant increase of PDCD4 protein in fetal cerebral cortex along with inhibition of methyl-cap associated eIF4A, compared to iso-caloric controls. Increased PDCD4 also occurred fractions of remaining brain regions, suggesting that PDCD4 mediates inhibitory effects of ethanol on protein synthesis in PCNs and other developing brain regions. Alcohol induced dysregulation of protein synthesis was mediated by PDCD4. Furthermore, an ETOH-induced PDCD4 up-regulation influenced the translation of selective mRNA subsets which was evident from the other factors involved in alcohol-induced neurotoxic phenomena, suggesting that targeting multiple translational checkpoints instead of independent regulatory points would be a promising pharmacological strategy in FAS (Xu et al., 2008; Narasimhan et al., 2011).

FAS and Cancer Predisposition: Varela-Rey (2013) reported that cancer is one of the most significant diseases associated with chronic drinking, particularly of the upper aerodigestive tract, liver, colorectum, and the breast. Several factors, including the actions of acetaldehyde, the first and primary metabolite of ethanol, and oxidative stress contribute to alcohol-induced carcinogenesis. However, aberrant patterns of DNA methylation, an important epigenetic mechanism of transcriptional control, could also be part of the pathogenetic mechanisms that lead to alcohol-induced cancer development. Alcohol abuse is associated with aberrant DNA methylation in various types of cancer. However, most studies have relied on examining individual genes or a limited number of CpG loci. Genome-wide DNA methylation analyses may yield maps of changes in DNA methylation in alcohol-associated carcinogenesis, which could be useful in pharmacoepigenetics, as biomarkers for cancer detection, prognosis, and treatment response.

Treatment of FAS: Currently treatment options for FAS are limited. Usually choline, folate, and vitamin A are prescribed depending on the severity of FASD symptoms. Sari et al (2013) reported that PAE can induce fetal brain growth deficits at different embryonic stages of development, hence these investigators examined the neuroprotective effects against alcohol-induced apoptosis at mid-gestation period using activity-dependent neurotrophic factor (ADNF)-9; a peptide derived from activity-dependent neurotrophic factor, and NAP, a peptide derived from activity-dependent neuroprotective protein. NAP and ADNF-9 prevented alcohol-induced weight reduction of fetal brains. NAP or ADNF-9 prevented alcohol-induced increase in TUNEL-positive cells in primordium of the cingulate cortex and ganglionic eminence, suggesting therapeutic potential of NAP and ADNF-9 against alcohol intoxication during pregnancy. NAP or ADNF-9, administered alongside PAE from embryonic days 7 to 15, prevented alcohol-induced fetal brain weight reduction and TUNEL-positive cells in primordium of the cerebral cortex and ganglionic eminence suggesting their therapeutic potential against alcohol intoxication during pregnancy.

Tourette syndrome is a heterogeneous neuropsychiatric disorder comprised of multiple motor and vocal tics that begin in early childhood and persist for at least a year. Chronic tic disorder is a related condition, with similar clinical and demographic characteristics, consisting of either only chronic motor or only vocal tics, but not both. Tourette syndrome has a prevalence of 0.3-0.8%, whereas chronic tic disorder has a prevalence of 1-3%. These disorders can cause significant physical and psychosocial morbidity in childhood, and in severe cases produce lifelong disability. Tourette syndrome and chronic tic disorder have a genetic component, and together these disorders have among the highest familial recurrence risks of all neurodevelopmental disorders. Despite the heritabilities, twin and family studies have demonstrated a role for non-genetic factors in the pathogenesis of Tourette syndrome and chronic tic disorder. Mathews et al (2014) reported that Tourette syndrome and chronic tic disorder are heritable but their etiology is complex. Although environment plays a role in their development, existing studies of non-genetic risk factors are inconsistent. Maternal alcohol and cannabis abuse, inadequate maternal weight gain and parity were associated with Tourette syndrome or Tourette syndrome/chronic tic disorder. These investigators examined the association between pre- and perinatal ethanol exposures and Tourette syndrome/chronic tic disorder in 6090 children using logistic regression. Alcohol abuse in the third trimester of pregnancy, remained significant and could be considered a prenatal risk factor for these disorders. PAE and Tourette syndrome genetic susceptibility alleles are also under investigation.

Mitochondria-Targeted Therapeutics in FAS: Maternal as well as paternal mitochondrial genetics and epigenetics are impaired in FAS as a consequence of fetal ethanol exposure, leading to CB formation due to extensive mitochondrial degeneration in highly susceptible developing hippocampal and cerebellar Purkinje neurons. Recently we have reported CB as a universal biomarker of cell injury (Sharma and Ebadi 2014). CB is a pleomorphic, multi-lamellar, electron-dense membrane stack which is formed as a consequence of oxidative and nitrative stress and/or toxins including ethanol and mitochondrial genome knock out aging (RhO_{mgko}) cells. CB is sensitive pre-apoptotic, biomarker which is formed in a highly susceptible proliferative cell as a consequence of compromised mitochondrial bioenergetics (Sharma et al., 2013; Sharma and Ebadi 2014a, Sharma and Ebadi 2014b). We introduced charnolophagy to describe the degenerated mitochondrial autophagy (*usually named as mitophagy to characterize endoparasitism*). It is known that all mitochondrial diseases in the developing embryo are originated from the maternal mtDNA, whereas paternal mtDNA is degenerated in the zygote soon after fertilization by mitophagy. Usually mitophagy occurs in the zygote soon after the paternal nuclear DNA hybridizes with the maternal nuclear DNA. However the mtDNA is single stranded, naked intron less, labile structure without any structural and functional support of histones and protamines; hence can be readily destroyed by free radicals attack. CB formation occurs as a consequence of ethanol-induced compromised mitochondrial bioenergetics and can be prevented and/or eliminated by nutritional rehabilitation, physiological zinc, and MTs (Sharma et al 2013). Specific CB antagonists and charnolophagy agonists may be developed to prevent or treat neurodegenerative and cardiovascular complications at an early pre-zygotic phase of fetal development with minimum or absolutely no adverse effects on the craniofacial growth and development of FAS.

Usually CB is phagocytosed by charnolophagy due to enhanced lysosomal activity in severe undernutrition. Hence, specific CB antagonists and charnolophagy agonists will have therapeutic potential in preventing and treating neurodegenerative and cardiovascular diseases, whereas cancer stem cell specific CB agonists and charnolophgy antagonists will have therapeutic potential in preventing predisposition to carcinogenesis during early pre-zygotic phase of FAS. These specific mitochondrially-targeted drugs will have minimum or no adverse effects and will be useful to prevent/treat not only FAS but also early fetal exposure to general anesthetic agents, antiepileptic drugs, and environmental toxins.

FAS is unpredictable because of various factors including CB pathogenesis. Depending on the amount of acute or chronic ethanol abuse; acetaldehyde-induced mitochondrial degeneration results in lysosomal-sensitive or resistant CB formation. Lysososomal-sensitive CB during acute phase of ethanol exposure can be readily subjected to charnolophagy, resulting in cellular recovery and hence FAS escape; whereas lysosomal-resistant CB during chronic phase inhibits charnolophagy, resulting in the formation of intra-neuronal inclusions and apoptosis due to the release of toxic, Cyt-C, heme iron sulfur proteins, AIF, BID, BAX due to CB sequestration, causing cellular degeneration and FAS victimization with typical cranio-facial and neurobehavioral anomalies. Nutritional rehabilitation, physiological zinc, and MTs may provide protection by serving as anti-apoptotic, anti-inflammatory free radical scavengers (Sharma et al., 2013; Sharma and Ebadi 2014a, Sharma and Ebadi 2014b).

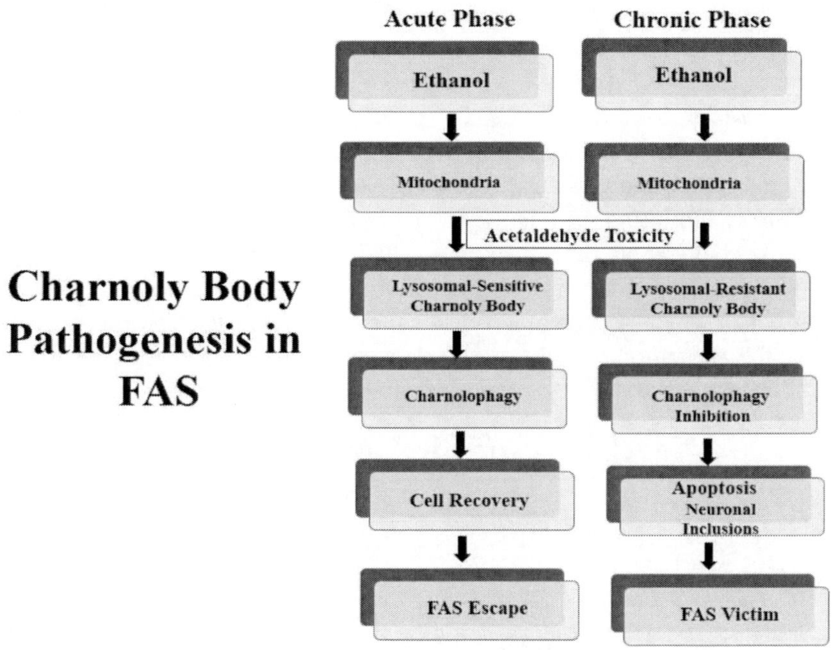

Figure 3. A flow diagram illustrating CB pathogenesis in FAS.

Charnolophagy in FAS: We have proposed charnolophagy as an elimination process of degenerated mitochondrial membranes of CBs during nutritional stress (Sharma and Ebadi 2014). If chornologphagy is delayed or inhibited due to chronic intrauterine toxic exposure of ethanol, anesthetic agents, and/or antiepileptic agents, it can have deleterious consequences and may induce spontaneous death of the zygote due to apoptosis as a result of CB sequestration.

Depending on the quantity and frequency of ethanol consumed, the deleterious effects will appear in a FASD victim as illustrated in Figure 3. It seems that the paternal charnolophagy occurs in the oocyte soon after fertilization as it is highly critical and temporally-sensitive event for the survival and normal development of the zygote. Delayed charnolophagy after fertilization can release apoptotic factors from the degenerating paternal mitochondria.

This will also depend on how efficiently paternal CB is eliminated by the oocytes during pre-zygotic phase. Ethanol can significantly delay this naturally-occurring efficient process of CB elimination through charnolophagy in the zygote. Absence or delayed chronolophagy may have deleterious consequences on the nuclear and mitochondrial DNA epigenetics in the developing fetus.

In addition, ethanol is converted to acetaldehyde by alcohol dehydrogenase. Acetaldehyde is highly toxic, causes oxidative stress, and free radical overproduction. Thus nutritional stress and ethanol augment CB formation by inhibiting protein synthesis in the zygote. Moreover genetic and epigenetic changes in the maternal as well as paternal nuclear DNA and mtDNA, can be induced by nutritional stress and/or environmental neurotoxins, which can compromise the mitochondrial bioenergetics to enhance CB formation.

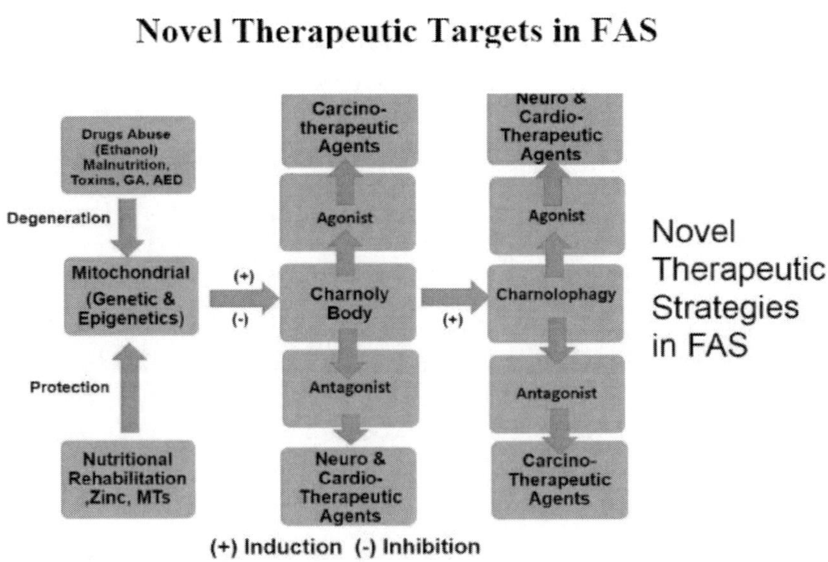

Figure 4. A flow diagram illustrating novel therapeutic strategies in FAS.

Prenatal ethanol exposure, and environmental toxins result in the formation of pleomorphic, electron-dense multi-lamellar membrane stacks collectively named as CB. CB formation can be inhibited by nutritional rehabilitation, physiological zinc, and MTs by serving as free radical scavengers. CB is degraded by increased lysosomal activity.

The structural degradation of CB by lysosomes is called charnolopahgy to represent CB autophagy (*also named as mitophagy or endoparasitism*). Hence CB and charnolophagy-targted novel therapeutic drugs may be developed as specific agonists or antagonists for the early prevention and/or treatment of neurodegenerative disorders, cardiovascular disorders, and cancer in FAS victims with minimum or absolutely no adverse effects (Figure 4).

Future Prospects: Deleterious consequences of FAS are well documented, and, as a leading cause of intellectual disabilities, FAS has significant societal and public health implications.

Among environmental factors; provocative factors, socio-behavioral permissive factors, and biological provocative factors could play a significant role in the pathogenesis of FAS. Alcohol exposure affects the development of the brain during critical periods of differentiation and growth, resulting in cognitive and behavioral deficits. Detailed epidemiological studies of mitochondrial epigenetics and the exact role of gerontogenes in FAS are needed.

Whether methylation of the mitochondrial transcription factor–A promoter is influenced by FAS also requires further attention. Similarly the exact molecular mechanism of epigenetic changes involved in ethanol-mediated CB formation needs to be established. It remains unknown whether ethanol can influence iron-sulfur protein-mediated mitochondrial epigenetics in FAS. It is now known that hypermethylation of the promoter regions of IGF-1 and leptin genes can induce gene silencing to cause diabetes and obesity later in life of FASD victims.

Hence prevention and treatment of alcohol-related problems from a developmental perspective is extremely important. Particularly, major complications, such as craniofacial anomalies, delayed eye-blink conditioning, ophthalmic complications, neurobehavioral impairments, late onset obesity, diabetes, cardiovascular diseases, and cancer vulnerability may be prevented by developing specific CB and chronolophagy-targeted drugs to prevent FAS during pre-zygotic phase.

ACKNOWLEDGMENTS

Authors express their sincere thanks to Kallol Guha, President, Saint James School of Medicine, Bonaire for his moral support and encouragement.

Conflict of Interest

There is no conflict of interest in this manuscript.

REFERENCES

Arain, M; Haque, M; Johal, L; Mathur, P; Nel, W; Rais, A; Sandhu, R; Sharma, S. (2013) Maturation of the adolescent brain. Neuropsychiatric *disease and treatment.,* 9, 449-461.

Astley, S.J; Larren, S.K. (1995) A fetal alcohol syndrome screening tool. *Alcohol Clin. Exp. Res.*, 19; 1565e71: 1995.

Bailey, B.A; Sokol, R.J. (2011) Prenatal Alcohol Exposure and Miscarriage, Stillbirth, Preterm Delivery, and Sudden Infant Death Syndrome. *Alcohol Res. Health.*, 34, 86–91.

Bakhireva, L.N; Savage, D.D. (2011) Focus On: Biomarkers of Fetal Alcohol Exposure and Fetal Alcohol Effects. *Alcohol Res. Health.*, 2011; 34(1): 56–63.

Balaraman, S; Tingling, J.D; Tsai, P.C; Miranda, R.C. (2013) Dysregulation of microRNA Expression and Function Contributes to the Etiology of Fetal Alcohol Spectrum Disorders. *Alcohol Res.*, 35, 18–24.

Balk, J; Schaedler, T.A. (2014) Iron Cofactor Assembly in Plants. *Annu. Rev. Plant. Biol.*, Jan 29.

Byun, H.M., Baccarelli, A.A. (2014) Environmental exposure and mitochondrial epigenetics: study design and analytical challenges. *Hum. Genet.,* 133, 247-257.

Carter, R.C; Jacobson, J.L; Sokol, R.J; Avison, M.J; Jacobson, S.W. (2013) Fetal alcohol-related growth restriction from birth through young adulthood and moderating effects of maternal prepregnancy weight. *Alcohol Clin. Exp. Res.,* 37, 452–462.

Chabenne, A; Moon, C; Ojo, A; Khogali, A; Nepal, B; Sharma, S. (2014) Biomarkers in Fetal Alcohol Syndrome (Recent Update) *Biomarkers & Genomic Medicine*. 1-11. *(in press)*

Chartier, K; Caetano, R. (2010) Ethnicity and Health Disparities in Alcohol Research. *Alcohol Res. Health.,* 33, 152-160.

Chartier, K.G; Vaeth, P.A.C; Caetano, R. (2010) Focus On: Ethnicity and the Social and Health Harms From Drinking. *Alcohol Res. Health.,* 33, 152–160.

Coles, C.D. (2011) Discriminating the Effects of Prenatal Alcohol Exposure From Other Behavioral and Learning Disorders. *Alcohol Res. Health.,* 34, 42–50.

Coplan, J.D; Fathy, H.M; Abdallah, C.G; Ragab, S.A; Kral, J.G; Mao, X; Shungu, D.C; Mathew, S.J. (2013) Reduced hippocampal N-acetyl-aspartate (NAA) as a biomarker for overweight. *NeuroImage Clinical.*, 4, 326-335.

Creeley, C.E; Dikranian, K.T; Johnson, S.A; Farber, N.B; Olney, J.W. (2013) Alcohol-induced apoptosis of oligodendrocytes in the fetal macaque brain. *Acta. Neuropathol. Commun.*, 23.

Creeley, C.E; Olney, J.W. (2013) Drug-Induced Apoptosis: Mechanism by which Alcohol and Many Other Drugs Can Disrupt Brain Development: *Brain Sci.*, 3, 1153–1181.

Dobson, C. C; Mongillo, D.L; Brien, D.C; Stephila, R; Poklewska-Koziell, M; Winterborn, A; Holloway, A.C; Brien, J.F' and Reynolds, J.N. (2012) "Chronic PAE Increases Adiposity and Disrupts Pancreatic Morphology in Adult Guinea Pig Offspring." *National Center for Biotechnology Information*. U.S. National Library of Medicine, Web. 05 Mar. 2014.

Doig, J; McLennan, J.D; Gibbard, W.B. (208) Medication effects on symptoms of attention-deficit/hyperactivity disorder in children with fetal alcohol spectrum disorder. *J. Child Adolesc. Psychopharmacol.*, 18, 365-371.

Donovan, J.E. (2014) The Burden of Alcohol Use: Focus on Children and Preadolescents. *Alcohol Res.*, 35, 186–192.

France, K.E; Donovan, R.J; Bower, C; Elliott, E.J; Payne, J.M; D'Antoine, H; Bartu, A.E. (2014) Messages that increase women's intentioins to abstain from alcohol during pregnancy: results from quantitative testing of advertising concepts. *BMC Public Health*, Jan 13, 2014.

Frankel, F; Paley, B; Marquardt, R; O'Connor, M. (2006) Stimulants, neuroleptics, and children's friendship training for children with fetal alcohol spectrum disorders. *J. Child Adolesc. Psychopharmacol.*, 16, 777-789.

Graham, D.M; Crocker, N; Deweese, B.N; Roesch, S.C; Coles, C.D; Kable, J.A; May, P.A; Kalberg, W.O; Green, A.S; Limesand, S.W. (2010) Remembering development –epigenetic responses to fetal malnutrition. *J. Physiol.*, 588.9, 1379–1380.

Hannigan, J.H; Chiodo, L.M; Sokol, R.J; Janisse, J; Ager, J.W; Greenwald, M.K; Delaney-Black, V. (2010) A 14-year retrospective maternal report of alcohol consumption in pregnancy predicts pregnancy and teen outcomes. *Alcohol., 44*, 583-594.

Haycock, P.C. (2009) Fetal alcohol spectrum disorders: the epigenetic perspective. *Biol. Reprod.,* 81, 607-617.

Hepper, P. G; Dornan, J.C; Lynch. C. (2012) ("Fetal Brain Function in Response to Maternal Alcohol Consumption: Early Evidence of Damage." *National Center for Biotechnology Information*. U.S. National Library of Medicine, 36 Dec. 2012. Web. 05 Mar. 2014.

Hoyme, H.E; May, P.A; Kalberg, W.O; Kodituwakku, P; Gossage, J.P; Trujillo, P.M; Buckley, D.G; Miller, J.H; Aragon, A.S; Khaole, N; Viljoen, D.L; Jones, K.L; Robinson, L.K. (2005) A practical clinical approach to diagnosis of fetal alcohol spectrum disorders: clarification of the 1996 institute of medicine criteria. *Pediatrics*. 115, 39-47.

Hutson, J. R; Stade, B; Lehotay, D.C; Collier, C.P; Kapur, B.M. (2012) "Folic Acid Transport to the Human Fetus Is Decreased in Pregnancies with Chronic Alcohol Exposure." *National Center for Biotechnology Information*. U.S. National Library of Medicine, 29 May 2012.

Jia, Y; Li, R; Cong, R; Yang, X; Sun, Q et al. (2013) Maternal Low-Protein Diet Affects Epigenetic Regulation of Hepatic Mitochondrial DNA Transcription in a Sex-Specific Manner in Newborn Piglets Associated with GR Binding to Its Promoter. *PLoS ONE.,* 8, e63855.

Jones, K.L; Smith, D.W; Ulleland; C.N. Streissguth AP. (1973) Pattern of malformation in offspring of chronic alcoholic mothers. *Lancet.,* 7815, 1267–1271.

Jones, K.L; Smith DW. (1973) Recognition of the fetal alcohol syndrome in early infancy. *Lancet.* 302, 999–1001.

Jousse, C; Parry, L; Lambert-Langlais, S; Maurin, A.C; Averous, J; Bruhat, A; Xarraro, V; Tost, J; Latteron, P; Chen, P; Jockers, R; Launay, J.M; Mallet, J; Fafoumoux, P. (2011) Perinatal undernutrition affects the methylation and expression of the leptin gene in adults: implication for the understanding of metabolic syndrome. *FASEB J.*, 25, 3271–3278.

Karhunen, P. J; Erkinjuntti, T; Laippala, P. (1994) "Moderate alcohol consumption and loss of cerebellar Purkinje cells. *British Med. Journal.*, 309, 1663-1667.

Kietzman, H.W; Everson, J.L; Sulik, K.K; Lipinski, R.J. (2014) The Teratogenic Effects of PAE Are Exacerbated by Sonic Hedgehog or Gli2 Haploinsufficiency in the Mouse. *PLoS One.*, 2014; 9, e89448.

Kim, S.G; Jong, H.S; Kim, T.Y; Lee, J.W; Kim, N.K; Hong, S.H; Bang, Y.J. (2004) Transforming growth factor-beta 1 induces apoptosis through Fas ligand-independent activation of the Fas death pathway in human gastric SNU-620 carcinoma cells. *Mol Biol Cell.*, 15, 420-434.

Kobor, M.S; Weinberg, J. (2011) Focus On: Epigenetics and Fetal Alcohol Spectrum Disorders. *Alcohol Res. Health.*, 34, 29–37.

Kruman, II; Fowler, A.K. (2014) Impaired one carbon metabolism and DNA methylation in alcohol toxicity. *J. Neurochem.*, Feb 12.

Kumpfer, K.L; Fowler, M.A. (2007) Parenting skills and family support programs for drug-abusing mothers. *Semin. Fetal. Neonatal. Med.*, 12, 134-142.

Laker, R.C; Wlodek, M.E; Connelly, J.J; Yan, Z. (2013) Epigenetic origins of metabolic disease: The impact of the maternal condition to the offspring epigenome and later health consequences. *Food Science and Human Wellness*. 2, 1-11.

Landgraf, M. N; Nothacker, M; Kopp, I.B;. Heinen. F. (2014) "The Diagnosis of Fetal Alcohol Syndrome." *National Center for Biotechnology Information*. U.S. National Library of Medicine, 18 Oct. 2013.

Lehle, S; Hildebrand, D.G; Merz, B; Malak, P.N; Becker, M.S; Schmezer, P; Essmann, F; Schulze-Osthoff, K; Rothfuss, O. (2013) LORD-Q: a long-run real-time PCR-based DNA-damage quantification method for nuclear and mitochondrial genome analysis. *Nucleic Acids Res.* Dec 26.

Livy, D.J; Miller, E.K; Maier, S.E; West, J.R. (2013) Fetal alcohol exposure and temporal vulnerability: effects of binge-like alcohol exposure on the developing at hippocampus. *Neurotoxicol. Teratol.* 25, 447-458.

Lutz, U.C. (2008) Alterations in homocysteine metabolism among alcohol dependent patients—Clinical, pathobiochemical and genetic aspects. *Current Drug Abuse Reviews.*, 1, 47–55.

Masten, A.S; Faden, V.B; Zucker, R.A; Spear, L.P.A. (2009) Developmental Perspective on Underage Alcohol Use. *Alcohol. Res. Health.*, 32, 3–15.

Mathews, C.A; Scharf, J.M; Miller, L.L; Macdonald-Wallis, C; Lawlor, D.A; Ben-Shlomo, Y. (2014) Association between pre- and perinatal exposures and Tourette syndrome or chronic tic disorder in the ALSPAC cohort. *Br. J. Psychiatry.*, 204, 40–45.

Mattson, S.N; Riley; E.P. (2011) The Quest for a Neurobehavioral Profile of Heavy Prenatal Alcohol Exposure. *Alcohol Res. Health.*, 34, 51–55.

Mattson, S.N; Roesch, C.S; Glass, L; Deweese, B.N; Coles, C.D; Kable, J.A; May, P.A; Kalberg, .W.O; Sowell, E.R; Adnams, C.M; Jones, K.L; Riley, E.P. (2013) Further Development of a Neurobehavioral Profile of Fetal Alcohol Spectrum Disorders. *Alcohol Clin. Exp. Res.,* 37, 517–528.

May, P.A; Gossage, J.P. (2011) Maternal Risk Factors for Fetal Alcohol Spectrum Disorders: Not As Simple As It Might Seem. *Alcohol Res. Health.*, 34, 15–26.

McCarthy, N; Wetherill, L; Lovely, C.B; Swartz, M.E; Foroud, T.M; Eberhart, J.K. (2013) Pdgfra protects against ethanol-induced craniofacial defects in a zebrafish model of FASD. *Development.,* 140, 3254–3265.

Menendez, J.A; Alarcón, T; Joven, J. (2014) Gerometabolites: The pseudohypoxic aging side of cancer oncometabolites. *Cell Cycle.,* 13(5).

(2014) Messages that increase women's intentions to abstain from alcohol during pregnancy: results from quantitative testing of advertising concepts. *BMC Public Health.*, 14, 30.

Miranda, R.C; Pietrzykowski, A.Z; Tang, Y; Sathyan, P; Mayfield, D; Keshavarzian, A; Sampson, W; Hereld, D. (2010) MicroRNAs: Master Regulators of Ethanol Abuse and Toxicity? Alcoholism: *Clinical and Experimental Research.*, 34, 575–587.

Moffett JR, Arun P, Ariyannur PS, Namboodiri AMA. N-Acetyl aspartate reduction in brain injury : Impact on post-injury neurogenetics, lipid synthesis, and protein acetylation. Frontiers in Neurogenetics. 5; 2013: 1-19.

Moskalev, A.A; Aliper, A.M; Smit-McBride, Z; Buzdin, A; Zhavoronkov, A. (2014) Genetics and epigenetics of aging and longevity. *Cell Cycle.*, 13, (7).

Muralidharan, P; Sarmah, S; Zhou, F.C; Marrs, J.A. (2013) Fetal Alcohol Spectrum Disorder (FASD) Associated Neural Defects: Complex Mechanisms and Potential Therapeutic Targets . *Brain Sci.* 3, 964-991.

Murawski, N.J; Stanton, M.E. (2010) Variants of contextual fear conditioning are differentially impaired in the juvenile rat by binge ethanol exposure on postnatal days 4–9. *Behav Brain Res.*, 212, 133–142.

Narasimhan, M; Rathinam, M; Riar, A; Patel, D; Mummidi, S; Yang, H.S; Colburn, N.H; Henderson, G.I; Mahimainathan, L. (2013) Programmed Cell Death 4 (PDCD4): A Novel Player in Ethanol Mediated Suppression of Protein Translation in Primary Cortical Neurons and Developing Cerebral Cortex. *Alcohol Clin. Exp. Res.*, 37, 96–109.

Nguyen, T.T; Ashrafi, A; Thomas, J.D; Riley, E.P; Simmons, R.W. (2013) Children with Heavy Prenatal Alcohol Exposure have Different Frequency Domain Signal Characteristics when Producing Isometric Force. *Neurotoxicol. Teratol.*, 35, 14–20.

NIAAA Director's Report on Institute Activities to the 133rd Meeting of the National Advisory Council on Alcohol Abuse and Alcoholism. June 2013.

Nuñez, S.C; Roussotte, F; Sowell, E.R. (2011) Focus on: Structural and Functional Brain Abnormalities in Fetal Alcohol Spectrum Disorders. *Alcohol Res. Health.,* 34, 121–132.

O'connor, M.J; Frankel, F; Paley, B; et al. (2006) A controlled social skills training for children with fetal alcohol spectrum disorders. *journal of consulting and clinical psychology.,* 74, 639–648.

O'Leary-Moore, S.K; Parnell, S.E; Godin, E.A; Sulik, K.K. (2011) Focus On: Magnetic Resonance–Based Studies of Fetal Alcohol Spectrum Disorders in Animal Modals. *Alcohol Res. Health.,* 34, 99–105.

Paley, B; O'Connor, M.J. (2011) Behavioral Interventions for Children and Adolescents With Fetal Alcohol Spectrum Disorders. *Alcohol Res. Health.*, 34, 64–75.

Pandhare, J; Addai, A.B; Mantri, C.K; Hager, C; Smith, R.M; Barnett, L; Villalta, F; Kalams, S.A; Dash, C. (2014) Cocaine Enhances HIV-1-Induced CD4+ T-Cell Apoptosis: Implications in Disease Progression in Cocaine-Abusing HIV-1 Patients. *Am. J. Pathol.* Jan 31.

Park, K.S; Kim, S.K; Kim, M.S; Cho; E.Y; Lee, J.H; Lee, K.U; Pak, Y.K; Lee, H.K. (2003) Fetal and Early Postnatal Protein Malnutrition Cause Long-Term Changes in Rat Liver and Muscle Mitochondria. *J. Nutr.,* 133, 3085–3090.

Peng, H; Yang, M; Chen, Z.Y; Chen, P; Guan, C.X; Xiang, X.D; Cai, S; Chen, Y; Fang, X. (2013) Expression and methylation of mitochondrial transcription factor a in chronic obstructive pulmonary disease patients with lung cancer. *PLoS One,*. 8, e82739.

Pfinder, M. (2014) Anthropometric and Health-Related Behavioral Factors in the Explanation of Social Inequalities in Low Birth Weight in Children with Prenatal Alcohol Exposure. *Int. J. Environ. Res. Public Health.,* 11, 849–865.

Philibert, R.A.; Gunter, T.D.; Beach, S.R.; et al. (2008) MAOA methylation is associated with nicotine and alcohol dependence in women. *American*

Journal of Medical Genetics Part B Neuropsychiatric Genetics., 147B, 565–570.

Popova, S; Lange, S; Burd, L; Rehm, J. (2014) Canadian Children and Youth in Care: The Cost of Fetal Alcohol Spectrum Disorder. *Child Youth Care Forum*., 43, 83–96.

Popova, S; Yaltonskaya, A; Yaltonsky, V; Kolpakov, Y; Abrosimov, I; Pervakov, K; Tanner, V; Rehm, J. (2014) What Research Is Being Done on Prenatal Alcohol Exposure and Fetal Alcohol Spectrum Disorders in the Russian Research Community? *Alcohol Alcohol.* 49, 84–95.

Qi, Y; Zhang, M; Li, H; Dai, L; Liu, H; G. Chen. G. (2014) "Result FMicroRNA-29b Regulates Ethanol-induced Neuronal Apoptosis in the Developing Cerebellum through Sp1/Rax/PKRilters." *National Center for Biotechnology Information.* U.S. National Library of Medicine, 19 Feb. 2014.

Raineki, C; Hellemans, K.G.C; Bodnar, T; Lavigne, K.T; Ellis, L; Woodward, T.S; Weinberg, J. (2014) Neurocircuitry Underlying Stress and Emotional Regulation in Animals Prenatally Exposed to Alcohol and Subjected to Chronic Mild Stress in Adulthood. *Front Endocrinol (Lausanne)* 5, 5.

Resendiz, M; Chen, Y; Öztürk, N.C; Zhou, F.C. (2013) Epigenetic medicine and fetal alcohol spectrum disorders. *Epigenomics.,* 5, 73-86.

Riley, E.P; McGee, C.I. (2013) Fetal alcohol spectrum disorders: an overview with emphasis on changes in brain and behavior. E*xperimental Biology and Medicine (Maywood).,* 230, 357–365.

Rudy, J.W; O'Reilly, R.C. (2001) Conjunctive representations, the hippocampus, and contextual fear conditioning. *Cogn. Affect Behav. Neurosci.,*1, 66-82.

Russo, D; Purohit, V; Foudin, L; Salin, M. (2004) Workshop on Alcohol Use and Health Disparities 2002: a call to arms. *Alcohol*., 32, 37-43.

Sari, Y; Weedman, J.M; Nkrumah-Abrokwah, M. (2013) Neurotrophic Peptides, ADNF-9 and NAP, Prevent Alcohol-Induced Apoptosis at Midgestation in Fetal Brains of C57BL/6 Mouse. *J. Mol. Neurosci.* 49, 150–156.

Sawant, O.B; Lunde, E.R; Washburn, S.E; Chen, W.J.A; Goodlett, C.R; Cudd, T.A. (2013) Different Patterns of Regional Purkinje Cell Loss in the Cerebellar Vermis as a Function of the Timing of PAE in an Ovine Model. *Neurotoxicol. Teratol*., 35, 7–13.

Scott, D.M; Taylor, R.E. (2007) Health-Related Effects of Genetic Variations of Alcohol-Metabolizing Enzymes in African Americans. *Alcohol Res. Health*., 30, 18–21.

Shankar, K; Ronis, M.J.J; Badger, T.M. (2007) Effects of Pregnancy and Nutritional Status on Alcohol Metabolism. *Alcohol Res. Health.* 30, 55–59.

Shankar, K.; Hidestrand, M.; Liu, X.; et al. (2006) Physiologic and genomic analyses of nutrition-ethanol interactions during gestation: Implications for fetal ethanol toxicity. *Experimental Biology and Medicine.,* 231,1379–1397.

Shannon, E; Washburn, S.E; Tress, U; Emilie, R; Lunde, E.R; Chenn, W.J.A; Cudd, T.A. (2013) The role of cortisol in chronic binge alcohol-induced cerebellar injury: Ovine Model. *Alcohol.*, 47, 10.

Sharma, S; Ebadi, M. (2014a) CB as a Universal Biomarker of Cell Injury. Biomarkers and Genomic Medicine. (*in press*)

Sharma, S. (2014b) Molecular Pharmacology of Environmental Neurotoxins. In Kainic Acid: Neurotoxic Properties, Biological Sources, and Clinical Applications. Nova Science Publishers. New York. (*in press*)

Sharma, S; Nepal, B; Moon, C.S; Chabenne, A; Khogali, A; Ojo, C; Hong, E; Goudet, R; Sayed-Ahmad, A; Jacob, A; Murtaba, M; Firlit, M. (2014c) Psychology of Craving. *Open Jr. of Medical Psychology.*, 3, 120-125.

Sharma, S; Ebadi M. (2014d) Significance of Metallothioneins in Aging Brain. *Neurochemistry International.*, 65, 40-48.

Sharma, S; Ebadi, M. (2014e) Antioxidant Targeting in Neurodegenerative Disorders. Ed. I. Laher, Springer Verlag. Germany. Chapter 85, 1-30. (*in Press*)

Sharma, S; Moon, C.S; Khogali, A; Haidous, A; Chabenne, A; Ojo, C; Jelebinkov, M; Kurdi, Y; Ebadi, M. (2013a) Biomarkers of Parkinson's Disease (Recent Update). *Neurochemistry International.,* 63, 201-229.

Sharma, S; Rais, A; Sandhu, R; Nel, W; Ebadi, M. (2013b) Clinical significance of metallothioneins in cell therapy and nanomedicine. *International Journal of Nanomedicine.*, 8, 1477–1488.

Sharma, S; Ebadi, M. (2008) SPECT Neuroimaging in Translational Research of CNS Disorders. *Neurochem Internat.* 52, 352-362.

Sharma, S.K; Yashpal, K; Fundytus, M.E; Sauriol, F; Henry, J.L; Coderre, T.J. (2003) Alterations in brain metabolism induced by chronic morphine treatment: NMR Studies in Rat CNS. *Neurochem. Res.,* 28, 1369-1373.

Sonuga-Barke, E.J. (2005) Causal models of attention-deficit/hyperactivity disorder: from common simple deficits to multiple developmental pathways. *Biol. Psychiatry.*, 57, 1231-1238.

Sookoian, S; Gianotti, T.F; Burgueno, A.L; Pirola, C.J. (2013) Fetal metabolic programming and epigenetic modifications: a systems biology approach. *Pediatric Research.*,73, 531-542.

Sowell, E.R; Jones, K.L; Riley, E.P; Mattson, S.N. (2013) The CIFASD. Prenatal Alcohol Exposure, ADHD, and Sluggish Cognitive Tempo. *Alcohol Clin. Exp. Res.*, 37, E338–E346.

Starkman, B.G; Sakharkar, A.J; Pandey, S.C. (2012) Epigenetics—Beyond the Genome in Alcoholism. *Alcohol Res.* 34, 293–305.

Sudheendran, N; Bake, S; Miranda, R.C; Larin, K.V. (2013) Comparative assessments of the effects of alcohol exposure on fetal brain development using optical coherence tomography and ultrasound imaging. *J. Biomed. Opt.*, 18, 020506.

Suttie, M; Foroud, T; Wetherill, L; Jacobson, J.L; Molteno, C.D; Meintjes; E.M; Hoyme, H.E; Khaole, N; Robinson, L.K; Riley, E.P; Jacobson, S.W; Hammond, P. (2013) Facial Dysmorphism Across the Fetal Alcohol Spectrum. *Pediatrics.*, 131, e779–e788.

Thomas, J.D; Warren, K.R; Hewitt, B.G. (2010) Fetal Alcohol Spectrum Disorders: From Research to Policy. *Alcohol Res. Health.* 33, 118–126.

Ungerer, M; Knezovich, J; Ramsay, M. (2013) In Utero Alcohol Exposure, Epigenetic Changes, and Their Consequences. *Alcohol Res.*, 35, 37–46.

Valenzuela, C.F; Puglia, M.P; Zucca, S. (2011) Focus On: Neurotransmitter Systems. *Alcohol Res. Health.* 34, 106–120.

Varela-Rey, M; Woodhoo, A; Martinez-Chantar, M.L; Mato, J.M; Lu, S.C. (2013) Alcohol, DNA Methylation, and Cancer. *Alcohol Res.,* 35, 25–35.

Vaurio, l; Crocker, N; Mattson, S.N. (2010) Fetal alcohol spectrum disorders. in: Davis, A.S., ed. *the handbook of pediatric neuropsychology.* New York: Springer Publishing Company, 2010, pp. 877–886.

Veazey, K.J; Muller, D; Golding, M.C. (2013) Prenatal Alcohol Exposure and Cellular Differentiation: A Role for Polycomb and Trithorax Group Proteins in FAS Phenotypes?. *Alcohol Res.* 35, 77–85.

Volk, B; Maletz, J; Mall, G; C. Klein, C; Berlet, H.H. (1981) Impaired Maturation on Purkinje Cells in the Fetal Alcohol Syndrome of the Rat." *Acta Neuropathologica.,* 54, 19-29.

Wagner, J.L; Klintsova, A.Y; Greenough, W.T; Goodlett, C.R. (2013) Rehabilitation Training Using Complex Motor Learning Rescues Deficits in Eyeblink Classical Conditioning in Female Rats Induced by Binge-Like Neonatal Alcohol Exposure. *Alcohol Clin. Exp. Res.*, 37, 1561–1570.

Wang, L.L; Zhang, Z; Li, Q; Yang, R; Pei, X; Xu, Y; Wang, J; Zhou, S.F; Li, Y. (2009) Ethanol exposure induces differential microRNA and target gene expression and teratogenic effects which can be suppressed by folic acid supplementation. *Hum. Reprod.*, 24, 562-579.

Ware, A.L; O'Brien, J.W; Crocker, N; Deweese, B.N; Roesch, S.C; Coles, C.D; Kable, J.A; May, P.A; Kalberg, W.O; Sowell, E.R; Jones, K.L; Riley, E.P; Mattson, S.N. (2013) The CIFASD. The Effects of Prenatal Alcohol Exposure and Attention-Deficit/Hyperactivity Disorder on Psychopathology and Behavior. *Alcohol Clin. Exp. Res.*, 37, 507–516.

Warren, K.R; Hewitt, B.G.(2010) NIAA: Advancing Alcohol Research for 40 years. *Alcohol Res Health.*, 33, 5–17.

Xu, Y; Tang, Y; Li, Y. (2008) Effect of folic acid on prenatal alcohol-induced modification of brain proteome in mice. *Br. J. Nutr.*, 99, 455-461.

Zakhari, S. (2013) Alcohol metabolism and epigenetics changes. *Alcohol Res.*, 35, 6-16.

Zamora, L.Y; Lu, Z. (2013) Alcohol-Induced Morphological Deficits in the Development of Octavolateral Organs of the Zebrafish (*Danio rerio*). *Zebrafish.*, 10, 52–61.

Zhou, F.C; Mason, S ( ) Genetics and Epigenetics of Fetal Alcohol Syndrome. Frontiers in Genetics.

Zucker, R.A; Donovan, J.E; Masten, A.S; Mattson, M.E; Moss, H.B. (2009) Developmental Processes and Mechanisms: Ages 0–10. *Alcohol Res. Health.*, 32, 16–29.

In: Substance Abuse
Editor: Jeffrey Raines

ISBN: 978-1-63321-949-6

Chapter 4

COCAINE AND KIDNEY, AN UNUSUAL TARGET?

Hortensia Álvarez Díaz,[1*] M.D., Ana Isabel Mariño Callejo,[1] M.D., José Francisco García Rodríguez,[1] M.D. Ph.D., Laura Rodríguez Pazos,[2] M.D. Ph.D., Inmaculada Gómez Buela,[3] M.D. and Ana María Bermejo Barrera,[4] Ph.D.

[1]Infectious Diseases Unit. Department of Internal Medicine. University Hospital of Ferrol. Health Area of Ferrol. SERGAS. A Coruña, Spain

[2]Department of Dermatology. University Hospital of Ferrol. Health Area of Ferrol. SERGAS. A Coruña, Spain

[3]Department of Internal Medicine. University Hospital of Ferrol. Health Area of Ferrol. SERGAS. A Coruña, Spain

[4]Institute of Forensic Science " Luis Concheiro". Forensic Toxicology Services. Faculty of Medicine. University of Santiago de Compostela. A Coruña, Spain

[*] Corresponding author. Email: hortensia.alvarez.diaz@sergas.es.

Abstract

Objective: To report renal damage induced by cocaine itself, highlighting a special condition when cocaine is contaminated with levamisole.

Background: Levamisole is a veterinary antihelminthic agent, previously used to treat nephrotic syndrome, various autoimmune disorders and cancers in humans (colon and breast). It has been detected in seized cocaine samples and a levamisole-induced vasculopathy (LIV) has been described.

Discussion: There is evidence to support the existence of cocaine-induced renal changes, through multifactorial pathophysiology: vasoconstrictive effects and nonspecific glomerular, interstitial and tubular cell lesions. Levamisole has been detected in adulterated cocaine and a synergistic action resulting in increased nicotinic and dopaminergic effects, has been suggested. A typical serologic profile with ANCA-positivity differentiates cocaine-levamisole vasculopathy, mainly focused on skin, but can also appear involving kidney.

Conclusions: Kidney, as end organ involvement, is an uncommon presentation of ANCA-positive vasculitis induced by levamisole-adulterated cocaine. High index of suspicion should be considered in cocaine users with skin lesions and abnormal renal function.

Keywords: Cocaine, levamisole, ANCA-positive vasculitis, kidney

Background

Levamisole is a veterinary antihelminthic agent, previously used to treat nephrotic syndrome, various autoimmune disorders and cancers in humans (colon and breast). Because of its adverse side effect profile, levamisole was withdrawn for use in humans in United States in 1999 but is still available for veterinary use. United States Drug Enforcement Agency first detected levamisole in cocaine in April 2005 [1] and first report of cocaine/ levamisole-induced vasculopathy (LIV) was in June 2010. [2]

According to 2009 estimates, approximately two thirds of the cocaine entering United States was contaminated with levamisole. [3] In Europe, levamisole has been detected in seized cocaine samples in United Kingdom, Italy and Spain. During second semester of 2009, surveillance programme results suggest a widespread cocaine consumption in Spain, with levamisole ranging 3-20%. [4]

Levamisole may have an inhibitory action on monoamine oxidase and catechol-O-methyltransferase, the enzymes that metabolize catecholamine neurotransmitters. It is theoretically possible that cocaine and levamisole may have a synergistic action at nicotinic acetylcholine receptors resulting in increased nicotinic and dopaminergic effects. Recent reports have suggested that, due to its ability to act as a hapten, levamisole may cause increased formation of antibodies to various antigens and therefore lead to an immune response. [5]

Cocaine itself has been reported to be associated with an antineutrophil cytoplasmic antibodies (ANCA)-positive pseudovasculitis. [3]

LIV is a diagnosis of exclusion, but this entity should be strongly considered in patients with a history of cocaine abuse who present with a tetrad of: cutaneous manifestations consisting of palpable retiform purpura (lesions tend to be stellate with a bright erythematous border and necrotic appearing center [6]) or bullae, with ear involvement (the most pathognomonic site), arthralgias, leukopenia, and positive ANCA in high titers (although not specific for the condition), when other infectious or idiopathic vasculitides have been excluded. [7] Biopsy findings range from leukocytoclastic and thrombotic vasculitis to vascular occlusion without true vasculitis. Although neutropenia is an expected and well-recognized association with LIV, it is not necessary to make the diagnosis, nor is it an inevitable consequence of levamisole exposure. [2]

The time from last cocaine use to onset the condition may be relatively rapid, but many of these affected individuals are chronic, habitual cocaine users, suggesting a large cumulative exposure to cocaine and, by association, levamisole, possibly over an extended period of time. [8]

CASE REPORT GUIDED ISSUE DESCRIPTION

In a previous published paper, we described a case report about nephrotic syndrome developed in the setting of ANCA-positive vasculitis induced by levamisole-adultered cocaine. [9]

A 36-year-old Caucasian man with history of antibodies to hepatitis C infection (negative hepatitis C virus RNA and negative HIV serology), smoking and intravenous use of cocaine and brown heroin, on treatment with methadone, presented to the hospital with purpuric skin lesions on extremities and earlobes. The patient had been admitted to the hospital four months before, due to intravenous drug-induced cellulitis and abscess on his forearms and legs. He had received treatment with amoxicillin-clavulanic acid, and skin lesions had improved. At that time, the patient had reported anorexia and weight loss and blood tests had revealed leukopenia and iron deficiency anemia (attributable to inadequate diet and malnutrition). A transthoracic echocardiogram had ruled out infectious endocarditis. One month before the current presentation, purpuric lesions on extremities and earlobes had appeared and a skin punch biopsy had been performed. The histopathologic findings were suggestive of mixed cryoglobulinemia. Blood tests showed polyclonal hypergammaglobulinemia and deterioration of renal function (serum creatinine 1.6mg/dl, normal range of 0.9-1.3mg/dl). Previous laboratory tests performed in the past (six years before), revealed creatinine 1.1mg/dl and inactive urinary sediment.

The patient reported last cocaine use, fifteen days before current admission. His complaints were: anorexia, weakness and loss of functional independence with confinement to bed, sore throat, dysphagia, arthralgias, myalgias and impairment of skin lesions, evolving to expand and become ulcers, leading to wound infection.

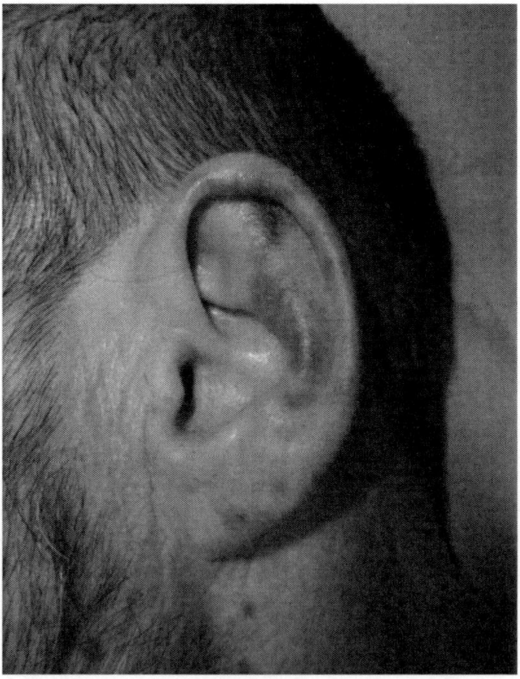

Picture 1. Skin lesions on helix and earlobe.

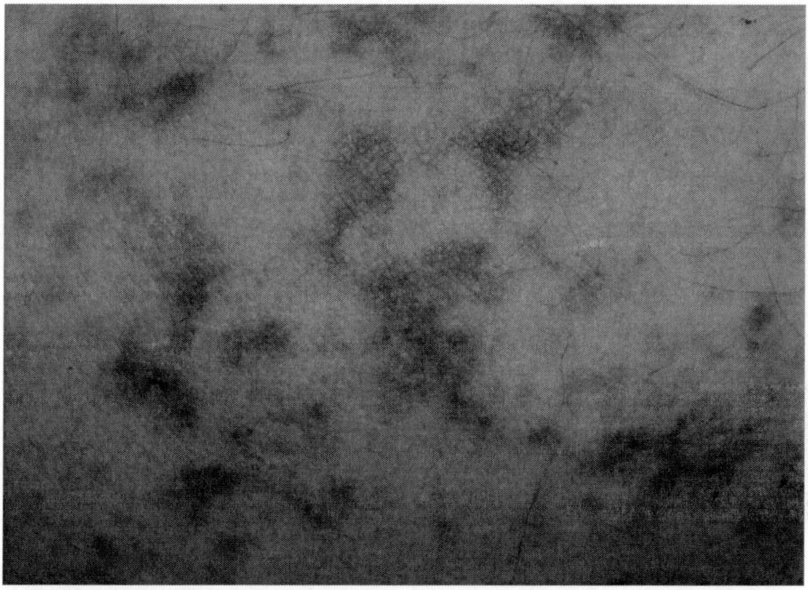

Picture 2. Rash detail: retiform pattern.

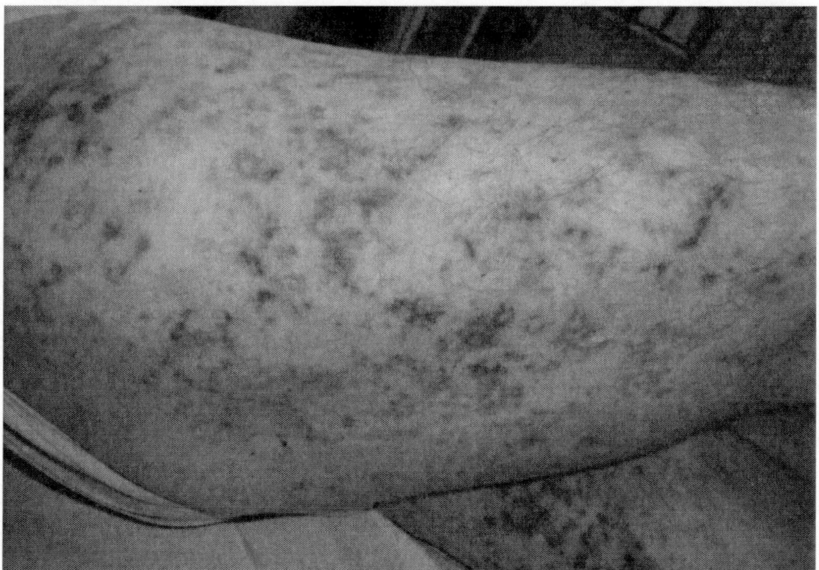

Picture 3. Rash on lower extremities.

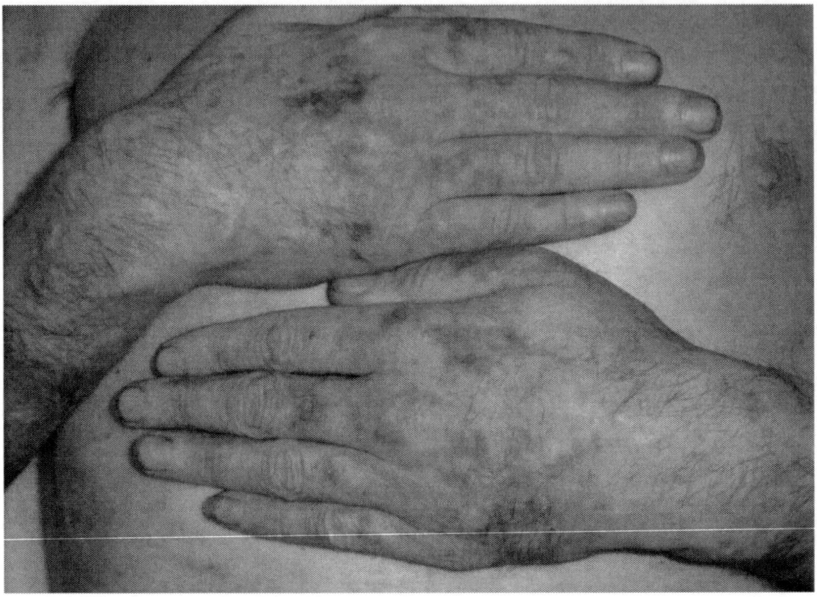

Picture 4. Rash on upper extremities.

On physical examination, the patient was afebrile and skin revealed a purpuric and violaceous, non-blanching rash in a retiform pattern with areas of necrosis and infected ulcers, located on helix and earlobes, upper and lower extremities [Pictures 1, 2, 3 and 4]. There were no mucosal lesions or peripheral lymphadenopathy, no heart murmur or rub. A hepatosplenomegaly was revealed.

Investigations

Laboratory testing showed a white blood cell (WBC) count of 2720 per mm3 (normal range of 4300-11000 per mm3), hemoglobin 5.6 g/dl (normal range of 12.5-17.5g/dl); hepatic function was normal; renal function revealed serum creatinine 2.71mg/dl, glomerular filtration rate (GFR) 28ml/min per 1.73m2; urinary sediment showed hematuria and 4750mg of protein excretion in 24hours-urine collection. Erythrocyte sedimentation rate was 121mm per hour and C-reactive protein 200mg/dl.

Test for cryoglobulin was negative; anti-nuclear antibody (ANA) positive at 1:80 dilution with a homogeneous pattern; complement C3 89mg/dl and C4

14 mg/dl (normal range of 19-152mg/dl and 16-43mg/dl, respectively); enzyme-linked immunosorbent assay (ELISA) for antiproteinase 3 antineutrophil cytoplasmic antibodies (PR3-ANCA) was negative at 3 AU/ml (normal 0-5 AU/ml) and for antimyeloperoxidase (MPO-ANCA) was positive at 145 AU/ml (normal 0-5 AU/ml). Anti-glomerular basement membrane antibodies were negative. Anticardiolipin antibodies (ACA) were normal (IgG 2GPL/ml and IgM 2MPL/ml, normal range of 0-10 and 0-7MPL/ml, respectively).

In our patient population, testing for anti- human neutrophil elastase (HNE) antibodies, was not available.

The skin punch biopsy performed one month before current admission (suggestive of mixed cryoglobulinemia), was revised and demonstrated pathologic findings consistent with leukocytoclastic vasculitis. Serum cryoglobulins and hepatitis C virus RNA were negative. Syphilis and hepatitis B serology were negative and tuberculin skin test was 0mm.

An ultrasound scan showed slightly enlarged kidneys and no other remarkable findings were present.

In spite of a renal biopsy was not performed, the renal damage was suggestive of nephrotic syndrome induced by probable glomerulonephritis.

The patient provided a cocaine sample for personal use and an analysis was performed using mass spectrometry–gas chromatography. Levamisole was detected in cocaine sample.

Treatment

The patient received a three weeks course of amoxicillin-clavulanic acid, for infected skin ulcers. In addition, six packed red cell transfusion was required, due to severe anemia.

Considering signs of inflammation and end organ damage (nephrotic syndrome induced by probable glomerulonephritis) in a toxic context, three bolus of intravenous methylprednisolone, were administered, followed by oral prednisone 1mg/Kg per day. Sulfamethoxazole-trimethoprim was started for *Nocardia* and *Pneumocystis jiroveci* prophylaxis. An angiotensin converting enzyme (ACE) inhibitor was added to decrease protein loss in the urine.

The patient was discharged with tapering down of prednisone.

Outcome and Follow-Up

Three months later, the patient denied cocaine use since last admission. On physical examination, he had gained weight and was fully active, skin lesions had disappeared and he reported only migrating joint pains. WBC count had normalized. Renal function had improved, reaching serum creatinine of 1.83mg/dl (GFR 45ml/min per 1.73m2) and 1915 mg of protein excretion in 24hours-urine collection. Complement C4 was normal and MPO-ANCA decreased to 83 AU/ml.

Tapering off prednisone is ongoing. Patient counseling has been provided to avoid cocaine use and therefore progression of renal damage can be reversed or at least, slowed or stopped.

Discussion

Apart from neutropenia, ANCA-positive vasculitis induced by levamisole-adultered cocaine has been reported to be limited to the skin, without evidence of the involvement of other organ systems.[1] Moreover, Tran et al. suggested that the absence of end organ involvement with isolated skin manifestations, along with a typical serologic profile, differentiates cocaine-levamisole cutaneous vasculopathy from idiopathic systemic vasculitis. [10]

However, rare clinical findings in LIV include renal and pulmonary involvement. [2] Mc Grath et al., described 30 patients with ANCA-positivity associated with levamisole contaminated-cocaine use. Abnormal urinalysis (defined as dipstick proteinuria, hematuria, or the presence of cellular casts on microscopy) was present in eight patients at diagnosis. Two developed severe acute kidney injury, one of them underwent renal biopsy, revealing pauci-immune focal necrotizing and crescentic glomerulonephritis; neither required renal replacement therapy. Despite improved renal function with immunosuppressive treatment, both were left with significant chronic kidney disease (estimated GFR < 30ml/min per 1.73m2). There was little definitive evidence of combined pulmonary-renal disease in this cohort. All cases had positive anti-MPO antibodies. By immunofluorescence, all cases were perinuclear antineutrophil cytoplasmic antibodies (p-ANCA) positive. The presence of hypocomplementemia with ANA and anti-ds DNA antibodies, raised the question of drug-induced lupus in a subset of these patients. Lack of documentation of levamisole in patient samples is a limitation of this study. [8]

Differential diagnosis includes infectious or primary vasculitis. In the study of Graf et al., three patients had antibodies to hepatitis C (none with detectable cryoglobulins), as our case presented above. ELISA revealed multiple antibodies to neutrophil elastase, lactoferrin, cathepsin G, PR3 and MPO. [1] The finding of multiple ANCA positivity is a strong indication of a drug-induced vasculopathy as opposed to other primary vasculitides. Positivity for anti-HNE antibodies is an indication of the cocaine use associated with LIV. [2]

On the other hand, cocaine and heroin themselves, could induce renal damage. There is evidence from in vitro cellular and animal studies to support the existence of cocaine-induced renal changes, through multifactorial pathophysiology: vasoconstrictive effects (inhibition of catecholamine reuptake at the presynaptic nerve terminal, increase of endothelins, activation of the renin-angiotensin-aldosterone system, increase of cellular oxidative stress and platelet aggregation) and nonspecific glomerular, interstitial and tubular cell lesions. Case reports of renal infarction, anti-glomerular basement membrane antibody-mediated glomerulonephritis or acute interstitial nephritis, have been described in cocaine users. Also, opioids could amplify cocaine-induced expression of tissue inhibitors of metalloproteinase-2, resulting in mesangial matrix accumulation. Focal segmental glomerulosclerosis and membranoproliferative glomerulonephritis have been found in renal biopsy of heroin users. Otherwise, chronic skin suppurative infections could lead to development of renal amyloidosis, in a similar manner to those who inject subcutaneous drugs ("skin popping"). [10] However, in our patient described above, despite the absence of renal biopsy, the typical skin lesions and serologic spectrum, in addition to detection of levamisole in cocaine sample, suggest cocaine-levamisole induced vasculitis causing renal injury revealed as nephrotic syndrome. [11]

Jenkins et al. reported the first case of vasculitis after levamisole snorting that was proven by urine toxicology. [12] The short half-life of levamisole (5.6 hours) and only a small amount of the parent drug (<5 %) is detected in urine, limits the utility of detection of this substance in specifying the cause of this syndrome; so, in a patient known to have used cocaine and with a high index of clinical suspicion, detection of levamisole should not be considered essential for diagnosis. [2]

The natural course of LIV may be self-limited. [3] There is a lack of evidence that systemic corticosteroids modify the clinical course of LIV. Discontinuation of levamisole is a critical part of the treatment. Nonetheless, in individual patients with striking signs of inflammation, corticosteroids might be considered. [2]

Conclusion Applied in Clinical Practice

- To our knowledge, report described above, could be the first one related to nephrotic syndrome induced by levamisole-adultered cocaine, proven by cocaine sample toxicology. Lack of renal biopsy is a limitation of this report.
- End organ involvement is an uncommon presentation of ANCA-positive vasculitis induced by levamisole-adultered cocaine. High index of suspicion for kidney involvement in this setting, should be considered in cocaine users with skin lesions and abnormal renal function.
- It is noteworthy to make differential diagnosis with other infectious or idiopathic vasculitis, considering that discontinuation of levamisole-cocaine can improve the clinical course of condition, without immunosuppressive therapy.

References

[1] Graf J., Lynch K., Yeh C. et al. Purpura, cutaneous necrosis and antineutrophil cytoplasmic antibodies associated with levamisole-adulterated cocaine. *Arthritis Rheum*. 2011;63(12):3998-4001.

[2] Pearson T., Bremmer M., Cohen J. et al. Vasculopathy related to cocaine adultered with levamisole: A review of the literature. *Dermatology Online Journal* 2012;18 (7).

[3] Arora N. Cutaneous vasculopathy and neutropenia associated with levamisole-adulterated cocaine. *Am. J. Med. Sci*. 2013;345(1):45-51.

[4] Ventura M., Caudevilla F. and Vidal C. Grupo Investigadores SELECTO. Cocaína adulterada con levamisol: posibles implicaciones clínicas. [Levamisole-adulterated cocaine: potential clinical implications]. *Med. Clin*. (Barc). 2011;136(8):365-368.

[5] Arora N., Jain T., Bhanot R. et al. Levamisole-induced leukocytoclastic vasculitis and neutropenia in a patient with cocaine use: an extensive

case with necrosis of skin, soft tissue, and cartilage. *Addiction Science and Clinical Practice* 2012;7:19.

[6] Geller L., Whang T., Mercer S. et al. Retiform purpura: a new stigmata of illicit drug use? *Dermatology online Journal* 2011;17(2):7.

[7] Poon SH., Baliog CR., Sams RN. et al. Syndrome of cocaine-levamisole-induced cutaneous vasculitis and immune-mediated leukopenia. *Semin. Arthritis Rheum.* 2011; 41(3):434-444.

[8] Mc Grath M., Isakova T., Rennke H. et al. Contamined cocaine and antineutrophil cytoplasmic antibody-associated disease. *Clin. J. Am. Soc. Nephrol.* 2011;6: 2799-2805.

[9] Álvarez Díaz H., Mariño Callejo A.I., García Rodríguez J.F. et al. ANCA-positive vasculitis induced by levamisole-adulterated cocaine and nephrotic syndrome: the kidney as an unusual target. *Am. J. Case Rep.* 2013; 14: 557-561.

[10] Tran H., Tan D. and Marnejon T. Cutaneous vasculopathy associated with levamisole-adulterated cocaine. *Clin. Med. Res.* 2013;11(1):26-30.

[11] Jaffe J. and Kimmel P. Chronic nephropathies of cocaine and heroin abuse: a critical review. *Clin. J. Am. Soc. Nephrol.* 2006;1:655-667.

[12] Jenkins J., Babu K., Hsu-Hung E. et al. ANCA-positive necrotizing vasculitis and thrombotic vasculopathy induced by levamisole-adultered cocaine: A distinctive clinicopathologic presentation. *J. Am. Acad. Dermatol.* 2011;e14-16.

In: Substance Abuse
Editor: Jeffrey Raines

ISBN: 978-1-63321-949-6

Chapter 5

COPING AND AUTONOMIC DYSFUNCTION ACT IN TANDEM WITH ALCOHOL-RELATED SUBCLINICAL ATHEROSCLEROSIS: THE SABPA STUDY

L. Malan[1,*], W. Oosthuizen[1], J. D. Scheepers[1], M. Möller-Wolmarans[2] and N. T. Malan[1]

[1]Hypertension in Africa Research Team (HART), North-West University, Potchefstroom, South Africa

[2]Unit for Drug Research and Development, Division of Pharmacology, School for Pharmacy, North-West University, Potchefstroom, South Africa

ABSTRACT

Introduction: Alcohol abuse is among the Westernized world's most common lifestyle factors contributing to sensitization of vascular structure and pathology. Gamma glutamyl transferase (γ-GT), as a marker of alcohol abuse, may indicate increased sensitization and vascular disease risk when using chronic defense coping (DefS). DefS was contradicted as a promoter of health, as it was related with dissociation between self-reported behavioral ("in-control") albeit physiological ("loss-of–control") responses. Therefore, we aimed to assess if DefS may

---

* Tel.: +27 18 2992438, Fax: +27 18 2991053, E-mail: Leone.Malan@nwu.ac.za.

mask autonomic dysfunction and induce alcohol-related subclinical atherosclerosis.

Methods: A black African male teacher cohort with similar socioeconomic standing and without atrial fibrillation (N=101) from the North-West Province of South Africa, was recruited and investigated. Fasting blood values, 24h ambulatory blood pressure (ABPM) and -ECG, Coping Strategy Indicator (CSI) scores and ultrasound left carotid intima media far wall scanning values, were obtained. The standard deviation between successful R-R intervals (SDNN) was utilized as a marker of time-domain 24h heart rate variability (HRV). Multivariate regression analyses were computed.

Results: A hypertensive state in the men was evident at a much lower ROC γ-GT cut point than the suggested MERCK cut-point of 78 U/L [55.7 U/L, sensitivity/specificity 60%/86% (AUC 0.78; 95% CI: 0.67; 0.88]. Hereafter, males were stratified into low (<55.7 U/l) and high (≥ 55.7 U/l) γ-GT groups. Overall, the high γ-GT group, revealed a poorer lifestyle profile, mean higher 24h ABPM, depressed 24h HRV and more 24h silent ischemic events (14 vs. 2) compared to their low γ-GT counterparts ($P \leq 0.01$). HRV responses were inversely associated with γ-GT when utilizing DefS ($r = -0.28$; $P = 0.015$). Additionally, ABPM predicted 24h silent ischemia (OR 1.11; $P \leq 0.01$) whereas 24h silent ischemia predicted a trend for structural vascular disease in the DefS African men (OR 1.06; $p \leq 0.06$).

Conclusion: DefS revealed behavioral "in-control" responses directly opposing or *masking* physiological "loss-of-control" responses, underpinning a dissociative response. Alcohol, which is a central nervous system depressant, enhanced vasoconstriction in the vasculature. Indeed, alcohol abuse was related to depressed heart rate variability, when utilizing DefS, sensitizing the vasculature, induced silent ischemia and ultimately structural vascular remodeling. The detrimental effects of DefS acting in tandem with autonomic dysfunction augment alcohol-related ischemia and may increase the risk for early sub-clinical atherosclerosis.

Keywords: Africans; gamma glutamyl transferase, alcohol abuse; cardiovascular health; defence coping

INTRODUCTION

Adapting to an urban environment and the stress associated with it lead to lifestyle changes, possibly in an attempt to cope. This includes increased alcohol intake and in some cases misuse thereof. [1] Alcohol abuse is a well-known risk-factor for an array of conditions, including coronary heart disease, diabetes and hypertension. [2] Contradicting research demonstrated that alcohol can be beneficial for overall cardiovascular health, [3] but the majority of prospective studies demonstrate that these positive effects are only found in low to moderate levels of consumption. [3]

A biomarker for alcohol abuse, γ-glutamyl transferase (γ-GT), has been described as a strong predictor of cardiometabolic disease, vagal-impaired heart rate variability (HRV) responses as well as the development of the metabolic syndrome. [4, 5] The use of γ-GT as marker for alcohol abuse is limited and often questioned, due to the fact that fatty liver disease and oxidative stress cannot be ruled out in elevated γ-GT levels. [6] However, supportive evidence for γ-GT as behavioral adjustment to psychosocial stress in Africans has been demonstrated. [7] It was also found that γ-GT correlated well with other markers for alcohol abuse. [7]

Another important factor in the development of cardiovascular disease (CVD) is the effect of daily stress and how each individual reacts to and copes with such stress. [8] Different coping styles exist, each exhibiting a different psychological stress response. A defensive active coping (DefS) style describes an active problem-solving focused person, who reports to be in control in stressful times [9] which mainly provokes a β-adrenergic cardiac response. [8] An emotional avoidance coping style refers to a person who reports loss of control [10] who will rather avoid the problem than face it head on [9] and which mainly provokes an α-adrenergic vascular response. [11] Whilst social support, another coping style, is mostly known to mediate good cardiovascular health. [9]

Overall poorer health is associated with an emotional avoidance coping style. [12] Conversely, we revealed intensified risk for the development of CVD when using the DefS style. [11, 13] Additionally, studies showed that Africans, when compared to their Caucasian counterparts, had elevated α-adrenergic vascular reactivity responses during exposure to acute mental stress. [11, 14]

They also revealed poorer overall cardiometabolic health, and four times more African than Caucasian males reported that they were under severe stress. [15] Behaviorally, African men reported the use of a DefS style – which should be a health promoter [9], but contradictorily they showed augmented α-adrenergic stress responses, enhanced after- and preload to the heart and ultimately reduced function of the heart. [11] These findings may underpin a mechanism where dissociation between physiological and behavioral stress responses are demonstrated during chronic stress. [15, 16].

Therefore, we intend to take it one step further by hypothesizing that alcohol abuse may be a contributing factor to cardiovascular risk in a male cohort when habitually utilizing DefS. Our findings may contradict DefS as a health promoter as associations between alcohol abuse, autonomic dysfunction and sensitization of the vasculature may predict ultimate poorer cardiovascular health in an urban African male cohort.

METHODS

Study Design and Participants

This sub-study forms part of the Sympathetic Activity and ambulatory Blood Pressure in Africans (SABPA) study. The target population study included Caucasian and African teachers from the Dr Kenneth Kaunda Education District of the North West province in South Africa from 2008 to 2009. The participants were selected to ensure similar socio-economic status and professional environments although their cultural characteristics may differ greatly. [16]

All eligible teachers between the age of 20 and 62 years were invited to participate in the study. Original exclusion criteria included users of α- or β-blockers, psychotropic substance abusers, atrial fibrillation, participants with tympanum temperature above 37.5°C, and those who have donated blood or received vaccinations within the 3 months prior to the study. Participants signed informed consent forms prior to the execution of the study. The SABPA study was approved by the Ethics Review Board of the North-West University (Potchefstroom Campus: NWU-0003607S6), and the conducting of the procedures all complied with the guidelines of the Declaration of Helsinki. [17] The total sample size comprised 101 African male participants and females were excluded as a limited sample exceeded the cut point for alcohol abuse.

Cardiovascular Measures

On working days, ambulatory blood pressure- (ABPM), electrocardiogram- (ECG) and accelerometer measurements were recorded (Cardiotens CE120®, Meditech, Budapest, Hungary and Actical®, Mini Mitter, Montreal, Quebec). The apparatuses were fitted respectively onto the non-dominant arm and the hip of each participant at approximately 07:00. A suitably-sized cuff, be it non-obese or obese, was used for each participant. The Cardiotens CE120® device was programmed to measure the participants' blood pressure (BP) at intervals of 30 minutes between 08:00 and 22:00 and at intervals of 60 minutes from 22:00 until 06:00 the next morning [18] with a successful mean inflation rate of 75.5 %. The silent ischemia/ambulatory ischemic events profile was assessed by two-channel ECG recordings (Cardiotens CE120®) according to a pre-set program for 20 seconds at 5 minute intervals. A silent ischemic event was recorded according to the following criteria (also known as the 1-1-1 rule), namely: horizontal or descending ST-segment depression by 1 mm; duration of the ST-segment episode lasts for 1 minute, and there was a 1 minute interval from the preceding episodes.

Heart rate variability (HRV) responses have been computed to obtain SDNN [4], which is a prognostic tool for cardiovascular outcome and may be defined as the standard deviation of the normal-to-normal (NN) intervals between adjacent QRS complexes, which equal the square root of variance. Since variance is mathematically equal to the total power of spectral analysis, the SDNN reflects all cyclic components responsible for variability in the period of recording. SDNN is regarded as the best overall prognostic tool, for values <50 ms are indicative of highly depressed HRV, those between 50-100 ms indicate moderately depressed HRV and those >100 ms are classified as normal. [4] SDNN values are closely related to the high frequency (parasympathetic) component of the power spectrum and thus reflect vagus nerve-mediated autonomic control of the heart. [4] The software program automatically filters out ventricular, supraventricular as well as artifacts in RR intervals, and outliers were manually removed.

Participants were instructed to note if they experienced any abnormal disturbances like syncope, nausea or visual impairment on a 24h diary card. After these devices were fitted, the participants carried on with their normal daily activities. At 16:30 they were transported to the North-West University's Metabolic Unit Research Facility for an overnight stay and familiarized with the experimental set-up. Hereafter, they completed a psychosocial battery, supervised by registered clinical psychologists. Later they received a standardized dinner and were requested to go to bed at 22:00, fasting overnight for other clinical measures to be performed the following day.

Participants were woken at 06:00 the next morning and the devices were removed as soon as the last ABPM was recorded. Hypertension was regarded as an average ambulatory BP of ≥ 130 mmHg and/or ≥ 80 mm Hg. [19]

Anthropometric measurements and an eight-hour fasting urine sample were obtained, and lastly blood samples were collected by a registered nurse. A General Socio-demographic and Health Questionnaire was used to gain information regarding the participants' family medical history and lifestyle habits such as smoking and alcohol usage.

Coping Assessment

The Coping Strategy Indicator (CSI) has a Cronbach reliability index of 0.84 - 0.93 and was used to identify each participant's chronic coping style successfully.[9] The CSI is a self-report measure consisting of 33 items which determine whether a person uses the problem solving, avoidance or seeking social support coping style in difficult times. The 33 items in the questionnaire are divided into three sub-sets of 11 items each. The participant answers each item using a three-point Lickert scale, 3 being "a lot", 2 "a little", and 1 "not at all". They choose 1, 2 or 3 as an answer while keeping in mind a stressful event they have encountered over the last six months. The accumulated score of the answers indicate the use of a certain coping style. A total score of ≥ 26 indicates above mean usage of the problem solving or DefS style, ≥ 23 indicating above mean use of the social support style, and ≥ 19 indicating above mean use of the avoidance style. [9]

Lifestyle Factors and Anthropometric Measurements

Physical activity was measured using the Actical® omnidirectional accelerometer which was fitted on the hip of the participant. Set to 15 second intervals, this device measured movement of the participant whilst they engaged in normal daily activities. The data was then converted into 1-second intervals for analysis. γ-GT levels were measured as marker for alcohol abuse, [7, 20] and for each participant's smoking habits, cotinine was measured.

All anthropometric measurements were obtained by ISAK (International Society for the Advancement of Kinanthropometry) level 2 accredited anthropometrists using calibrated instruments (Precision health scale, A & D Company, Tokyo, Japan; Invicta Stadiometer IP 1465, Invicta, London, UK), with subjects in minimal clothing and without shoes. Measurements were performed with standardized methods and in triplicate to ensure accuracy. Body mass index (BMI) was calculated by dividing the participants' weight (kg) by their length (m^2). The body surface area (BSA) in m^2 was calculated according to the Mosteller formula. [21] Intra- and inter-observer variability was less than 10%.

Measurements of Target Organ Damage

The left common carotid intima media thickness of the far wall (L-CIMTf) was determined using the SonoSite Micromaxx ultrasound system (SonoSite Inc., Bothell, WA, USA) and utilizing a 6-13 MHz linear array transducer according to the Rudi Meijer protocol. [22] LIMT-f was measured to identify sub-clinical arterial wall thickening. Urinary albumin and creatinine, as an index of kidney function, were determined with the sequential multiple analyzer computer (Konelab 20i TM, Thermo Scientific, Vantaa, Finland).

Biochemical Measures

Fasting blood samples from the antebrachial vein branches were obtained by a registered nurse using a sterile winged infusion set. Liver enzymes were analyzed with the enzyme rate method, C-reactive protein (CRP) levels with the turbidimetric method and the timed-end-point method was used to determine blood glucose, cholesterol, high density lipoprotein (HDL) and triglycerides levels. All the above variables were measured using the Unicel DXC 800 analyzer (Beckman and Coulter, Germany). Serum cotinine levels were measured using the homogeneous immunoassay on the Modular ROCHE automized analyzer (Konelab 20i; Thermo Scientific, Vantaa, Finland). The enzymatic colorimetric test and Cobas® Integra 400 plus (Roche, Basel, Switzerland) were used to determine serum creatinine. Glycated haemoglobin was measured with the Cobas® Integra 400 (Roche, Switzerland), using the turbidimetric inhibition immunoassay method.

Statistical Analyses

Analyses were done using Statistica version 12.0 (Statsoft Inc., Tulsa, USA, 2011). Non–Gaussian distributed variables were logarithmically transformed, after which independent t-tests were computed to describe the baseline characteristics of the entire group. Together with this, Chi-square (X^2) tests were used to determine prevalence for medications and pathology including ABPM hypertension, diabetes and also the treatment thereof, as well as HIV status.

Thereafter, a non-parametric receiver-operating characteristic (ROC) curve [23] was computed together with the area under the curve (AUC) to explore the association between γ-GT and ambulatory hypertension cut points. [19] Sensitivity and specificity values were computed to determine the cut points that would maximize the sum of the number of true positive and true negative predictions.

The male cohort was stratified according to the suggested cut point for γ-GT. Sensitivity and specificity values were once again calculated to highlight the odds of γ-GT predicting pathological ambulatory hypertension.

Interaction effect analyses were repeated for each of the three dichotomized coping strategies using the following mean cut points: DefS (≥ 26), avoidance (≥19) and social support (≥ 23). Main effects interactions between γ-GT x coping for cardiovascular risk markers were computed. Independent t-tests identified confounders for the two-way analysis of covariance (ANCOVA) tests. The ANCOVA's were adjusted for determined confounders. Multiple linear regression analyses in ethnic-gender groups were performed. Unadjusted linear associations between HRV and γ-GT in Defs groups were computed and presented in scatterplots. Odds ratios (OR's) with 95% Confidence Intervals (CI's) were calculated in several models to highlight the odds of independent risk markers (lifestyle, BP) to predict silent ischemia and structural vascular disease marker, L-CIMTf in high γ-GT as well as in high γ-GT DefS groups. Age, CRP, Cholesterol, BP were added as independent confounders in the L-CIMTf models. Significant values were noted as $p \leq 0.05$..

RESULTS

Table 1 demonstrates baseline characteristics of the entire African male cohort. It also shows the prevalence of certain pathology and medications taken by the participants.

Overall, levels exceeding cut points of γ-GT and cardiometabolic values were evident including ambulatory blood pressure (SBP and or DBP 130/80, triglycerides (≥1.7mmol/l), CRP (≥ 3 mg/l), HbA1c (pre-diabetic ≥ 5.7%) and glucose (5.6 mmol/l).

Table 1. Baseline characteristics of African male cohort (mean ± SD)

Variables	African males (N = 101)
Age, (years)	43.18 ± 8.17
Lifestyle factors:	
Body mass index, (kg/m2)	27.72 ± 5.78
Body surface area, (m2)	1.94 ± 0.23
Waist circumference, (cm)	93.56 ± 15.49
Cotinine, (ng/ml)	35.46 ± 65.01
Physical activity, (kcal/24h)	2714.85 ± 800.12
γ-Glutamyl transferase , (U/l)	84.84 ± 91.70
Aspartate aminotransferase : Alanine aminotransferase (AST:ALT)	1.63 ± 1.03
Psychological variables:	
Defensive problem solving score	28.21 ± 4.18
Social support score	24.87 ± 5.37
Avoidance score	21.00 ± 3.62
Biochemical variables:	
HbA1c, (%)	6.24 ± 1.23
C-reactive protein, (mg/l)	5.19 ± 8.23
Triglycerides, (mmol/l)	1.81 ± 1.59
Creatinine, (μmol/l)	77.22 ± 14.22
Total cholesterol, (mmol/l)	4.74 ± 1.17
High density lipoprotein, (mmol/l)	1.05 ± 0.37
Resting glucose, (mmol/l)	5.99 ± 2.02
Albumin:Creatinine (ACR)	1.72 ± 3.25
Cardiovascular variables:	
24hr SBP, (mmHg)	138 ± 16.01
24hr DBP, (mmHg)	88 ± 10.74
24h Heart rate, (beats/minute)	79 ± 11.36
SDNN (ms)	123.72 ± 45.59
Ischemic events, (n)	9.39 ± 20.84
L-CIMTf mean, (mm)	0.72 ± 0.18

Table 1. (Continued)

Variables	African males (N = 101)
Pathology and medications:	
*Hypertensive, n (%)	76 (75)
*Anti-hypertensive drugs, n (%)	20 (19.80)
*Anti-diabetic drugs, n (%)	7 (16.93)
*HIV infected, n (%)	13 (12.87)

Where: HbA1c, glycated haemoglobin; SDNN, standard deviation of the normal-to-normal (NN) intervals between adjacent QRS complexes; L-CIMTf, left carotid intima media thickness of the far wall. Values presented as arithmetic mean ± SD; *-values, presented as number of observations, n, and percentage of total group, (%).

ROC analysis was used to determine a suggested cut-point for γ-GT levels predicting ambulatory hypertension in 101 African men. Figure 1 illustrates where the AUC was most optimal for ambulatory hypertension, and also shows the cut-points according to the Youden index.

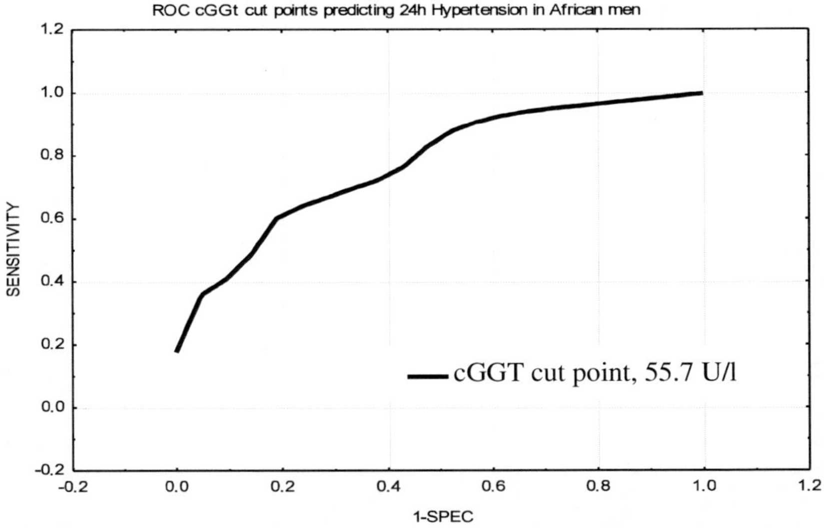

Figure 1. ROC curves depicting cGGT cut points for 24 Hypertension Prevalence in a cohort of 101 African males (AUC ± 95 % CI): 0.78 (0.67; 0.88).

The ROC cut point values that showed maximum sensitivity (60%) and specificity (86%) were found at 55.7 U/L with an AUC value of 0.78 (0.67; 0.88). Hereafter, the total group was stratified into low (<55.7U/L) and high (≥55.7 U/L) γ-GT levels.

Interaction effects were only evident for DefS and not for any other coping style. A single main effects (ROC γ-GT x DefS) interaction existed for ambulatory DBP [F (1, 95), 4.72: p=0.03].

Table 2, compares the low and high γ-GT groups, adjusting for the identified confounders, namely BSA and physical activity in the form of total energy expenditure (TEE). Significantly higher levels of triglycerides, aspartate aminotransferase: alanine aminotransferase ratio, ambulatory BP and ischemic events were revealed in the higher γ-GT group compared to the low group. Furthermore, significantly more participants (92%) suffer from hypertension in the high γ-GT group than in the low group (58%).

Table 2. Comparing mean cardiometabolic and coping responses in an African male cohort, stratified into low and high γ-GT levels (±95 % CI)

Variables	γ-GT levels (<55.7 u/l) N=50	γ-GT levels (≥55.7 u/l) N=51	P-value
Unadjusted lifestyle factors (mean ± SD):			
Body surface area, (m2)	1.86±1.12	2.00±1.12	0.002
Physical activity, (kcal/24h)	2429±1.28	2794±1.35	0.01
Adjusted for lifestyle factors (Body surface area; Physical activity):			
Age, (years)	42.23 (39.9, 44.4)	44.11 (41.9, 46.4)	0.26
Body mass index, (kg/m2)	26.83 (26.1, 27.6)	27.18 (26.4, 27.9)	0.52
Waist circumference, (cm)	90.84 (88.7, 93.0)	93.73 (91.6, 96.0)	0.07
Cotinine, (ng/ml)	29.13 (10.35, 48.0)	41.66 (23.0, 60.3)	0.36
γ-Glutamyl transferase, (u/l)	35.80 (31.5, 40.7)	108.27 (95.4, 122.9)	<0.001
AST:ALT	1.16 (1.0, 1.8)	1.27 (1.1, 1.5)	0.02
Psychological variables:			
Defensive problem solving score	27.38 (26.1, 28.7)	28.34 (27.0, 29.7)	0.32
Social support score	23.21 (21.6, 24.9)	25.19 (23.5, 27.0)	0.1
Avoidance score	20.38 (19.4, 21.5)	20.97 (20.0, 22.1)	0.45
Biochemical variables:			
HbA1c, (%)	5.97 (5.7, 6.3)	6.32 (6.0, 6.6)	0.10

Table 2. (Continued)

Variables	γ-GT levels (<55.7 u/l) N=50	γ-GT levels (≥55.7 u/l) N=51	P-value
C-reactive protein, (mg/l)	2.37 (1.7, 3.2)	3.19 (2.3, 4.4)	0.20
Triglycerides, (mmol/l)	1.07 (0.9, 1.3)	1.97 (1.7, 2.3)	<0.001
Creatinine, (μmol/l)	75.51 (71.7, 79.5)	76.44 (72.7, 80.4)	0.75
Total cholesterol, (mmol/l)	4.44 (4.2, 4.8)	4.77 (4.5, 5.1)	0.15
High density lipoprotein, (mmol/l)	1.01 (0.9, 1.1)	0.97 (0.9, 1.1)	0.57
Resting glucose, (mmol/l)	5.51 (5.1, 6.0)	6.0 (5.6, 6.5)	0.12
Albumin:Creatinine (ACR)	1.10 (0.9, 1.4)	0.94 (0.7, 1.2)	0.39
Cardiovascular variables:			
24hr SBP, (mmHg)	133 (129, 137)	141 (137, 145)	0.01
24hr DBP, (mmHg)	84 (82, 87)	90 (88, 93)	0.003
24h Heart rate, (beats/minute)	76 (73, 80)	80 (77, 84)	0.77
SDNN, (ms)	115.03 (102.4,127.7)	132.76 (119.8, 145.7)	0.06
Ischemic events, (n)	4.26 (2.22, 8.18)	13.75 (7.59, 24.91)	0.01
L-CIMTf mean, (mm)	0.70 (0.66, 0.76)	0.69 (0.65, 0.74)	0.78
Pathology and medication:			
*Hypertensive, n (%)	29 (58)	47 (92)	<0.01
*Anti-hypertensive drugs, n (%)	4 (8)	16 (31)	0.003
*Anti-diabetic drugs, n (%)	2 (4)	5 (10)	0.25
*HIV infected, n (%)	6 (12)	7 (14)	0.74

Abbreviations: HbA1c, glycated haemoglobin; SBP, systolic blood pressure; DBP, diastolic blood pressure; SDNN, standard deviation of the normal-to-normal (NN) intervals between adjacent QRS complexes; ; L-CIMTf, left carotid intima media thickness of the far wall. Values adjusted for body surface area and physical activity. *Values presented as number of observations, n, and percentage of total group.

In Figure 2, unadjusted associations between γ-GT and HRV became stronger when utilizing a DefS. OR's were calculated in Table 3 to determine the probability of high γ-GT levels and utilization of the DefS style predicting silent ischemia and increased structural wall remodelling. 24h SBP mostly predicted silent ischemic events in the high γ-GT as well as the high γ-GT plus DefS utilizing groups.

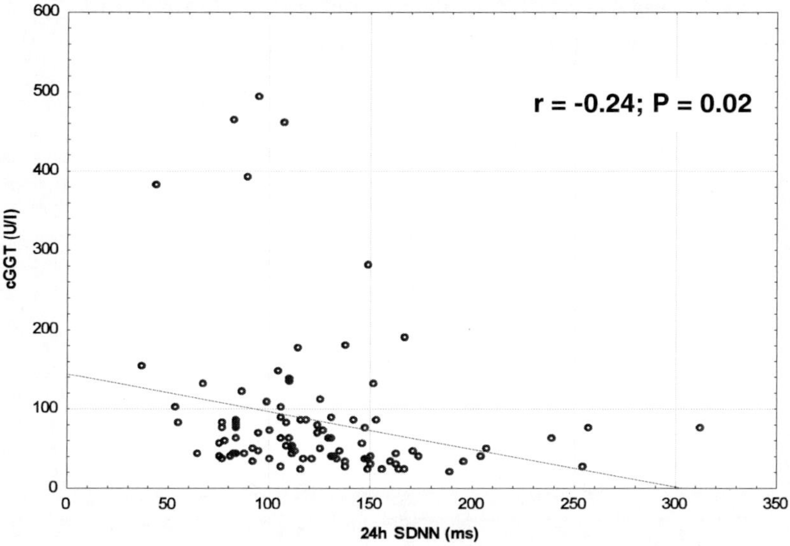

a

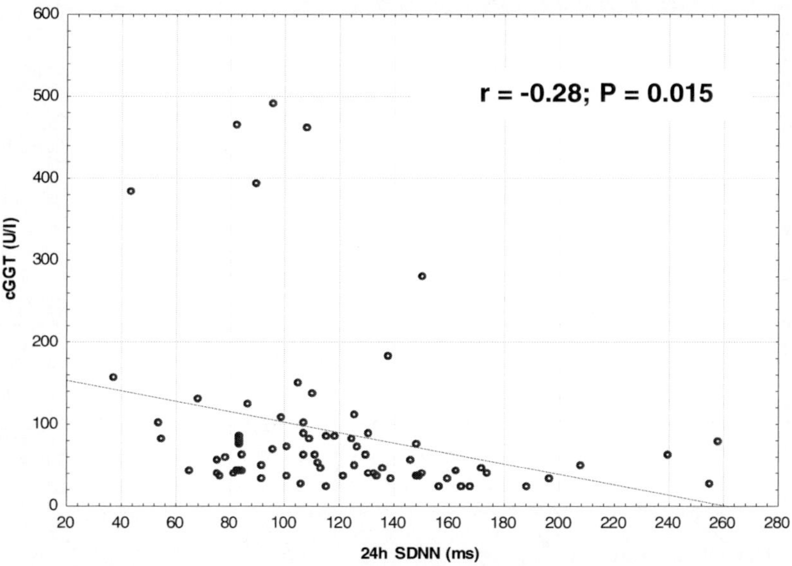

b

Figure 2. Unadjusted associations between heart rate variability and alcohol abuse (gamma glutamyl transferase) in all African men (Figure 2a); and (Figure 2b) in Defensive coping African men. Where: (SDNN, standard deviation of each successive R-R interval).

Table 3. Probability of ischemic events and increased structural vascular remodelling (L-CIMTf) in African men

	Prevalence of ischemic events				
Model 1	Nagelkerke R2	Odds Ratio	5th Percentile	95th Percentile	P
African Men – High γ-GT levels (>55.7U\l)					
24h SBP (mmHg)	0.30	1.09	1.03	1.12	<0.01
24h DBP (mmHg)	0.18	1.08	1.01	1.14	0.03
African Men – High γ-GT levels (>55.7U\l) + DefS					
24h SBP (mmHg)	0.36	1.11	1.03	1.18	<0.01
24h DBP (mmHg)	0.16	1.07	1.00	1.15	0.08
Model 2	L-CIMTf ≥ 0.9mm				
	Nagelkerke R2	Odds Ratio	5th Percentile	95th Percentile	P
African Men – High γ-GT levels (>55.7U\l)					
24h SBP (mmHg)	0.14	1.00	0.94	1.05	0.90
24h DBP (mmHg)	0.14	0.99	0.91	1.06	0.69
24h ischemic events (N)	0.14	1.01	0.98	1.04	0.41
African Men – High γ-GT levels (>55.7U\l) + DefS					
24h SBP (mmHg)	0.37	1.06	0.96	1.15	0.25
24h DBP (mmHg)	0.32	1.03	0.90	1.16	0.66
24h ischemic events (N)	0.37	1.06	1.00	1.11	0.06

Where: DefS, Defensive active coping; γ-GT, gamma glutamyl transferase and L-CIMTf, left carotid intima media thickness far wall. Confounders for Model 1 included body surface area and physical activity. Model 2 was adjusted for age, log CRP and cholesterol. Significant odds ratios presented where P values ≤ 0.05.

For African men with high γ-GT levels, 24h SBP predicted silent ischemia with an OR of 1.09 (95% CI: 1.03 – 1.12). The prediction is stronger in the group with high γ-GT levels if utilizing DefS, where 24h SBP predicted ischemia with an OR of 1.11 (95% CI: 1.03 - 1.18). 24h DBP also predicted ischemia in the high γ-GT as well as the high γ-GT plus DefS utilizing groups, with OR's of 1.08 (95% CI: 1.01 - 1.14) and 1.07 (95% CI of 1.00 - 1.15) respectively. Independent of confounders, silent ischemia in these men (high γ-GT + DefS), predicted a trend for structural vascular disease, namely L-CIMTf (OR 1.06; $p \leq 0.06$).

DISCUSSION

The main aim of this study was to assess whether alcohol abuse may be a contributing factor to cardiovascular risk factors in a male cohort when habitually utilizing DefS. The primary finding of our study demonstrated early sensitization of the vasculature in African men where an inverse relationship between autonomic dysfunction and alcohol abuse was demonstrated. High γ-GT levels with a cut point of 55.7 U/L predicted ambulatory hypertension. The significant interaction between γ-GT and DefS for ambulatory DBP enhances the notion of higher vascular responsiveness in the African male cohort. This is further supported by the interaction between alcohol abuse and DefS, where silent ischemia predicted a trend for structural vascular changes in L-CIMTf (≥ 0.90mm). The detrimental effects of DefS and autonomic dysfunction acting in tandem with alcohol-related ischemia seem to aggravate the risk for early sub-clinical atherosclerosis.

It is important to notice that pathology begins to manifest in the chosen group at a lower γ-GT cut point (55.7 U/L) than recommended by the Merck manual (78 U/L). [6] This may indicate early sensitization of the vasculature. Alcohol, which is a central nervous system depressant [6], will enhance vasoconstriction in the vasculature. Indeed, alcohol abuse was related to depressed heart rate variability when utilizing DefS, sensitizing the vasculature and may have induced silent ischemia and structural vascular remodeling. This can clearly be seen where 92% of the high γ-GT group demonstrated hypertension, despite the fact that only 31% of them are taking medication for the treatment thereof. This may suggest ethnic differences in pressor responsiveness and associated cardiometabolic risk. We, therefore, propose an ethnic specific γ-GT cut point indicating early vasculature responsiveness below the recommended cut point of 78 U/L. [6]

We need to mention that controversy exists over the use of γ-GT as marker for long term alcohol abuse, as non-alcoholic liver disease can also contribute to elevated levels thereof. [7] Therefore, we included another marker of liver pathology, namely the AST:ALT ratio. Assessing the ratio, a value <1 indicates liver pathology, which is not alcohol related, such as non-alcoholic fatty liver disease. [24] Thus, the > 1 ratio found in our high γ-GT group justifies the use of γ-GT as alcohol marker for the purposes of this study. [7]

Independently, both alcohol and DefS responses may be associated with pathology through various mechanisms, such as the well-known vasopressor effect of alcohol, [25] which is further worsened by DefS-induced endothelial dysfunction, especially in African men. [15, 16] The notion of alcohol as coping strategy and vagal-impaired response [16, 26, 27] have been demonstrated in African men, and our current data support alcohol abuse associated with autonomic dysfunction specifically depressed heart rate variability. [16] The current sub study support the above findings as an alcohol abuse ROC cut point predicted subclinical atherosclerosis in an African cohort utilizing DefS. The interaction between alcohol abuse and DefS [26, 27] for ambulatory DBP, underscores cardiac overload and α-adrenergic vascular sensitization and -vulnerability in these males.

Conversely, the higher prevalence of hypertension and usage of anti-hypertensive drugs in the high γ-GT African male group were confirmed in previous studies. This undercores that alcohol is a great risk factor in the development and progression of hypertension, and we recommend the restriction of alcohol in the treatment of hypertension. [5, 19, 28] High concentrations of alcohol are generally known to cause vasoconstriction of blood vessels. This can be due to the fact that alcohol inhibits endothelial-dependent vasodilation, and as previously mentioned – endothelial dysfunction. [29, 30] The higher number of ischemic events found in the high γ-GT group emphasizes higher central demand and compensatory increased autonomic activity, resulting in enhanced vasoconstrictive responsiveness, [29, 30] Ultimately reduced oxygen supply to the heart may increase the risk for coronary artery disease. [31, 32] It is however, also true that low to moderate consumption of alcohol leads to vasodilation, rather than vasoconstriction. [33] Therefore, recommended ethnic-culturally different cut points are needed as it seems that alcohol effects may vary considerably depending on the amount consumed and ethnicity of the user.

It seems clear that the majority of studies confirmed the alcohol-induced increased BP responses. It was demonstrated that arterial stiffening was significantly associated with consumption of large amounts of alcohol. [34] Subsequent pressor responses may induce elevated coronary artery disease risk. [35] Indeed, Hamer et al. computed odds ratios in African males of the SABPA study, where γ-GT was shown to indicate a risk of 3.1 (95% CI 0.6 - 15.5, independent of other confounders, predicting early structural vascular changes. [1] We take it one step further by demonstrating that an OR of 1.11

(95% CI 1.03 - 1.18) for silent ischemia may induce early structural vascular changes in high γ-GT, DefS African men.

Regarding the metabolic profile, it was evident that the high γ-GT group showed significantly increased levels of triglycerides, which confirm the findings of other studies where alcohol was directly linked to hypertriglyceridemia. [36, 37] Alcohol abuse is known to up-regulate hepatic fatty acid absorption, associated with the development of steatosis. [38] Triglycerides are then deposited into the liver and accumulate in the hepatocytes, which may also be evident in our own African group as significantly elevated levels of triglycerides were found in the high γ-GT group. This may be linked to central obesity and other cardiovascular risk factors. [39, 40] Literature describing the effects of alcohol usage on waist circumference shows that high consumption of alcohol shows an increase in weight gain, and as a result, an expansion of waist circumference or central obesity. [41] Cautiously, we want to speculate that the central obesity tendency (93%) in the high γ-GT group might also be stress related. Indeed, Björntorp & Rosmond confirmed this phenomenon in participants adapting to, or coping with psychosocial stress. [42] They demonstrated an association between psychosocial stress and increased corticoid receptor binding in abdominal adipose tissue that reflected increased cortisol and central obesity. [42] We cannot, however, declare the actual extent of alcohol abuse, as self-reporting alcohol intake may not always reflect actual intake.

What our result do show is that the high γ-GT group had significantly more silent ischemia, which are in line with previous fndings. It was suggested that dissociation between behavioral and physiological responses in DefS African men facilitates vascular hyper-responsiveness and sensitivity to even the smallest of challenges. [43] Indeed, DefS facilitated autonomic nervous system dysfunction, which was associated with higher blood pressure and sub-clinical structural vascular disease. This may further attribute to the vulnerable cardiovascular profile in the African male cohort, partly explaining why the prevalence of CVD amongst urban Africans is escalating at an alarming rate. It is suggested that this may be enforcing adaptation of their African collectivistic cultural lifestyles to a Westernized lifestyle and behavior. It may be that they turn to, amongst other things, alcohol as coping mechanism in order to cope with this transition or challenges in an individualistic westernized environment. [1] Limitations in the study included the controversial use of γ-GT as true marker of alcohol abuse. Another limitation is the absence of another group to compare the data with, for example their Caucasian counterparts. The motivation behind this limitation is the fact that too few Caucasian males showed levels of γ-GT ≥ 55.7 U/L. Expanding analyses to other ethnic-cultural groups in prospective studies may confirm the detrimental effect of alcohol abuse on the vascular system and subsequent CVD's or events.

In conclusion, alcohol abuse directly causes myocardial damage [43] due to the toxic effects it has on myocytes, and has been associated with an increased incidence of atherosclerotic coronary artery disease. [1] Our findings thus underscores a vulnerable cardiometabolic and vagal-impaired profile in an African male cohort. It emphasizes a mechanism of defense coping and sensitized autonomic responses during chronic or taxing circumstances. The detrimental effect of excessive alcohol usage subsequently induces reduced perfusion and early structural vascular remodeling. Our data support previous findings where DefS revealed self-reported behavioral "in-control" responses directly opposing or *masking* physiological "loss-of-control" responses, underpinning a dissociative response. Thus, an ethnic cultural specific cut point of 55.7U/L of γ-GT is suggested to reveal the level at which alcohol intake may drive increased risk for silent ischemia and a tendency for early structural vascular pathology.

ACKNOWLEDGMENT

The authors would like to thank the participants for their involvement in the study, and the Department of Education, North West Province, South Africa for approving their participation. We would also like to thank, Chrissie Lessing (RN) and Mrs Tina Scholtz for their technical assistance and support. This research was partly funded by The Metabolic Syndrome Institute, France; ROCHE Diagnostics; Medical Research Council; National Research Foundation (NRF), North West University, and the Dr Kenneth Kaunda District of the North West Department of Education, South Africa. The funding organizations played no role in the design and conduct of the study; collection, management, analysis and interpretation of the data; preparation, review, or approval of the manuscript.

Conflict of Interest Statement

The authors declare no conflicts of interest.

REFERENCES

[1] Hamer M., Malan L., Schutte A. E., Huisman H. W., van Rooyen J. M., Schutte R., et al. Conventional and behavioral risk factors explain differences in sub-clinical vascular disease between black and Caucasian South Africans: The SABPA study. *Atherosclerosis,* 2011; 215(1): 237-42.

[2] Grønbæk M. The positive and negative health effects of alcohol- and the public health implications. *J. Intern. Med.,* 2009; 265(4): 407-20.

[3] Hvidtfeldt U. A., Tolstrup J. S., Jakobsen M. U., Heitmann B. L., Grønbæk M., O'Reilly E., et al. Alcohol intake and risk of coronary heart disease in younger, middle-aged, and older adults. *Circulation,* 2010; 121(14): 1589-97.

[4] Thayer J. F., Åhs F., Fredrikson M., Sollers J. J. *et al.* A meta-analysis of heart rate variability and neuroimaging studies: Implications for heart rate variability as a marker of stress and health. *Neurosci. Biobehav. Rev.,* 2012; 36:747-56.

[5] Beilin L. J., Puddey I. B. Alcohol and hypertension: an update. *Hypertension,* 2006; 47(6): 1035-8.

[6] Porter R. S. The Merck manual of diagnosis and therapy. 19 ed: Wiley; 2011.

[7] Hastedt M., Büchner M., Rothe M., Gapert R., Herre S., Krumbiegel F., et al. Detecting alcohol abuse: traditional blood alcohol markers compared to ethyl glucuronide (EtG) and fatty acid ethyl esters (FAEEs) measurement in hair. *Forensic Sci. Med. Pathol.,* 2013; 9(4): 471-7.

[8] Henry J. P., Stephens P. M., Ely D. L. Psychosocial hypertension and the defence and defeat reactions. *J. Hypertens.*, 1986; 4(6): 687-8.

[9] Amirkhan J. H. A factor analytically derived measure of coping: The Coping Strategy Indicator. *J. Pers. Soc. Psychol.*, 1990; 59(5): 1066-74.

[10] Gerin W., Pickering T. G., Glynn L., Christenfeld N., Schwartz A., Carroll D., et al. An historical context for behavioral models of hypertension. *J. Psychosom. Res.,* 2000; 48(4): 369-77.

[11] Malan L., Schutte A. E., Malan N. T., Wissing M. P., Vorster H. H., Steyn H. S., et al. Coping mechanisms, perception of health and cardiovascular dysfunction in Africans. *Int. J. Psychophysiol.*, 2006; 61(2): 158-66.

[12] Rhenen W., Schaufeli W., Dijk F. H., Blonk R. B. Coping and sickness absence. *Int. Arch. Occup. Environ. Health*, 2008; 81(4): 461-72.

[13] Malan L., Malan N. T., Wissing M. P., Seedat Y. K. Coping with urbanization: A cardiometabolic risk?: The THUSA study. *Biol. Psychol.*, 2008; 79(3): 323-8.

[14] Van Rooyen J., Kruger H., Huisman H., Wissing M., Margetts B., Venter C., et al. An epidemiological study of hypertension and its determinants in a population in transition: the THUSA study. *J. Hum. Hypertens.*, 2000; 14(12): 779-87.

[15] de Kock A., Malan L., Hamer M., Malan N. T. Defensive coping and subclinical vascular disease risk – associations with autonomic exhaustion in Africans and Caucasians: The SABPA study. *Atherosclerosis,* 2012; 225(2): 438-43.

[16] Malan L., Hamer M., Schlaich M. P., Lambert G., Ziemssen T., Reimann M., et al. Defensive coping facilitates higher blood pressure and early sub-clinical structural vascular disease via alterations in heart rate variability: The SABPA study. *Atherosclerosis,* 2013; 227(2): 391-7.

[17] World Medical Association. World Medical Association Declaration of Helsinki: ethical principles for medical research involving human subjects. *J. Indian Med. Assoc.*, 2009; 107: 403-5.

[18] Kohara K., Nishida W., Maguchi M., Hiwada K. Autonomic nervous function in non-dipper essential hypertensive subjects: evaluation by power spectral analysis of heart rate variability. *Hypertension,* 1995; 26(5): 808-14.

[19] Mancia G., Fagard R., Narkiewicz K., Redon J., Zanchetti A., Bohm M., et al. 2013 ESH/ESC Guidelines for the management of arterial hypertension: The Task Force for the management of arterial hypertension of the European Society of Hypertension (ESH) and of the European Society of Cardiology (ESC). *Eur. Heart J.,* 2013; 34(28): 2159-219.

[20] Topic A., Djukic M. Diagnostic characteristics and application of alcohol biomarkers. *Clin. Lab.*, 2013; 59(3-4): 233-45.

[21] Mosteller R. D. Simplified calculation of body-surface area. *N. Engl. J. Med.*, 1987; 317(17): 1098.

[22] Liang Y., Teede, H., Kotsopoulos, Shiel, L., Cameron, J., Dart, A., McGrath, B. Non-invasive measurements of arterial structure and function: repeatability, interrelationships and trial sample size. *Clin. Sci.,* 1998; 95: 669-79.

[23] Zweig M. H., Campbell G. Receiver-operating characteristic (ROC) plots: a fundamental evaluation tool in clinical medicine. *Clin. Chem.,* 1993; 39(4): 561-77.

[24] Niemelä O., Alatalo P. Biomarkers of alcohol consumption and related liver disease. *Scand. J. Clin. Lab. Invest.*, 2010; 70(5): 305-12.

[25] Bau P. F., Bau C. H., Rosito G. A., Manfroi W. C., Fuchs F. D. Alcohol consumption, cardiovascular health, and endothelial function markers. *Alcohol,* 2007; 41(7): 479-88.

[26] Bourdillon M. Christianity and wealth in rural communities in Zimbabwe. *Zambezia XI (i),* 1983: 37-53.

[27] Sjöberg L., Samsonowitz V. Coping strategies and relapse in alcohol abuse. *Drug Alcohol Depend.,* 1985; 15(3): 283-301.

[28] Jackson R., Stewart A., Beaglehole R., Scragg R. Alcohol consumption and blood pressure. *Am. J. Epidemiol.,* 1985; 122(6): 1037-44.

[29] Criscione L., Powell J. R., Burdet R., Engesser S., Schlager F., Schoepfer A. Alcohol suppresses endothelium-dependent relaxation in rat mesenteric vascular beds. *Hypertension,* 1989; 13(6): 964-7.

[30] Brizzolara A. L., Morris D. G., Burnstock G. Ethanol affects sympathetic cotransmission and endothelium-dependent relaxation in the rat. *Eur. J. Pharmacol.*, 1994; 254(1): 175-81.

[31] Opie L. H. Heart physiology: from cell to circulation. 4 ed. Philadelphia: Lippencott Williams & Wilkinss; 2004.

[32] Neunteufl T., Katzenschlager R., Hassan A., Klaar U., Schwarzacher S., Glogar D., et al. Systemic endothelial dysfunction is related to the extent and severity of coronary artery disease. *Atherosclerosis*, 1997; 129(1): 111-8.

[33] Kawano Y. Physio-pathological effects of alcohol on the cardiovascular system: its role in hypertension and cardiovascular disease. *Hypertension Res.,* 2010; 33(3): 181-91.

[34] Sierksma A., Muller M., van der Schouw Y. T., Grobbee D. E., Hendriks H. F., Bots M. L. Alcohol consumption and arterial stiffness in men. *J. Hypertens.*, 2004; 22(2): 357-62.

[35] Matsumoto C., Tomiyama H., Yamada J., Yoshida M., Shiina K., Nagata M., et al. Association of blood pressure levels with the effects of alcohol intake on the vasculature in Japanese men. *Hypertension Res.,* 2009; 32(2): 127-32.

[36] Bessembinders K., Wielders J., van de Wiel A. Severe hypertriglyceridemia influenced by alcohol. *Alcohol and alcohol*, 2011; 46(2): 113-6.

[37] Toft U., Pisinger C., Aadahl M., Linneberg A., Lau C., Jørgensen T. The effect of sustained, long-term changes in alcohol intake on cardiovascular risk. *Prev. Med.,* 2012; 2(4): 444-51.

[38] Zhong W., Zhao Y., Tang Y., Wei X., Shi X., Sun W., et al. Chronic alcohol exposure stimulates adipose tissue lipolysis in mice: role of reverse triglyceride transport in the pathogenesis of alcoholic steatosis. *Am. J. Pathol.*, 2012; 180(3): 998-1007.

[39] Purohit V., Gao B., Song B.-J. Molecular mechanisms of alcoholic fatty liver. *Alcohol Clin. Exp. Res.,* 2009; 33(2): 191-205.

[40] Steinberg H. O., Tarshoby M., Monestel R., Hook G., Cronin J., Johnson A., et al. Elevated circulating free fatty acid levels impair endothelium-dependent vasodilation. *J. Clin. Invest.,* 1997; 100(5): 1230.

[41] Han T., Bijnen F., Lean M., Seidell J. Separate associations of waist and hip circumference with lifestyle factors. *Int. J. Epidemiol.*, 1998; 27(3): 422-30.

[42] Björntorp P., Rosmond R. Obesity and cortisol. *Nutrition*, 2000; 16(10): 924-36.

[43] Malan L., Hamer M., Schlaich M. P., Lambert G. W., Harvey B. H., Reimann M., et al. Facilitated defensive coping, silent ischaemia and ECG left-ventricular hypertrophy: the SABPA study. *J. Hypertens.,* 2012; 30(3): 543-50.

Reviewed by:

Prof YK Seedat, M.D. (NU Irel); PhD (Med Sci) (hc) (UDW); MD (hc) (Univ Free State); FRSSAf; Hon FCM (SA); FRCP (London); FRCP (Irel); FACP; FCP (SA); FACC, FCCP ; FCPS (PAK); FICA Fellow of the University of KwaZulu Natal, Nelson R Mandela School of Medicine, Faculty of Health Sciences, University of Kwa Zulu Natal. Tel: +27 31 266 1501; Fax: + 2786 665 3216. E-mail: seedaty1@ukzn.ac.za. Email: seedaty1@gmail.com

Dr AS Uys (Ph.D.), Junior Subject Specialist, Hypertension in Africa Research Team (HART), Faculty of Health Sciences, North-West University, Potchefstroom Campus. Tel: +27 18 299 2400; Fax: +27 18 2991053. E-mail: lisa.uys@nwu.ac.za

In: Substance Abuse
Editor: Jeffrey Raines

ISBN: 978-1-63321-949-6

Chapter 6

ALCOHOL CONSUMPTION AND ALCOHOLISM MORTALITY IN RUSSIA

Y. E. Razvodovsky*
Grodno State Medical University, Grodno, Belarus

Background: Alcohol is increasingly implicated in the mortality crisis observed in Russia since the collapse of the communist system.

Objective: The aim of this study was to examine the aggregate-level relation between the alcohol consumption and alcoholism mortality rates in Russia.

Method: Age-standardized sex-specific male and female alcoholism mortality data for the period 1970-2005 and data on overall alcohol consumption were analyzed by means ARIMA (autoregressive integrated moving average) time series analysis.

Results: Alcohol consumption was significantly associated with both male and female alcoholism mortality rates: a 1 liter increase in overall alcohol consumption would result in a 23.1% increase in the male alcoholism mortality rate and in 27.1% increase in the female mortality rate.

Conclusions: The findings from the present study have important implications in regards alcohol-related mortality prevention indicating that a restrictive alcohol policy can be considered as an effective measure of prevention in countries with higher rate of alcohol consumption.

---

* Author for correspondence: Grodno State Medical University, 80 Gorky Street, Grodno 230009, Belarus. tel.: + 375 0152 70 18 84, fax: +375 0152 43 53 41, e-mail: razvodovsky@tut.by yury razvodovsky@mail.ru.

The harmful use of alcohol was identified as one of the major contributing factor to mortality globally (WHO 2011). Alcohol consumption caused a considerable disease burden in Europe: 6,1% of all the deaths could be attributed to this factor, with most of the burden in Eastern European region (Anderson & Baumberg, 2006; Moskalewicz, Razvodovsky, & Wieczorek, 2009). Its contribution is especially striking in Russia, where alcohol may be responsible for more than 30% of all deaths (Nemtsov, 2002), while a case-control study in Izhevsk suggests that 43% of all deaths of male in the 25-54 years age range were attributed to hazardous drinking (Leon, Saburova, Tomkins, Andreev, Kiryanov, McKee, & Shkolnikov, 2007). A more recent study in the Siberian city of Barnaul based on proxy information on alcohol consumption and other lifestyle factors from families of adults who died in 1990-2001 showed that alcohol was responsible for 59% of all male and 33% of all female deaths at ages 15-54 years (Zaridze, Maximovitch, Lazarev, Igitov, Boroda, Boreham, Boyle, Peto, & Boffetta, 2008). Collectively, this research evidence suggests that alcohol is a major contributor to premature deaths toll in Russia. Alcohol is also increasingly implicated in the massive fluctuations in Russian mortality over the past several decades, but the nature of this phenomenon is still poorly understood by a research community.

The most important cause of the health burden in Europe is alcohol dependence (alcoholism), accounting for more than 70% of the overall alcohol-attributable net mortality before age 65 (Anderson & Baumberg, 2006). Alcohol dependence is a maladaptive pattern of alcohol misuse, defined as a cluster of physiological, behavioral, and cognitive phenomena in which the use of alcohol takes on a much higher priority for a given individual than other behaviors that once had greater value, is one of the most severe consequences of problem drinking (ICD-10).

Russia has the highest prevalence of alcoholism in Europe, which may be explained by high overall population drinking and prevalence of irregular heavy drinking episodes (binge drinking) (Nemtsov & Razvodovsky, 2008; Stickley, et al., 2007).

Overall, in 2005 close to 11 million people in Russia suffered from alcohol dependence (Anderson & Baumberg, 2006). This is a good reason to expect positive association between alcohol consumption and alcoholism mortality at the aggregate level in Russia. In present study we will test the hypothesis of the close aggregate level link between alcohol and alcoholism mortality in Russia using data on overall alcohol consumption and sex-specific alcoholism mortality rate between 1970 and 2005.

METHODS

Data

The data on age-adjusted sex-specific alcoholism mortality rates per 1000.000 of the population are taken from the Russian State Statistical Committee (*Rosstat*). The Rosstat's cause of death classification has undergone several changes in recent decades. Until 1988 the cause of death classification was based upon the Soviet nomenclature which had a limited number of causes of death in comparison with the International Classification of Diseases (ICD) system. From 1989-1998 Rosstat used a coding scheme that was based on ICD-9. From 1999 a new coding system based on ICD-10 was introduced. Rosstat issued a table of correspondence between its classification system and ICD-9 and ICD-10 and it has been claimed that the Russian system of coding is compatible with ICD codes.

Realizing the difficulties associated with measuring alcohol consumption at the population level in Russia, we employed an alternative measure of overall alcohol consumption relative to Nemtsov's estimates (Nemtsov, 2000). Estimation of alcohol consumption per capita was based on a set of indicator of alcohol-related harm which was adjusted for the effect of recorded alcohol consumption employing ARIMA (autoregressive integrated moving average) model (Razvodovsky, 2013b). More specifically, we calculated the level of unrecorded alcohol consumption as the difference between observed changes in the harm indicator and changes that would be expected on the bases of alcohol sales. The harm indicator series used was alcohol poisoning mortality rate because this indicator depends almost entirely on alcohol consumption (Babor, et al., 2010). It should be noted that in Russia the fatal alcohol poisoning rate is likely to be a good measure of heavy episodic drinking (Stickley, et al., 2007). Therefore, a common approach is to use the fatal alcohol poisoning rate as an indicator of binge drinking in these countries (Razvodovsky, 2009).

Statistical Analysis

To examine the relation between changes in the alcohol consumption and alcoholism mortality across the study period a time-series analysis was performed using the statistical package "Statistica". The dependent variables were the annual alcoholism mortality and the independent variable was aggregate overall alcohol consumption. Bivariate correlations between the raw data from two time-series can often be spurious due to common sources in the trends and due to autocorrelation (Norström & Skog, 2001). One way to reduce the risk of obtaining a spurious relation between two variables that have common trends is to remove these trends by means of a 'differencing' procedure, as expressed in formula:

$$\nabla x_t = x_t - x_{t-1}$$

This means that the annual changes '∇' in variable 'X' are analyzed rather than raw data. The process whereby systematic variation within a time series is eliminated before the examination of potential causal relationships is referred to as 'prewhitening'. This is subsequently followed an inspection of the cross-correlation function in order to estimate the association between the two prewhitened time series. It was Box and Jenkins (1976) who first proposed this particular method for undertaking a time series analysis and it is commonly referred to as ARIMA modeling. We used this model specification to estimate the relationship between the time series alcoholism mortality and alcohol consumption rates in this paper. In line with previous aggregate studies (Norström & Skog, 2011; Razvodovsky, 2012) we estimated semi-logarithmic models with logged output. The following model was estimated:

$$V LnM_t = a + I3 VA_t + VN_t$$

where V means that the series is differenced, M is alcoholism mortality rates, a indicates the possible trend in alcoholism mortality due to other factors than those included in the model, A is the alcohol consumption, β is the estimated regression parameter, and N is the noise term. The percentage increase in alcoholism mortality rate associated with a 1-litre increase in alcohol consumption is given by the expression: $(\exp(\beta_1)-1)*100$. The temporal structure of the error term was estimated by using autoregressive (AR) or moving average (MA) parameters in the model. A diagnostic test for residual correlation is given by the Box-Ljung Q-test, which indicates whether the model has been adequately fitted.

A change in aggregate level drinking is expected to have an immediate effect on acute forms of alcohol-related problems (such as fatal alcohol poisoning), as well as a long-term effect on chronic problems (liver cirrhosis) (Norström & Ramstedt, 2005). As alcoholism is attributed to the chronic rather from acute alcohol-related problems, we should expect that the alcoholism mortality response to changes in aggregate level alcohol consumption will be distributed over several years (Norström & Skog, 2011). In order to deal with the time-lag problem we inspected the cross-correlations between two time series at different lags.

RESULTS

According to official statistics, the male alcoholism mortality rate increased 1.6 times (from 44.0 to 72.3 per 1000.000 of population) and female mortality rate increased 2.3 times (from 7.5 to 17.5 per 1.000.000 of population) in Russia from 1970 to 2005. Across the whole period the male alcoholism mortality rate was 4.8 times higher than the female rate (51.3 vs. 10.8 per 1 000.000) with a rate ratio of 5.9 in 1970 decreasing to 2.8 by the 2005. The trends in the sex-specific alcoholism mortality rates are displayed in Figures 1. As can be seen, the pattern of alcoholism mortality for men and women was uniform. For both sexes the time series alcoholism mortality rates fluctuated greatly over the period: decreased from 1972 to 1976, increased from 1976 to 1981, decreased markedly from 1981 to 1983 (by 15.0% and 21.5% for men and women respectively), dropped sharply between 1984-1988 (4 times for men and 3.3 times for women), than started on an upward trend from 1988-1989, before jumping dramatically during 1992 to 1995 (4.9 times for men and 5.9 times for women). From 1995-1998 there was a fall in the rates before they again rising between 1998 and 2003 and than started to decrease in the most recent years.

Estimated alcohol consumption in Russia increased by 38.3% (from 12.0 to 16.6 litres per capita) between 1970 and 2005. The average per capita alcohol consumption figure was 13.2 litres with vodka being the drink overwhelmingly consumed. Estimates suggest that total alcohol consumption rose steadily between 1970 and 1980, decreased substantially from 1980 to 1984, fell sharply during Gorbachev's anti-alcohol campaign in the mid-1980s (between 1984 and 1987 alcohol consumption decreased by 44.3%), but then rose dramatically in the early 1990s to a temporary pick in 1994 – 17.3 litres. Following the repeal of state alcohol monopoly in 1992, the overall level of alcohol consumption grew to 16-17 litres per capita, the highest rate in the countries history.

The graphical evidence suggests that the temporal pattern of Russian alcoholism mortality for males and females fits closely with changes in estimated alcohol consumption and alcohol poisoning mortality (Figures 2,4,6,7).

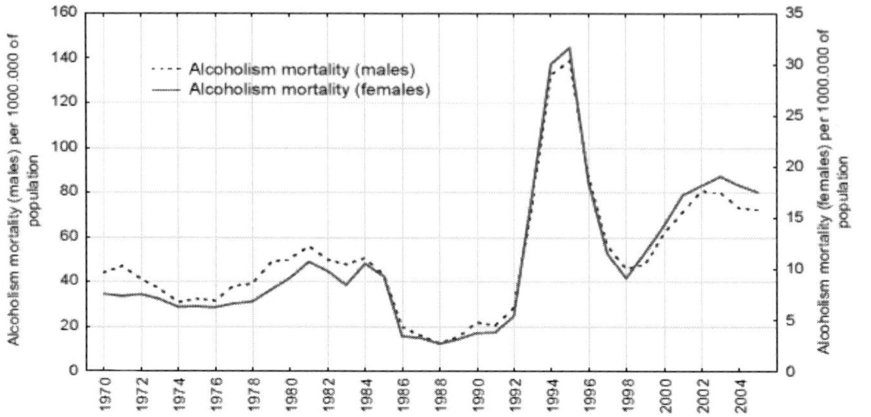

Figure 1. Trends in male and female alcoholism mortality rates in Russia between 1970 and 2005.

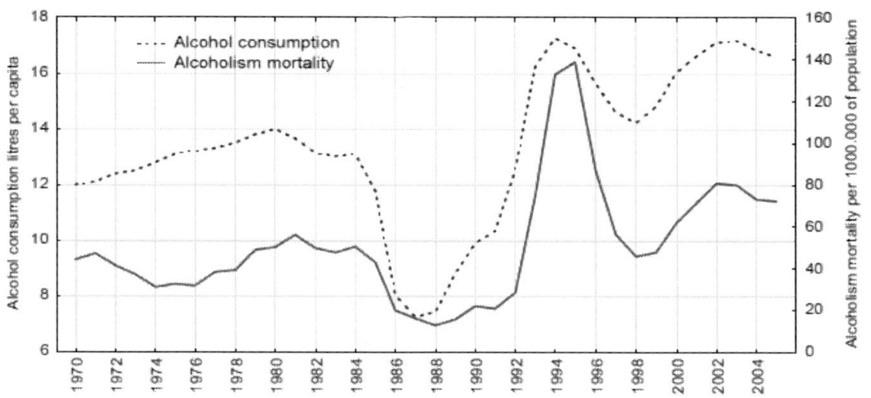

Figure 2. Trends in male alcoholism mortality rate and alcohol consumption per capita in Russia between 1970 and 2005.

As can be seen, there were sharp trends in the time series data across the study period. These trends were removed by means of a first-order differencing procedure (Figures 3,5). After prewhitening the cross-correlations between alcohol consumption and the alcoholism mortality time series were inspected. This indicated that there was a statistically significant cross-correlation between alcohol consumption and alcoholism mortality for males and females at lag zero (Table 1). The specification of the bivariate ARIMA model and outcome of the analyses are presented in Table 2.

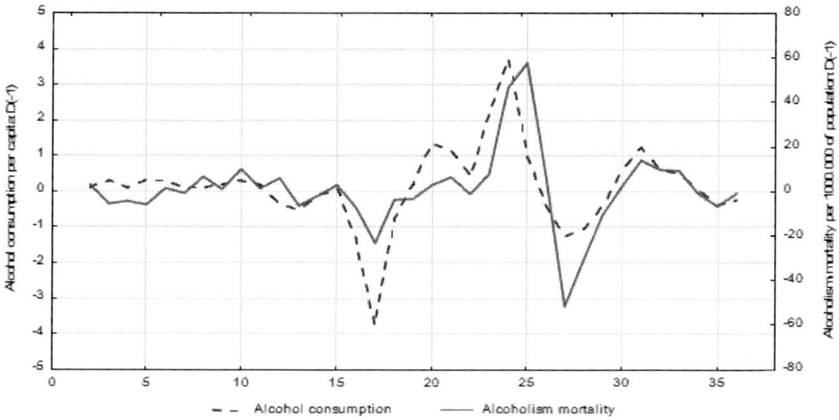

Figure 3. Trends in prewhitened male alcoholism mortality rate and alcohol consumption per capita in Russia between 1970 and 2005.

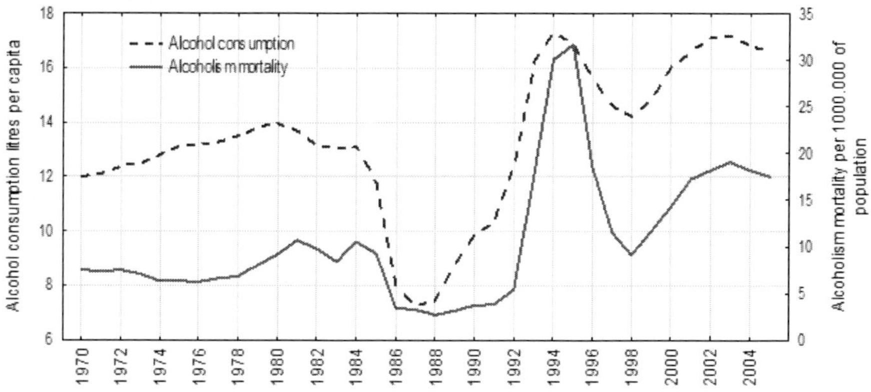

Figure 4. Trends in female alcoholism mortality rate and alcohol consumption per capita in Russia between 1970 and 2005.

According to the results, alcohol consumption is a statistically significant associated with both male and female alcoholism mortality rates, implying that a 1-litre increase in per capita consumption is associated with an increase in male mortality of 23.1% and female mortality of 27.1%.

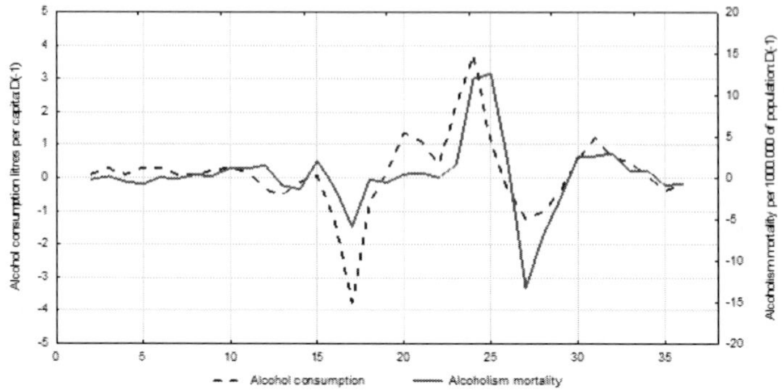

Figure 5. Trends in prewhitened female alcoholism mortality rate and alcohol consumption per capita in Russia between 1970 and 2005.

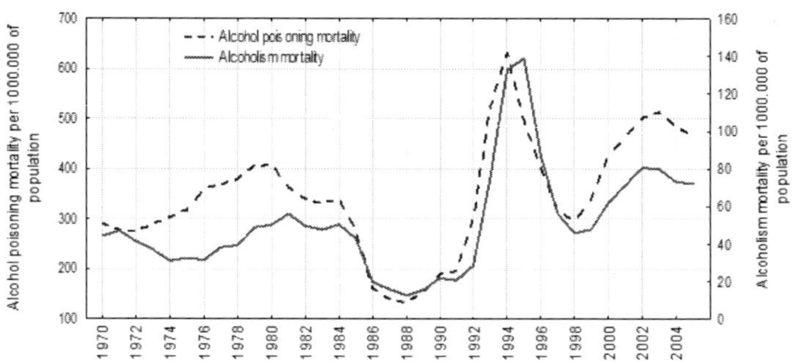

Figure 6. Trends in male alcoholism and alcohol poisoning mortality rates in Russia between 1970 and 2005.

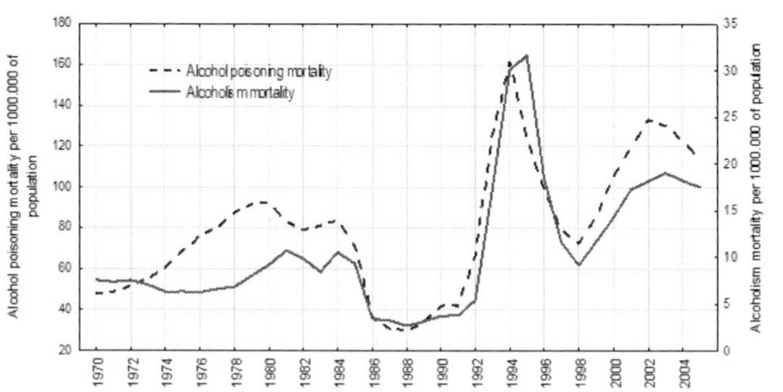

Figure 7. Trends in female alcoholism and alcohol poisoning mortality rates in Russia between 1970 and 2005.

Table 1. The results of cross-correlation analysis between prewhitened time series. Effects of alcohol consumption per capita on alcoholism mortality rates

	Mortality males		Mortality females	
Lag	r	SE	r	SE
-3	-0.214	0.177	-0.236	0.177
-2	0.256	0.174	0.192	0.174
	Mortality males		Mortality females	
Lag	r	SE	r	SE
-1	0.295	0.172	0.324	0.172
0	0.699	0.169	0.704	0.169
1	0.229	0.172	0.221	0.172
2	-0.156	0.174	-0.167	0.174
3	-0.298	0.177	-0.299	0.177

Table 2. Estimated effects (bivariate ARIMA model) of overall alcohol consumption on alcoholism mortality rates

Parameter	Model	Estim.	St.Err.	p
Alcoholism mortality males	0.1.1*	0.231	0.023	0.000
Alcoholism mortality females	0.1.1	0.271	0.024	0.000

DISCUSSION

Before considering the implications of this study, it is necessary to discuss alcohol policy issues. Despite the fact that alcohol-control policies remained a low priority for the Soviet government between 1950 and 1985, there were brief campaigns addressing alcohol-related problems in 1972 and 1982. In 1972 a resolution by the CPSU Central Committee "About the Measures Restricting Alcohol Consumption" was passed. The main emphasis was placed upon education and propaganda, although restrictions upon the sale of alcohol were also introduced. According to the document, the production of vodka and the number of shops selling it were to be cut. The beginning of the 1980s was marked by a new attempt to fight alcohol-related problems. The new Soviet leaders, Andropov first and then Chernenko, took a number of measures aimed at restricting alcohol availability. It was done within a campaign to strengthen public order and discipline in the workplace.

In May 1985 Gorbachev launched the anti-alcohol campaign in response to the high level of alcohol consumption and alcohol-related problems. The campaign restricted the hours of alcohol sales, increased the price of alcohol, implemented purchase quotas, imposed tougher legal sanctions on home production and destroyed most of the vineyards across a number of Soviet republics. Major social, political and economic changes throughout the 1990s caused dramatic growth in alcohol consumption. Increasing alcohol consumption was one of the outcomes of collapse following 'shock therapy' economic reforms that left a majority of the population below the poverty level. In January 1992 the state alcohol monopoly was abolished as part of the economic liberalization, which led to the fragmentation of the alcohol industry. In November 1995 Federal Council adopted a law "On State Regulation of the Production and Sale of Ethyl Spirit and Alcohol Products", which again established a state monopoly on the production and sale of alcohol products and sharply limited imports of such products in to Russia. In February 1996 changes in the law "On Excise Taxes" were adopted. In 1997 a State Dumas Committee reported concern about mass drunkenness and proclaimed the parliament to start drafting a federal law 'On the principles of alcohol policy in the Russian federation'. The government's measures during these years led to decreases in alcohol consumption and the improved quality of alcoholic beverages.

Understanding the reasons the substantial fluctuations in alcoholism mortality rate in Russia over recent decades is very important from a public health perspective. There is evidence that the alcoholism mortality trends in Russia influenced by the four major factors: the campaign addressing alcohol-related problems in 1972, the brief Andropov's anti-alcohol campaign in the early 1980s, Gorbachev's anti-alcohol campaign 1985-88, severe socioeconomic crisis imposed by rapid societal transformation in the early 1990s, financial crisis and worsening economic situation in 1998.

It is widely accepted that the overall level of alcohol consumption is an important determinant of alcohol-related mortality in a population (Anderson & Baumberg, 2006). This is particularly true in relation to Russia where Gorbachev's anti-alcohol campaign was associated with a rapid reduction in the level of alcoholism mortality, while increasing consumption in the transition period has been linked to dramatic rise in mortality rate. A fairly close aggregate-level match between alcohol consumption and alcoholism mortality during the Andropov's and Gorbachev's anti-alcohol campaigns may be use as evidence for the hypothesis suggesting that a restrictive alcohol policy can be considered as an effective measure of alcohol-related mortality prevention.

The increase in alcohol consumption has contributed to the dramatic rise in alcoholism deaths between 1992 and 1995. The increase of alcohol consumption in this period was to a great extent due to increase of alcohol availability following the repeal of the state alcohol monopoly in January 1992 (Nemtsov & Razvodovsky, 2008).

Studies from many countries have shown an inverse relationship between alcohol prices and alcohol drinking and concluded that affordability of alcohol is one of the most important predictor of alcohol-related mortality (Rabinovich, Brutscer, Tiessen & Reding, 2009; Wagenaar, Todler & Komro, 2010; Osterberg, 2011). The results from ecological regression suggest that lower vodka prices were associated with statistically significant increase in Russian total mortality (Treisman, 2010). It is obvious, therefore, that the increase in heavy drinking in Russia during transition, which triggered the dramatic rise in alcoholism mortality, resulted also from an increase in the affordability of vodka. With price liberalization in 1992, vodka became much more affordable because of a sharp drop in the price of vodka relative to those of other goods and alcoholic beverages including beer (Nemtsov, 2009). By 1995, the real price of vodka fell to its lowest point, after which point the real vodka price recovered until 1999, and then the affordability trend turned down again (Nemtsov & Razvodovsky, 2008). The relative fall in price for vodka explains an apparent paradox – an increase in alcohol consumption against a background of economic crisis.

It should be emphasized that alcohol consumption per capita in 1995 not exceeded the level recorded in the 2003, while mortality rates in the mid-1990s exceeded the level of early 2000s significantly. This means that some additional factors, most probably related to the consumption of vodka, came into play in the yearly 1990s. It seems plausible that mortality crisis in the mid-1990s was to a great extent due to changed alcohol consumption structure, when 80% of all alcohol in Russia was consumed in the form of spirit (Razvodovsky, 2010). In 2003, according to official alcohol sales figured, strong beverages accounted for 41,2% of the total consumption (Razvodovsky, 2010).

Another potential reason for the detrimental effect of alcohol in the yearly 1990s was deterioration of his quality. The declining quality of alcoholic beverages also is an important factor in alcoholism mortality crisis during this period. According to the data from the State Statistics Service, 21.6% to 45.1%

of vodka sold during that period did not meet quality standards (Nemtsov, 2009).

Some put forward the "demographic echo" or "catching-up" hypothesis suggesting that excess deaths in the early of 1990s are the deaths of alcohol dependent individuals, whose lives were saved during the anti-alcohol campaign (Brainerd & Cutler, 2005). The Russian alcoholism mortality crisis in the mid-1990s could therefore be the combined results of increase in availability/affordability of alcohol, deterioration of his quality, change in alcohol consumption structure, lagged "catch-up" mortality and reversion of the long-run trend.

There are several potential factors behind the decrease in alcohol consumption and alcoholism mortality rate between 1995 and 1998. They include better regulation of the alcohol market that may have resulted in a relative increase in prices for vodka compared to those for food products (Nemtsov, 2000). In this period the government affected the alcohol market through a struggle against production of illegal vodka. Thus, only in 1995, agencies of the Ministry of Internal Affairs closed more than 2.300 underground workshops producing contrafactual vodka (Nemtsov, 2009). It also appears likely that changes in the structure of alcohol consumption (switch from predominant consumption of spirits to the consumption of beer) have had a positive impact on bringing down the death rate from alcoholism in Russia between 1995 and 1998. Another possible factor in the decrease in alcohol consumption was impoverishment and decrease in the purchasing capacity of the population due to unpaid or delayed salaries (Nemtsov, Davydov & Razvodovsky, 2009). An important factor in the decrease in mortality from alcoholism that began in 1995 may have been the excess deaths in the cohort of alcoholics in previous years. The subsequent rise in alcohol consumption and alcoholism mortality rates from 1998 may be associated with the increase in affordability of alcohol (Nemtsov & Razvodovsky, 2008).

The results of present study are important because despite the growing literature on alcohol and mortality in Russia there has been no prior time-series analysis of alcohol and alcoholism mortality in the country. According to the results of time-series analysis there was a positive and statistically significant effect of per capita alcohol consumption on alcoholism mortality in Russia at lag zero. These findings clearly indicate that population drinking and alcohol-related mortality are positively related phenomena in Russia. It is important to point out, that the size of the bivariate association between alcohol consumption and alcoholism mortality rates for women is higher than for men. It seems plausible that women are more sensitive to an increased risk of alcohol-related mortality even at the relatively low levels of alcohol consumption. More specifically, women appear to suffer alcohol-related physical and psychical illnesses at lower levels of exposure to alcohol and to a greater degree than men. Further, there are some indications that Russian women are drinking more now which are likely to be a factor in the narrowing of the male-female alcohol-related mortality rate ratio. In his recent study, based on the results of RLMS Perlman (2010) highlighted that frequent heavy drinking almost doubled among women between 1994 and 2004.

It should be emphasis that the results suggest a fairly quick response of alcoholism mortality rates to changes in population drinking. The instantaneous response in mortality rates from chronic alcohol-related diseases seem quite surprising when considering the long latency period at the individual level. There are several reasonable explanations for this seeming inconsistency. It is well recognized, that alcoholism mortality is the classical indicator of harmful effect of chronic heavy drinking and also associated with episodic heavy drinking, thus reflecting the acute and chronic consequences of heavy drinking (Babor et al., 2010). Therefore, the contemporaneous association between the two variables may support the point that binge drinking is an important determinant of alcoholism mortality in Russia. Further, Norström and Skog (2001) argue that in a population there exists a reservoir of heavy drinkers who are near the critical threshold-value for a dying from chronic alcohol-related consequences. In case when these high risk individuals increase alcohol consumption during a given year, they will exceed the threshold value and die from alcohol-related diseases. This is the reason why the immediate impact on chronic alcohol related mortality can be registered from marked changes in aggregate consumption.

There is assumption that alcohol dependent individuals might be particularly sensitive to reduction in affordability of alcohol because: (i) they consume nearly 80% of all alcohol, (ii) they spend a great amount of budget on alcohol, (iii) they usually have a low income (Wagenaar, Todler & Komro, 2010). Indeed, the results from present study suggest a close aggregate-level link between alcohol availability and alcoholism mortality and support the idea that high availability of alcohol is associated with increasing in binge drinking and that heavy drinkers are sensitive to availability of alcohol.

Before concluding, several potential limitations of this study must be mentioned. In particular, estimating unrecorded consumption of alcohol in Russia is a challenge, because of the diversity of this fraction of alcohol consumption that ranges from samogon through legal non-beverage alcohol (medical tincture) to counterfeit vodka produced from technical spirits

(Stickley, Razvodovsky & McKee, 2009). We relied on estimated overall level of alcohol consumption across the period. However, the accuracy of assessment of actual alcohol consumption using indirect methods depends significantly on whether the level of alcohol consumption is the only factor influencing the index chosen as the indicator of alcohol-related problems. This represents an essential drawback of such methods, because many other factors influence the level of alcohol-related problems (Razvodovsky, 2010).

Some researchers argue that alcohol unlikely provide the universal explanation for the mortality fluctuations during 1980s in Russia (Wasserman, Varnik & Eklund, 1994). They believe that the decrease in mortality rate in Russia in the mid-1980s could have been related to the political and social liberalization during the period known as "perestroika", which gave rise to social optimism and new hope. However, in his seminal work Nemtsov (2003) argue that “so-called national optimism was more likely a projection of the emotions of the more intelligent sections of the population than of the Russian population as a whole”.

Further, there was the risk of omitted variable bias in this work. While some experts have underlined the importance of binge drinking as the main reason for the alcohol-related mortality crisis in Russia in the 1990s, other has called attention to the effect of the psychosocial distress of economic and political reforms (Leon & Shkolnikov, 2005). The collapse of the USSR in 1991 and growth of consumer prices in 1992 were followed by declining of living standards majority of population. However, close aggregate level association between alcohol consumption and alcoholism mortality rates strongly supports an alcohol related hypothesis and suggests that rather that playing major causal role, psychosocial distress may represent a confounding factor.

Finally, it is likely that increase in alcoholism mortality in Russia in the mid-1990s is a consequence of deterioration in the quality of health care system, following the collapse of Soviet Union in late 1991. As command economy collapsed, the public health system faced a financial crisis. Left without proper funding, health care system was unable to maintain needed level of medical care (Brainerd & Cutler, 2005). A process of destruction of the narcological service that began in 1989 continued in the early 1990s (Nemtsov, 2009). Furthermore, in 1991 the Law on the Militia has been adopted, which called for the closing of all Medical-Labor clinics by June 1994 (Nemtsov, 2000). As a result, up to 150.000 of the most advanced alcoholics were released. However, the importance of these factors is clearly modest compared to alcohol, thus limiting their potential influence.

In conclusion, this is the first time-series analysis of overall level of alcohol consumption and alcoholism mortality rate in Russia, which has shown that population drinking is the strong predictor of alcoholism mortality rate at the aggregate level. The outcomes of this study provide indirect support for the hypothesis that unfavorable mixture of higher overall level of alcohol consumption and binge drinking pattern is a major risk factor for alcoholism mortality in Russia. The findings from the present study have important implications as regards alcohol-related mortality prevention indicating that a restrictive alcohol policy can be considered as an effective measure of prevention in countries where higher rate of alcohol consumption per capita.

Conflict of Interest

None declared.

References

Anderson, P., & Baumberg, B. (2006). *Alcohol in Europe*. London: Institute of Alcohol Studies.

Andreev, E.M., Nolte, E., Shkolnikov, V.M., Varavicova, E., & McKee. M. (2003). The evolving pattern of avoidable mortality in Russia. *International Journal of Epidemiology*, 32, 437-446.

Babor TF, Caetano R, Casswell S, Edwards G, Giesbrecht N, Graham K. et al. Alcohol: No Ordinary Commodity: *Research and Public Policy.* Oxford University Press. 2010.

Bobak, M., McKee, M., Rose, R., Marmot. M., 1999. Alcohol consumption in a sample of the Russian population. *Addiction.* 94, 857–866.

Box, G.E.P., Jenkins, G.M., 1976. Time Series Analysis: forecasting and control. London. Holden-Day Inc.

Brainerd, E., & Cutler, D. M. (2005). Autopsy on an Empire: Understanding mortality in Russia and the former Soviet Union. *Journal of Economic Perspective*, 19(1), 107-130.

Leon, D. A., & Shkolnikov, V. M. (2005). Social stress and the Russian mortality crisis. *Journal of American Medical Association,* 279, 790-91.

Leon, D., Saburova, L., Tomkins, S., Andreev E., Kiryanov N., McKee M. & Shkolnikov V. (2007). Hazardous alcohol drinking and premature mortality in Russia: a population based case-control study. *Lancet*, 369, 2001-2009.

Moskalewicz, J., Razvodovsky, Y. & Wieczorek, P. (2009). East-West disparities in alcohol-related harm within European Union. Paper presented at the KBS Annual Conference, Copenhagen, 1-5 June, 2009.

Nemtsov A.V. Alcohol-related human losses in Russia in the 1980s and 1990s. *Addiction*, 2002;97: 1413-1425.

Nemtsov AV. Alcohol History of Russia: The Latest Period. – M.: Book House "Librokom", 2009.

Nemtsov, A.V. & Razvodovsky, Y.E. (2008). Alcohol situation in Russia, 1980-2005. *Social and Clinical Psychiatry*, 2, 52-60.

Nemtsov, A.V., 2000. Estimates of total alcohol consumption in Russia, 1980-1994. *Drug and Alcohol Dependence*. 58, 133–142.

Nemtsov, A.V., Davydov, K.E., Razvodovsky, Y.E. (2009). Comparative analysis of the alcohol situation in Belarus and Russia. *Narcologia*, 1, 52-60.

Nicholson, A., Bobak, M., Murphy, M., Rose, R. & Marmot, M. (2005). Alcohol consumption and increased mortality in Russian men and women: a cohort study based on the mortality of relatives. *Bulletin of the World Health Organization*, 83, 812-819.

Norström, T., 1989. The use of aggregate data in alcohol epidemiology. British *Journal of Addiction*. 84, 969–977.

Norström, T., Ramstedt, M., 2005. Mortality and population drinking: a review of the literature. *Drug and Alcohol Review*. 24, 537–547.

Norström, T., Razvodovsky, Y., 2010. Per capita alcohol consumption and alcohol-related harm in Belarus, 1970–2005. *European Journal of Public Health*. 20(5), 564-568.

Norström, T., Skog, O.J., 2001. Alcohol and mortality: methodological and analytical issue in aggregate analysis. *Addiction*. 96, 5–17.

Osterberg, E.L. (2011). Alcohol tax changes and the use of alcohol in Europe. *Drug and Alcohol Review*, 30 (2), 124-129.

Perlman, F.J.A. (2010). Drinking in transition: trends in alcohol consumption in Russia 1994–2004. *BMC Public Health*, 10, 691.

Rabinovich, L., Brutscer, P.B., de Vries, H., Tiessen, J., Clift, J., & Reding, A. (2009). *The affordability of alcohol beverages in the European Union*. RAND Corporation.

Razvodovsky YE. Noncommercial Alcohol in Belarus. LAP LAMBERT Academic Publishing GmbH & Co. KB, Saarbrucken. – 2012.

Razvodovsky YE. Unrecorded alcohol consumption: quantitative methods of estimation. *Alcoholism*. 2010: 46(1): 15-24.

Razvodovsky, Y. E. (2009). Alcohol consumption and mortality in Russia and Belarus. *Medical News*, 16, 41-46.

Razvodovsky, Y.E. (2010). Beverage specific alcohol sale and mortality in Russia. *Alcoholism*, 46(2), 63-75.

Razvodovsky, Y.E., 2012. Estimation of alcohol attributable fraction of mortality in Russia. *Adicciones*. 24(3), 247–252.

Razvodovsky, Y.E., 2013. Estimation of the level of alcohol consumption in Russia. *ICAP Periodic Review Drinking and Culture*. 8, 6-10.

Rehm J., Room R., Monteiro M., Gmel G., Graham K., Rehn N., Sempost C.T., Jernigan D. Alcohol as a risk factor for global burden of disease. *Eur. Addict. Res.*, 2003;9:157-164.

Rehm, J., Sulkowska, U., Manczuk, M., Boffeta, P., Powles, J., Popova, S. & Zatonski, W. (2007). Alcohol accounts for a high proportion of premature mortality in central and Eastern Europe. *International Journal of Epidemiology*, 36, 458-67.

Rehm, J., Taylor, B. & Patra, J. (2006). Volume of alcohol consumption, pattern of drinking and burden of disease in the European region. *Addiction*, 101, 1086-95.

Stickley, A., Leinsalu, M., Andreew, E., Razvodovsky, Y.E., Vagero, D., McKee, M., 2007. Alcohol poisoning in Russia and the countries in the European part of the former Soviet Union, 1970-2002. *European Journal of Public Health*. 17(5), 444–449.

Stickley, A., Razvodovsky, Y., McKee, M., 2009. Alcohol and mortality in Russia: A historical perspective. *Public Health*. 123, 20-26.

Treisman, D. (2010). Death and price. The political economy of Russia's alcohol crisis. *Economics of Transition,* 18 (2), 281-331.

Wagenaar, A.C., Todler, A.L., & Komro, K.A. (2010). Effects of alcohol tax and price policies on morbidity and mortality: a systematic review. *American Journal of Public Health*, 100 (11), 2270-2277.

Wasserman, D., Varnik, A., & Eklund, G. (1994). Male suicides and alcohol consumption in the former USSR. *Acta Psychiatrica Scandinavica*, 89, 306-313.

WHO. (2011).Global status report alcohol and health. Switzerland. *WHO Press.*

Zaridze, D., Maximovitch, D., Lazarev, A., Igitov, V., Boroda, A., Boreham, J., Boyle, P., Peto, R. & Boffetta, P. (2008). Alcohol poisoning is a main determinant of recent mortality trends in Russia: evidence from a detailed analysis of mortality statistics and autopsies. *International Journal of Epidemiology*, 38, 143153.

In: Substance Abuse
Editor: Jeffrey Raines
ISBN: 978-1-63321-949-6

Chapter 7

Oxycodone: Abuse Prevention Especially in Cancer Patients

Yuko Kanbayashi, Ph.D. [1, 2*]
and Toyoshi Hosokawa, M.D., Ph.D. [2, 3]
Departments of [1]Hospital Pharmacy
[2]Pain Treatment & Palliative Care Unit, University Hospital
[3]Department of Pain Management & Palliative Care Medicine,
Graduate School of Medical Science,
Kyoto Prefectural University of Medicine, Kyoto, Japan

Abstract

Reformulated OxyContin® (oxycodone-HCl controlled release) tablets became available in the United States in August 2010. The original formulation of the OxyContin® used a delivery system that did not prevent crushing and dissolving of the tablet.

Cancer patients experience three kinds of pain: (1) cancer related pain, (2) pain due to their treatments (such as chemotherapy induced peripheral neuropathy), and (3) chronic non-cancer pain (such as post herpetic neuralgia). However, physicians sometimes dispense similar opioid prescriptions for patients with (2) and (3) according to the three-step analgesic ladder framework of the World Health Organization, as

* Corresponding Author: Yuko Kanbayashi PhD. Department of Hospital Pharmacy, Kyoto Prefectural University of Medicine Kawaramachi Hirokoji, Kamigyo-ku, Kyoto 602-8566, Japan. E-mail: ykokanba@koto.kpu-m.ac.jp; Tel: +81-75-251-5865; Fax: +81-75-251-5863.

well as for patients with (1). Thus, addiction or abuse of opioids in Japan has become a problem, especially in cancer survivors. Moreover, oxycodone consumption is increasing in Japan, as patients can be started on a low dose (5 mg tablet) that has few adverse effects.

This review discusses medical uses, potential adverse effects of oxycodone, and further reviews of recent pharmacotherapy for the prevention of its abuse, especially in cancer patients.

Keywords: Addiction, OxyContin, analgesics, drug administration routes, drug reformulation, opiate addiction, opiate dependence, opioid analgesics, oxycodone, prescription drug abuse, tamper resistant drugs

INTRODUCTION

Chronic non-cancer pain is a disabling chronic condition with a high prevalence rate around the world. Opioids are routinely prescribed for the treatment of chronic pain. During the last two decades, there has been a dramatic increase in the use of strong opioids for chronic non-cancer pain [1, 2]. As a result, many patients with chronic non-cancer pain now receive high doses of long-acting opioids on a long-term basis. Even so, chronic pain and related disability rates remain high, with the majority of chronic non-cancer pain patients dissatisfied with their treatments. These increasing trends in opioid use have also been accompanied by a steep increase in abuse, misuse, and both fatal and non-fatal overdoses involving the prescribed opioids [1-6]. Prescription opioid-related harm is a complex, multifactorial issue that requires a multifaceted solution [1-7]. In this respect, formulations of opioid analgesics designed to resist or deter abuse may be a useful component of a comprehensive opioid risk minimization program. One of the formulations under development is abuse-resistant opioids. In these agents, a physical barrier is created that prevents the user from tampering with the formulation. In contrast, formulations classified as abuse-deterrent opioids are not necessarily resistant to tampering, but do contain substances designed to make the formulation less attractive to abusers [1, 8].

An example of these changes is the reformulated OxyContin® (oxycodone-HCl controlled release) tablets (ORF) that were redesigned and approved for use in the United States in August 2010 [9]. The original formulation of OxyContin® tablets (OC) used a delivery system that was not resistant to crushing and dissolving, thereby making it easier to abuse [9-12].

Along with OC abuse, oral oxycodone consumption has also been increasing in conjunction with the decreased consumption of morphine in Japan. One of the possible reasons for this change is that patients can easily be started on a low dose (5 mg tablet) of the drug, as it has few adverse effects [13].

This review discusses the medical uses and potential adverse effects of oxycodone, and further reviews of recent pharmacotherapy for the prevention of its abuse, especially in cancer patients.

MEDICAL USES FOR CANCER PAIN

Pain is a highly prevalent and distressing symptom, and can be a major health problem that patients with cancer have to deal with. The incidence of pain in those receiving active treatment ranges from 24% to 60%, while it approaches 58% to 69% in patients with advanced cancer, and 33% in patients after curative therapy [14-16]. Cancer is also no longer considered a "terminal disease", as 50% to 65% of patients survive for at least 2 years. The number of cancer survivors is increasing all over the world, especially in developed countries. In Japan, the number of survivors is also gradually increasing. Unfortunately, many cancer survivors still experience chronic pain, which often leads to psychological distress due to decreased activity, motivation, and personal interactions, that can lead to an overall poor quality of life.

In 1986, the World Health Organization (WHO) designed a three-step analgesic ladder for use as a basic approach in treating cancer pain. This three-step treatment, which starts with nonopioid analgesics followed by weak opioids and then proceeds to strong opioids, has been used to guide the management of pain among cancer patients [14, 17]. Subsequently, the Agency for Healthcare Policy and Research (AHCPR) in 1994 [18], the American Pain Society (APS) in 2005 [19], and the National Comprehensive Care Network (NCCN) in 2000 and 2009 [14, 20, 21] further established and/or revised these guidelines to help with cancer pain management. During this time, there has been an increase in the availability of opioids, with adoption of the national policies developed to address cancer pain. In all of the recommended guidelines put forth for the treatment of cancer pain, opioids continue to be an important part of a physician's armamentarium.

Though opioids continue to be the mainstay for cancer pain treatments, there has been a paucity of literature proving the efficacy of its long-term use. Moreover, there is a growing concern about opioid abuse and addiction in cancer pain patients along with other adverse consequences similar to what has been seen in non-cancer pain patients [2-8, 14, 22].

Based upon the population studied and the criteria used, relevant literature indicates that the prevalence of addiction to opioids varies from 0% to 7.7% in cancer patients [14, 23].

Furthermore, there remains a concern regarding the long-term use of opioids in patients at risk for substance abuse and/or diversion. In addition, the use of opioids for chronic non-cancer pain continues to be debated due to worries about the adverse effects, the lack of long-term efficacy, and a growing concern over the abuse and addiction to opioids. With improved survival, the challenge of dealing with chronic cancer pain and pain among survivors has now become an issue. Despite the widespread use of opioids for cancer pain, there is little published evidence that supports their long-term efficacy [14, 24].

Additionally, when faced with complaints of uncontrolled pain, clinicians must consider a differential diagnosis of tolerance, disease progression, addiction, pseudoaddiction, chemical coping, or even criminal behavior [25-27]. Survivors who have chronic stable pain need to be treated with time-scheduled sustained-release (long-acting) opioids, and not by breakthrough pain-contingent immediate-release opioids.

The NCCN Guidelines for Adult Cancer Pain (available at NCCN org.) recommend using a detailed patient's evaluation or other tools to screen survivors for risk factors of aberrant opioid use or diversion of their pain medication [28]. Cancer patients experience three kinds of pain: (1) cancer related pain, (2) pain due to their treatments (such as chemotherapy induced peripheral neuropathy) [29-31], and (3) chronic non-cancer pain (such as post herpetic neuralgia) [32, 33]. However physicians sometimes dispense similar opioid prescriptions for patients with (2) and (3) according to the three-step analgesic ladder framework of the World Health Organization as well as for patients with (1). Thus, addiction or abuse of opioids in Japan has become a problem, especially in the cancer survivors.

OXYCODONE: ABUSE PREVENTION

Oxycodone Hydrochloride

Oxycodone hydrochloride is the hydrochloride salt of oxycodone, a methylether of oxymorphone and a semisynthetic opioid agonist with analgesic and antitussive properties. Since oxycodone binds to the mu-receptors in the central nervous system (CNS), it can mimic the effects of endogenous opiates. Depending on the dosage and variations in individual metabolism, this agent may cause euphoria, anxiolysis, miosis, sedation, physical dependence, constipation, and respiratory depression, in addition to its analgesia and depressive effect on the cough center in the medulla [34].

Oxycodone is primarily metabolized in the liver by cytochrome P450 3A4 and 2D6 to noroxycodone through N-demethylation and to oxymorphone through O-demethylation [35, 36]. Although oxymorphone is a minor metabolite, it is 100 times more potent than oxycodone. Noroxycodone is the most abundant metabolite, but it is relatively inactive and has been reported to be 3–4 times less potent than oxycodone [37]. Oxycodone and its two primary metabolites also undergo reductive metabolism to form α- and β-oxycodol, α- and β-noroxycodol, and α- and β-oxymorphol. Oxycodone and noroxycodone are excreted unchanged in the urine, whereas oxymorphone is excreted only as the glucuronide metabolite. Lalovic et al. [35] have reported on the pharmacokinetics of both the oxidative and reduction metabolic pathways. The concentrations of metabolites were found to be dose-dependent, with the N-demethylation pathway providing the major metabolite. Oxidative metabolites comprised nearly 50% of the oxycodone dose excreted in urine, with only 10% as the unchanged drug and 18% as the reduced metabolites.

New Formulation of ORF

Experienced abusers and recreational users commonly employ alternate routes of administration (e.g., injecting and snorting) in order to abuse oral opioid medications [9, 38-40]. Among these users, data suggest that the incidence of injecting oral oxycodone products ranges from 22 to 59%, while the incidence of intranasal administration ranges from 45 to 92% [39, 40]. In order to abuse the drug via these routes, users first need to tamper with and accelerate the release of the active opioid, which results in a high blood concentration as compared with oral delivery [41]. To reduce this abuse and misuse, particularly the injecting and snorting of these oral opioid analgesics, pharmaceutical manufacturers have begun to develop tamper-deterrent products [42].

It was originally thought there was reduced abuse liability for OC owing to the slow release of the oxycodone from the formulation, thereby resulting in a lack of an immediate rush or high [43, 44]. However, no abuse liability studies of the product that support this have been published. Furthermore, oxycodone extended release (ER) exhibits a biphasic absorption pattern that may lead to an initial immediate release of more than 30% of the oxycodone dose [43, 45]. It was later noted that the potency and formulation of the oxycodone ER may have actually made it more attractive for abuse. Furthermore, the controlled release formulation is easily compromised, and the original safety warning may have inadvertently provided this information to abusers [43, 44]. Current ER opioid formulations remain a frequent target for drug abusers, as the products can be easily compromised in order to release the full opioid dose [43, 46]. For example, the rate of absorption of oxycodone ER can be increased through various means of tampering such as chewing, crushing, snorting, or dissolving the product in water and then injecting the solution [43, 47]. In April 2010, the Food and Drug Administration (FDA) approved ORF, as it was designed to help discourage misuse and abuse of the medication [43, 48]. The original OC used a delivery system that allowed it to be crushed or dissolved. In 2009, it was estimated that nearly 1.7 million Americans had used the previous OC formulation nonmedically during the previous year [43, 49]. Although the new formulation is supposed to reduce misuse and abuse relative to the previous version, this will remain unknown until the results of the required post-market study are available [43, 50].

The FDA did determine that the ORF has abuse-deterrent properties. Therefore, the FDA approved new labeling that indicated that the product has physical and chemical properties that are expected to make abuse by injection difficult, thereby reducing abuse via the intranasal route. The FDA determined there were safety issues with the original OC and thus it was withdrawn from the market. As a result, the agency will not accept or approve any new abbreviated drug applications (generics) that rely upon the approval of the same product.

In addition, the FDA approved ORF manufactured by the Purdue Pharma Company provided it would perform post-marketing surveillance concerning the abuse deterrent effect. Initial results have suggested that abuses, misuse, and the risk of the diversion have been found to decrease in comparison with the original OC [51-54]. However, other studies have shown that while the abuse-deterrent formulation can successfully reduce the abuse of a specific drug, it also can generate an unanticipated outcome. In these cases, there is replacement of the abuse-deterrent formulation with an alternative opioid medication and heroin, which poses a much greater overall risk to public health than OC [55, 56]. Therefore, Cicero et al. concluded that these new abuse-deterrent formulations may not be the "magic bullets" that many hoped they would be in solving the growing problem of opioid abuse [55]. This issue will need to be investigated in detail in the future.

Conclusion

Similar to problems in other countries, addiction and abuse of opioids is becoming a problem in Japan, especially in cancer survivors. In order to prevent abuse in Japan, it is my opinion that policy changes requiring patients to switch to Reformulated OxyContin® tablets be enacted.

References

[1] Bannwarth B. Will abuse-deterrent formulations of opioid analgesics be successful in achieving their purpose? *Drugs.* 2012 10; 72:1713-23.

[2] Sehgal N, Colson J, Smith HS. Chronic pain treatment with opioid analgesics: benefits versus harms of long-term therapy. *Expert Rev. Neurother.* 2013; 13:1201-20.

[3] Sehgal N, Manchikanti L, Smith HS. Prescription opioid abuse in chronic pain: a review of opioid abuse predictors and strategies to curb opioid abuse. *Pain Physician.* 2012; 15 (3 Suppl):ES67-92.

[4] Stanos SP, Bruckenthal P, Barkin RL. Strategies to reduce the tampering and subsequent abuse of long-acting opioids: potential risks and benefits of formulations with physical or pharmacologic deterrents to tampering. *Mayo. Clin. Proc.* 2012; 87:683-94.

[5] Schneider MF, Bailey JE, Cicero TJ, Dart RC, Inciardi JA, Parrino M, Muñoz A. Integrating nine prescription opioid analgesics and/or four signal detection systems to summarize statewide prescription drug abuse in the United States in 2007. *Pharmacoepidemiol Drug Saf.* 2009 18: 778-790.

[6] Atluri S, Akbik H, Sudarshan G. Prevention of opioid abuse in chronic non-cancer pain: an algorithmic, evidence based approach. *Pain Physician.* 2012; 15 (3 Suppl):ES177-89.

[7] Sekhon R, Aminjavahery N, Davis CN Jr, Roswarski MJ, Robinette C. Compliance with opioid treatment guidelines for chronic non-cancer pain (CNCP) in primary care at a Veterans Affairs Medical Center (VAMC). *Pain Med.* 2013; 14:1548-56.

[8] Webster L, St Marie B, McCarberg B, Passik SD, Panchal SJ, Voth E. Current status and evolving role of abuse-deterrent opioids in managing patients with chronic pain. *J. Opioid. Manag.* 2011; 7:235-45.

[9] Perrino PJ, Colucci SV, Apseloff G, Harris SC. Pharmacokinetics, tolerability, and safety of intranasal administration of reformulated OxyContin (®) tablets compared with original OxyContin (®) tablets in healthy adults. *Clin. Drug Investig.* 2013; 33:441-9.

[10] Havens JR, Leukefeld CG, Deveaugh-Geiss AM, Coplan P, Chilcoat HD. The impact of a reformulation of extended-release oxycodone designed to deter abuse in a sample of prescription opioid abusers. *Drug Alcohol Depend.* 2014; 139:9-17.

[11] Harris SC, Perrino PJ, Smith I, Shram MJ, Colucci SV, Bartlett C, Sellers EM. Abuse potential, pharmacokinetics, pharmacodynamics, and safety of intranasally administered crushed oxycodone HCl abuse-deterrent controlled-release tablets in recreational opioid users. *J. Clin. Pharmacol.* 2014; 54:468-77.

[12] Sellers EM, Perrino PJ, Colucci SV, Harris SC. Attractiveness of reformulated OxyContin(R) tablets: assessing comparative preferences and tampering potential. *J. Psychopharmacol.* 2013; 27:808-16.

[13] Yoshimoto T, Hisada A, Yomiya K, Tomiyasu S, Hasegawa T, Murakami S, Matoba M. Efficacy and safety of compound oxycodone injection for cancer pain relief-a multicenter survey of prescriptions. *Gan To Kagaku Ryoho.* 2010; 37:871-8. [Article in Japanese]

[14] Koyyalagunta D, Bruera E, Solanki DR, Nouri KH, Burton AW, Toro MP, Bruel BM, Manchikanti L. A systematic review of randomized trials on the effectiveness of opioids for cancer pain. *Pain Physician.* 2012 ;15 (3 Suppl):ES39-58.

[15] van den Beuken-van Everdingen MH, de Rijke JM, Kessels AG, Schouten HC, van Kleef M, Patijn J. Prevalence of pain in patients with cancer: A systematic review of the past 40 years. *Ann. Oncol.* 2007; 18:1437-1449.

[16] Glare PA, Davies PS, Finlay E, Gulati A, Lemanne D, Moryl N, Oeffinger KC, Paice JA, Stubblefield MD, Syrjala KL. Pain in cancer survivors. *J. Clin. Oncol.* 2014; 32:1739-47.

[17] World Health Organization. Cancer Pain Relief. World Health Organization; Geneva, Switzerland; 1986.

[18] Management of cancer pain guideline overview. Agency for Healthcare Policy and Research Rockville, Maryland. *J. Natl. Med. Assoc.* 1994; 86:571-573, 634.

[19] Gordon DB, Dahl JL, Miaskowski C, McCarberg B, Todd KH, Paice JA, Lipman AG, Bookbinder M, Sanders SH, Turk DC, Carr DB. American Pain Society recommendations for improving the quality of acute and cancer pain management: American Pain Society Quality of Care Task Force. *Arch. Intern. Med.* 2005; 165:1574-1580.

[20] Benedetti C, Brock C, Cleeland C, Coyle N, Dube JE, Ferrell B, Hassenbusch S, 3rd, Janjan NA, Lema MJ, Levy MH, Loscalzo MJ, Lynch M, Muir C, Oakes L, O'Neill A, Payne R, Syrjala KL, Urba S, Weinstein SM. NCCN Practice Guidelines for Cancer Pain. *Oncology (Williston Park)* 2000; 14:135-150.

[21] Network NCC. NCCN Clinical Practice Guidelines in Oncology. Adult Cancer Pain Version 1.2009:1-40.

[22] Starr TD, Rogak LJ, Passik SD. Substance abuse in cancer pain. *Curr Pain Headache Rep.* 2010; 14:268-275.

[23] Hojsted J, Sjogren P. Addiction to opioids in chronic pain patients: A literature review. *Eur. J. Pain* 2007; 11:490-518.

[24] Quigley C. Opioids in people with cancer-related pain. Clin Evid (Online) 2008; 2008:2408. www.ncbi.nlm.nih.gov/pmc/articles/PMC2907984/

[25] Modesto-Lowe V, Girard L, Chaplin M. Cancer pain in the opioid-addicted patient: can we treat it right? *J. Opioid. Manag.* 2012; 8:167-75.

[26] Del Fabbro E. Assessment and Management of Chemical Coping in Patients with Cancer. *J Clin Oncol.* 2014; 32:1734-1738.

[27] Kwon JH, Tanco K, Hui D, Reddy A, Bruera E. Chemical coping versus pseudoaddiction in patients with cancer pain. *Palliat Support Care.* 2014; 13:1-5.

[28] Denlinger CS, Ligibel JA, Are M, et al. Survivorship: pain version 1.2014. *J. Natl. Compr. Canc. Netw.* 2014; 12:488-500.

[29] Kanbayashi Y, Hosokawa T, Kitawaki J, Taguchi T. Statistical identification of predictors for paclitaxel-induced peripheral neuropathy in patients with breast or gynaecological cancer. *Anticancer Res.* 2013; 33: 1153-6.

[30] Kanbayashi Y, Hosokawa T, Okamoto K, Konishi H, Otsuji E, Yoshikawa T, Takagi T, Taniwaki M. Statistical identification of predictors for peripheral neuropathy associated with administration of bortezomib, taxanes, oxaliplatin or vincristine using ordered logistic regression analysis. *Anticancer Drugs.* 2010; 21: 877-81.

[31] Kanbayashi Y and Hosokawa T. Predictors of Chemotherapy-Induced Peripheral Neuropathy, Peripheral Neuropathy - Advances in Diagnostic and Therapeutic Approaches, Dr. Ghazala Hayat (Ed.), Croatia: InTech; 2012

[32] Kanbayashi Y, Onishi K, Fukazawa K, Okamoto K, Ueno H, Takagi T, Hosokawa T. Predictive factors for postherpetic neuralgia using ordered logistic regression analysis. *Clin. J. Pain.* 2012; 28:712-4.

[33] Kanbayashi Y and Hosokawa T. Predictive Factors for Postherpetic Neuralgia and Recent Pharmacotherapies, Peripheral Neuropathy - A New Insight into the Mechanism, Evaluation and Management of a Complex Disorder, Dr. Nizar Souayah (Ed.), Croatia, InTech; 2013.

[34] National cancer institute, NCI Drug Dictionary, oxycodone hydrochloride, Available at: http://www.cancer.gov/drugdictionary?CdrID=508980 (accessed July 12, 2014).

[35] B. Lalovic, E. Kharasch, C. Hoffer, L. Risler, L.Y. Liu-Chen, and D.D. Shen. Pharmacokinetics and pharmacodynamics of oral oxycodone in healthy human subjects: role of circulating active metabolites. *Clin. Pharmacol. Ther.* 2006; 79: 461–479.

[36] B. Lalovic, B. Phillips, L.L. Risler, W. Howald, and D.D. Shen. Quantitative contribution of CYP2D6 and CYP3A to oxycodone metabolism in human liver and intestinal microsomes. *Drug Metab. Dispos.* 2004; 32: 447–454.

[37] J.K. Coller, L.L. Christrup, and A.A. Somogyi. Role of active metabolites in the use of opioids. *Eur. J. Clin. Pharmacol.* 2009; 65:121–139.

[38] Osgood ED, Eaton TA, Trudeau JJ, Katz NP. A brief survey to characterize oxycodone abuse patterns in adolescents enrolled in two substance abuse recovery high schools. *Am. J. Drug Alcohol Abuse.* 2012; 38:166–70.

[39] Katz N, Dart RC, Bailey E, Trudeau J, Osgood E, Paillard F. Tampering with prescription opioids: nature and extent of the problem, health consequences, and solutions. *Am. J. Drug Alcohol Abuse.* 2011; 37: 205–17.

[40] Young AM, Havens JR, Leukefeld CG. Route of administration for illicit prescription opioids: a comparison of rural and urban drug users. *Harm. Reduct. J.* 2010; 7:24.

[41] Lofwall MR, Moody DE, Fang WB, Nuzzo PA, Walsh SL. Pharmacokinetics of intranasal crushed OxyContin and intravenous

oxycodone in nondependent prescription opioid abusers. *J. Clin. Pharmacol.* 2012; 52:600–6.

[42] Hamed E, Moe D. Development of tamper deterrent formulations: state of the pharmaceutical industry. *Curr. Drug Abuse Rev.*2010; 3:139–46.

[43] Setnik B, Roland CL, Cleveland JM, Webster L. The abuse potential of Remoxy (®), an extended-release formulation of oxycodone, compared with immediate- and extended-release oxycodone. *Pain Med.* 2011; 12:618-31.

[44] US General Accounting Office. Prescription drugs, OxyContin abuse and diversion, and efforts to address the problem. 2003. http://www.gao.gov/new.items/d04110.pdf (accessed July 12, 2014).

[45] Mandema JW, Kaiko RF, Oshlack B, Reder RF,Stanski DR. Characterization and validation of a pharmacokinetic model for controlled-release oxycodone.*Br. J. Clin. Pharmacol.* 1996;42:747–56.

[46] Martins SS, Storr CL, Zhu H, Chilcoat HD. Correlates of extramedical use of OxyContin versus other analgesic opioids among the US general population. *Drug Alcohol Depend* 2009; 99:58–67.

[47] Webster LR. PTI-821: Sustained-release oxycodone using gel-cap technology. *Expert Opin. Investig. Drugs* 2007; 16:359–66.

[48] US Food and Drug Administration. FDA approves new formulation of OxyContin. 2010. http://www.fda.gov/newsevents/newsroom/PressAnnouncements/ucm207480.htm (accessed July 12, 2014).

[49] Substance Abuse and Mental Health Services Administration. Results from the 2009 national survey on drug use and health: volume II. Technical Appendices and Selected Prevalence Tables (Office of Applied Studies, NSDUH Series H-38B, HHS Publication No. SMA 10-4856 Appendices). Rockville, MD: Substance Abuse and Mental Health Services Administration; 2010.

[50] U.S. Food and Drug Administration. OxyContin— questions and answers. 2010. http://www.fda.gov/Drugs/DrugSafety/PostmarketDrugSafetyInformationforPatientsandProviders/ucm207196.htm (accessed July 12, 2014).

[51] U.S. Food and Drug Administration. FDA approves abuse-deterrent labeling for reformulated OxyContin 2013 http://www.fda.gov/newsevents/newsroom/pressannouncements/ucm348252.htm (accessed July 12, 2014).

[52] McNaughton EC, Coplan PM, Black RA, Weber SE, Chilcoat HD, Butler SF. Monitoring of Internet Forums to Evaluate Reactions to the

Introduction of Reformulated OxyContin to Deter Abuse. *J. Med. Internet. Res.*. 2014; 16:e119.

[53] Coplan PM, Kale H, Sandstrom L, Landau C, Chilcoat HD. Changes in oxycodone and heroin exposures in the National Poison Data System after introduction of extended-release oxycodone with abuse-deterrent characteristics. *Pharmacoepidemiol Drug Saf.* 2013; 22:1274-82.

[54] Severtson SG, Bartelson BB, Davis JM, Muñoz A, Schneider MF, Chilcoat H, Coplan PM, Surratt H, Dart RC. Reduced abuse, therapeutic errors, and diversion following reformulation of extended-release oxycodone in 2010. *J. Pain.* 2013; 14:1122-30.

[55] Cicero TJ, Ellis MS, Surratt HL. Effect of abuse-deterrent formulation of OxyContin. *N. Engl. J. Med.* 2012; 367:187-9.

[56] Coplan PM, Kale H, Sandstrom L, Landau C, Chilcoat HD. Changes in oxycodone and heroin exposures in the National Poison Data System after introduction of extended-release oxycodone with abuse-deterrent characteristics. *Pharmacoepidemiol Drug Saf.* 2013; 22:1274-82.

INDEX

A

B

C

D

E

F

I

J

K

L

M

N

O

P

Q

R

S

V

W

Y

Z

γ